Got Gold?

Get Gold!

The Everything Gold Answer Book.

Your Guide to Protecting your Wealth in the 21st Century Gold
Rush while Riding the Golden Bull and the Silver Stallion.

Jerry Western

Other books by Jerry Western:

The Precious Metals Mining Company Directory:
A Who's Who Guide of the Leading Gold and Silver Mining Plays

ISBN-10: 1461097967
ISBN-13: 978-1461097969

http://www.amazon.com/Precious-Metals-Mining-Company-Directory/dp/1461097967/ref=sr_1_10?s=books&ie=UTF8&qid=1305825659&sr=1-10#_

The Precious Metals Bull Market Model Portfolio: Investment Options for Riding the Silver and Gold Bull Market

ISBN-10: 146111148X
ISBN-13: 978-1461111481

http://www.amazon.com/Precious-Metals-Market-Model-Portfolio/dp/146111148X/ref=sr_1_9?s=books&ie=UTF8&qid=1305825805&sr=1-9

The Precious Metals Investment Guide: A Directory of Securities offering Investment Opportunities in Gold, Silver, and other Precious Metals

ISBN-10: 1461139503
ISBN-13: 978-1461139508

http://www.amazon.com/Precious-Metals-Investment-Guide-Opportunities/dp/1461139503/ref=sr_1_11?s=books&ie=UTF8&qid=1305825860&sr=1-11

Legal Notice / Disclaimer

This book is not and should not be construed as an offer to sell or the solicitation or an offer to purchase any investment. Western Outlook (Jerry Western) has based much of this book on information obtained from sources it believes to be reliable but which it has not independently verified; Western Outlook (Jerry Western) makes no guarantee, representation or warranty and accepts no responsibility or liability as to its accuracy or completeness. Expressions of opinion are those of Western Outlook (Jerry Western) only and are subject to change without notice. Western Outlook (Jerry Western) assumes no warranty, liability, or guarantee for the current relevance, correctness or completeness of any information provided within this book and will not be held liable for the consequence of reliance upon any opinion or statement contained herein or any omission. Furthermore, we assume no liability for any direct or indirect loss or damage or, in particular, for lost profit, which you may incur as a result of the use and existence of the information, provided within this book. By purchasing the Got Gold? Get Gold! book you are agreeing with this notice.

Nothing in this book should be taken as Financial or Investment Advice. Do Not make Investment Decisions based solely on the information presented here.

Do Your Own Due Diligence.

Full Disclosure: The author is not a financial planner and has no interest, financial or otherwise, in your buying or selling anything.

Full Disclosure: The author is long gold, silver, and their associated mining stocks.

Preface

The Gold and Silver markets are rockets primed and ready to explode skyward. All that's needed is the spark to start the ignition. Nobody knows what that spark will be or when it will come but surely it will come. This book has been written as an attempt to explain, in the simplest and easiest to understand way (I hope), why this is so. As I see it, the ignition and explosion is inevitable and imminent. I'm an unapologetic bull when it comes to gold and silver. After almost six years and literally thousands of articles read, both pro and con, I frankly can see no other outcome than the metals increasing in price, need, and want in the years to come. But imminent shouldn't be confused with immediate, though immediate is always a possibility and one day will prove true. This spark will probably take everyone by surprise, including myself and those deemed market experts. It could even be a spark that no-one has even contemplated or thought possible. However, I firmly believe that this is one of those rare instances when we can divine the likely direction of a market, though we can never know the timing nor magnitude. But if we play it right, direction is all we'll need.

When I started on my quest to understand these markets some six years ago, I made the mistake of confusing imminent with immediate. I could see all the signs back then and would never have thought that all these years later the rocket would still be on the launching pad. Surely, I thought, others could see and understand what I was discovering. Not so. I was an early adopter. Just because I could see and understand didn't mean that a) others were researching what I was, and b) they would come to the same conclusions as I, and c) bid up the metal. The problem is that opinion, consensus, and paradigm shift often happen at a glacial pace. A body of evidence needs to build and many data points need to be collected by the seeker (even if he isn't sure what he's seeking) in order to either enlighten the individual or change that person's opinion or view. It's like a supertanker turning at sea. It takes a long time to make a U-turn. Opinions and prejudices aren't often changed or turned on a dime. Since markets are nothing more than aggregated opinions, markets also tend to make very gradual shifts over years or decades. It's only rarely that we see quick changes in sentiment or opinion. Think of the market crashes of October 1929 and 1987 or the events of 9/11 for examples.

Please keep the above in mind when reading the rest of the book. Just because you are discovering a new data point for the first time doesn't mean everyone else is or that trend reversal is near (though it could be). Some trends have been moving in a certain direction for decades and it often takes years for markets, trends, or politics to reverse or take on a new direction. Don't be too quick to jump 'all-in' in one direction only to get whipsawed in the other. Construct a long term view. Take the example of one who discovered the Gold Bull Market in mid 2008. It looked great. Gold had been rising every year for 8 years running. Gold was trading at $1000/oz. Then it plunged to less than $700 in a matter of weeks and didn't recover to 4 digits until many months later. If you were new to the market and you had gone all-in at the intermediate top, you'd have been looking at a loss of more than a third of your portfolio in short order. Would you have had the fortitude to stay long in the market or would you have bailed for a hefty loss? Bull markets advance two steps forward and one step back. Almost nothing ever goes straight up or straight down in the short term. Markets take years to develop. Never be all-in or all-out on a whim. Stay the course for the long haul. To paraphrase the famous trader, Jesse Livermore: 'The greatest money is made by sitting tight and knowing you're right.' A bull market will make up any losses for you over time. It's probably best to average in over time but I wouldn't want to not be in the gold market at all at this time.

The generational bull market is now in tangible assets – commodities, energy, farmland, and precious metals among others. Certain individual stocks will advance and the stock indexes may advance over time as well. But they won't likely keep pace with inflation like commodities will – and you might just make a nice profit as well.

Who am I and why am I qualified to write this book?

I've been collecting coins for 34 years and have always had an interest in natural resources, geopolitics, money, ratios and percentages, and current events. I started researching the energy markets and inflation back in 2004 and that quickly led me to the precious metals markets and that's been my focus ever since. It's been both a hobby and a passion and I read and research continuously, occasionally publishing articles on Precious Metal Websites.

I do feel that I'm standing on the shoulders of giants though. While I have contributed my opinion and thoughts in various ways throughout the book, in reality, much of my thoughts and opinion have been formed and shaped by the hundreds of authors I've read and am deeply indebted to. My forte is to collect and distill the information I find into a simple, straightforward, understandable text for you, the reader. I have not invented the wheel, nor re-invented the wheel. What I've done is to introduce the wheel to a new audience and provide instructions in its use. This book is a compilation of my research of all things gold and silver. By liberally quoting the true gurus of the precious metals community, I've tried to bring out the best that those in the know have to offer. I've tried to cover the full spectrum of the basics that one needs to know to begin to have a true understanding of the value and power of gold (and silver). And the material within should be a fantastic starting point to learn how to protect your wealth by riding the golden bull.

Table of Contents

Chapter 4
Inflation   56

Chapter 5
It's Our Dollar but Your Problem   67

Chapter 6
The Precious Metals Markets   81

Chapter 7
Silver 'n Gold   112

Chapter 8
Precious Metal Ownership   122

Chapter 9
Precious Metals Equities   152

Chapter 10
Summary and Conclusion   181

A List of Links to Articles on the Coming Economic Collapse

If you only read or remember or understand one thing from this book, know this: Gold is money. Gold is the ultimate money. Gold is money when all other money fails. No matter what anyone may say to the contrary, the historic record indicates that gold is money and has always been. As the banker J.P. Morgan so famously put it, "Gold is money and nothing else." This quote can be taken in one of two ways. The first is that the primary function of gold is as money and that that is its only or most important function. The second is that gold is money and nothing else is, or that nothing else functions as money as good as gold. No matter how he meant it, he was correct. Gold is money and nothing else.

If you really understand that gold is money, that is all you really need to know, and you know what it is you need to do to protect yourself financially at this time. If not, the remainder of this book will try to convince you of the importance of gold and then you'll know what you need to do, that is, to get yourself some gold.

Therefore, if you do understand that gold is money and you own none, put down this book and go get some. If not, read on.

Chapter 1
The Current Bull Market in Precious Metals

"The Trend is Your Friend and the Trend in Gold is Up."
Jerry Western

The Current Bull Market in Precious Metals

The world is currently in the midst of a bull market in precious metals.
Gold has been in a bull market in U.S. Dollar terms since at least 2001
(as has silver and the other precious metals). Furthermore, the
advance has not been limited to the U.S. Dollar price, but is present in
all major world currencies, and seems likely to continue for some time.
As no market moves in a straight line, bull markets are characterized by
a succession of higher price highs and higher price lows, moving from
the lower left to the upper right on a chart; two steps forward – one step
back. But it is definitely a bull market.
That much we know.
Thus, the obvious questions we all seem to want answers to are three:
1.   Will the bull market in precious metals continue from here?

2.   If so, how long will it last?

and
3.   At that time, what will the ultimate high reach before the inevitable
bear returns?

In short, these answers are not conclusively knowable as the future is
uncertain. However, we can make inferences and educated guesses
by looking at the past and surveying the present. After all, history tends
to rhyme and there is nothing new under the sun.
A good deal of the content of this book is dedicated to providing
possible answers to these questions by surveying the current
circumstances, and examining the voluminous evidence, of this ongoing
bull market in precious metals.

Why a Bull Market Now?

First and foremost, since gold is money, it competes directly with currency, and is highly negatively (or inversely) correlated with the dollar and every other fiat currency (hint: all of them) in the world. Thus, holding gold is a hedge against the falling value of the dollar via inflation of the money supply. On a related note, the U.S. dollar is losing its status as the world reserve currency which will also exacerbate the inflation of dollars domestically at some point. More about this later. One needs to understand why an individual would desire to hold precious metals for the long term. For 5000 years of recorded history there have only been two things that people have consistently and continuously used as money: gold and silver. The main reason they have done so, and continue to do so, is because gold and silver act as a store of value. Each retains its value (read: purchasing power) over long periods of time; the more uncertain the economic times, the more the desire for safety. People become more interested in keeping what they have rather than in speculating. We are in the midst of uncertain economic times on both a national and a global scale.
There is now unprecedented continuous global currency debasement occurring due to worldwide reflationary policies in place attempting to stimulate economic growth and head off recessionary or depressionary forces. This is highly gold price positive.
Another huge factor is that precious metals are negatively correlated with all other major investment sectors. As the stock and housing markets have deflated, the metals have benefitted.
These are but a very few of the overarching circumstances present as the catalyst for this gold bull run. Much more is covered in sections to follow. In fact, this entire book is constructed as an argument for owning gold and there's something in each section that furthers that argument.

Commodity Cycles: How Long will the Bull Market Last?

All markets tend to fluctuate from bull to bear (or bubble to bust if you prefer) and back again over varying periods of time and for various reasons. Certain market sectors may be in alignment (stocks and bonds 1982-2000) at any given point in time or may be traveling in opposite directions, in a big picture/long term sense, spanning years or even decades. Those sectors traveling together are said to be positively correlated while those in opposition are said to be negatively correlated.

The dollar and gold normally move in opposite directions. When the dollar moves down, gold is normally up and vice versa. This has been a normal cycle. The dollar has been in a down trending market since the turn of the century. With dollars being created far in excess of expanding productivity and population, this trend seems likely to continue as each dollar created in excess degrades each existing dollar. Excess dollar creation has increased immensely in recent years. In actuality, it's not the value of gold which is increasing, it's the value of the dollar that is decreasing, thus necessitating more dollars to purchase a set amount of the metal. The metal doesn't change over time. It just is.

The last bull market in gold and silver lasted from 1971 until 1980. However, the price of gold was fixed at $35 per ounce until 1971. One could make a case that it started years earlier. The subsequent bear market in gold lasted about 2 decades, until the present bull began. The precious metals tend to run in sync with the general commodity cycles. Commodity cycles tend to last 15-20 years and sometimes up to 30 years. One reason for these cycles in commodities is due to the peculiarities of the mining industry.

Dr. Thomas Chaize has identified a 32.75 year cycle between production peaks in gold. Once a commodity deficit is recognized in the markets, production can't simply be increased quickly or easily. It takes 7-10 years for a promising piece of property to become a producing mine. By the time these mines are financed and built, the cycles is often turning and all of the new mines now create an over-supply and the market goes into a bear phase. This is one way to predict the length of a bull market. There are others.

Another is to measure the low-to-high price of gold during the last bull market. The price rose from $35 per ounce at the beginning of the seventies to $875 per ounce in January 1980. That's a 25 fold increase in price. The lowest low of the 1980's/1990's bear market was $255 (+- $1). Multiply that figure by 25 and see that this bull market may not be over until we reach or surpass $6375. Though only time will tell, this writer is of the opinion that we'll surpass that figure this time around for reasons presented in this book.

How long will the bull market last?

Let's let the experts tell us what they think.

"If you are a regular reader of my articles, then you know that I have been continually preaching the commodity pendulum. This is a series of massive swings in commodity prices (each lasting 10-20 years). The first swing was down (in real terms) from 1963-71. The second swing was up (in both real and nominal terms) from 1971-1980. The third swing was down again (both real and nominal) from 1980 to 1999. And the fourth swing was up (both real and nominal) from 2001 to the present."

Howard Katz "Commodities -- On the Move" 10/26/2009

"Note that Gold rose about six-fold the first eight years into the bull market (it began in 1970). Ultimately it rose 25-fold. The Nasdaq from 1982 to 1992 advanced about four fold. Ultimately it rose 29-fold. The Nikkei advanced less than three fold from 1970 to 1978. From 1970 to 1990 it gained 19-fold. Gold is nine years into its bull market and has advanced less than five fold. See a pattern here?" *Jordan Roy-Byrne*

"…a minimum 16 yr. bull market." *Aubie Baltin*

"If we measure gold in terms of its increasing purchasing power, we are only in about the third year of a 20-year run." *Bob Hoye*

The nature of cyclical bull markets is that there occurs a 'blow off' top at the completion of the bull move (Think Nasdaq circa 1999-2000). This means that the big gain comes in the latter stages of the bull. We've seen minor blow-offs in this bull but the big one should be ahead of us. Currently, there has been no 'recognition move' yet. The masses are still fast asleep. One day there will likely be a move to the upside in price that gets mass (media) attention. That move will likely be the beginning of the final move but that move may take months or years to complete.

This gold cycle shows no signs of doing anything but continuing. In fact, it is strengthening as it progresses.

Is Gold a Bubble?

Is gold a bubble like the real estate and dot com bubbles of the last two decades?

No. Gold is not a bubble at present (mid 2010) but likely will be at some point. The current bubble is in the dollar and the bond market. The U.S. government is artificially propping up both markets and has been doing so for some time. It swaps currency with foreign governments to purchase dollars on the Forex market and it has purchased more than half of recent bond offerings. Your government works diligently to prop up the value of the dollar, bond, treasury, and stock markets while suppressing the commodities markets. While the dollar price of gold has been steadily rising for over a decade, it is nowhere near being a bubble.

According to Davos Sherman Okst, in his writing "What's in Your Wallet?", June 24, 2010,

"0.8% of all global financial assets are invested in gold, gold shares, and ETFs. In 1932 it was 20%, in the 1980s 26%." And "TODAY? .8% POINT 8 Percent!" He goes on to say,

"IF 2% were allocated today, demand would amount to the total global mining output of 34 consecutive years. Gold in a bubble? I seriously don't think so." Bravo Mr. Okst!

Others have posted similar numbers. John Hathaway, Manager of the Tocqueville Gold Fund finds that the market cap of all above ground gold equals about 6% of global financial assets. In 1934 and 1982 he finds that it was between 20%-25%. Commentator Jordan Roy-Byrne says that market cap of all gold and gold assets was 15% in 1934 and 29% in 1980. Then we hear James Turk, founder of Goldmoney, telling us that in 1900 40% of invested money was in gold but today only about 1-2%.

Notice that most of the above commentators mention dates in the early 1930s and the early 1980s. What was happening back then? Of course, these were times of economic stress and uncertainty. The so-called Great Depression was going on in the 30s and the early 80s were right at the end of the last great inflation which coincided with the last great gold and silver bull market. People were putting a relatively large portion of their investable assets in the metals. They were doing so because of the protection and safety that the metals offered. The stock markets were in retreat in both these eras. People were afraid of losing what they had. They wanted safety and the metals provided it for them. This is what's going on in today's gold market. We have the same setup. I would guess that by the end of this current bull market we'll see similar percentages of wealth invested with the metals.

The above is a comparison of gold over time. Let's look at the current gold bull market versus stock bull markets. We'll start with a couple more quotes. The first is from Barton Biggs, from his book, Hedgehogging.

"In fact something like 80% of all the public money that was invested in mutual funds at the height of the bubble in the spring of 2000 went into tech funds." Wow. Remember that Nasdaq Tech Bubble of the late 90s? The public was really into that one. Where's the public in today's gold market? Nowhere to be seen. How can we have a bubble with the public?

Gold Market Commentator Andrew Mickey recently wrote:

"And they're certainly not even close to the 48% of all Americans owning stocks at the height of the stock bubble in 2000." Do 48% of the people you know own any form of gold? I'd say we have a long way to go.

People are selling gold (i.e. Cash4Gold) not buying it. That's the opposite of a bubble. Let me repeat, Americans are selling their gold at 'gold parties' not buying it. Someday they will – at the top – just like during the tech/internet mania – but not yet. In a later section, I'll be discussing signs of a top (bubble). None of those signs are evident today.

Reasons why Precious Metals will Appreciate from Here

This section is meant to be quick overview of prominent factors causing this gold bull run. It is certainly not exhaustive and most of the following is discussed in much greater detail in subsequent chapters. Here's a sampling of some quick facts. Briefly...

- Commodity Bull Markets tend to last 15 to 20 years. We're only in about the ninth or tenth year.

- The biggest gains normally come at the end of bull markets. While we may be more than half way through, the greatest percentage gains are ahead.

- Investment demand continues to rise in volume and percent. Gold investment demand increased 64% in 2008 and 118% in the second quarter of 2010. Retail investment demand was up 400+% in 2009 according to the World Gold Council (WGC).

- Precious metals are in a bull market in all major world currencies.

- The market capitalization of all above ground gold as a percentage of global financial assets is currently in the low single digits. During past times of economic turmoil, the percentage has been 20-40%.

- There is an ever more obvious shortage of physical gold and silver – both bars and coins.

- We're in the middle of a general commodities upswing.

- There has been a surge in open interest since mid-March 2010 in gold futures contracts.

- Investment demand is now overtaking jewelry demand as the most important or dominant demand (World Gold Council).

- There has been backwardation at the bullion exchanges. This is the first time this has happened in decades. It means that people want to take delivery of their metal sooner rather than later. Silver spent 47 straight days in Backwardation in 2009.

- Delivery and supply issues on the precious metal commodities exchanges.

- Worldwide economic disruption and monetary reflation currently underway.

- The need to diversify excessive global foreign exchange reserves.

- Nations are increasingly outspoken about the need to replace the dollar as the world reserve currency. Not only that, they're taking action.

- Foreign nations are increasingly losing their desire to buy U.S. Treasuries (or are not able to). In fact, they've become net sellers with the Federal reserve picking up the slack.

- Half of U.S. States and the Federal Government are technically bankrupt.

- Half of U.S. Homes are underwater. The broadest measure of unemployment is over 22%.

- Many gold and silver mines were closed for good during the last downturn in gold and silver and have yet to be reactivated. Supply is flat and mining costs are increasing.

- The World's Central Banks have stopped selling gold and are now buyers.

- The vast majority of people still have not invested in precious metals.

- Fractional Reserve Gold.

- Negative real interest rates.

- U.S. Deficit of 13+% of GDP for 2009. *(CBO)*

- Unfunded pension and health-care liabilities are over $99 Trillion. (Richard Fisher, president of the Dallas Federal Reserve Bank)

- Credit agencies have issued alerts regarding the U.S. AAA credit rating.

There are many more reasons, and too numerous to list all of them, but you get the picture.

It's not just the United States pursuing a policy of currency debasement. All other nations are on the same path. The result is that there is more than ten times the currency circulating world-wide than there was in the 1970's. This currency has to go somewhere. It went into the stock markets and then to housing and is still in U.S. debt. It's becoming more apparent that much is beginning to flow into precious metals. During the 1970s gold bull run, most of the global population had no way of participating. Those in the Communist Bloc did not participate. Only the U.S. and Europe, and to a lesser extent the Middle East, pushed gold and silver prices to the, then, all-time highs.

This time the entire world is participating. The global population is roughly double what it was then and probably 5 to 10 times more people have the ability to invest in the metals.

Because of globalization, the need to beat currency inflation, and the Internet, people now have a propensity to invest and speculate. They also have the ability.

As more and more people turn to gold and silver to protect their wealth, they will push the metals to greater heights than seen the last time around. By positioning yourself accordingly now, you will be in a position to protect yourself and quite possibly profit as well.

How You Can Profit from the Silver and Gold Bull Markets

Let's assume that you've come to the conclusion that gold is indeed in a bull market (it has been for 10 years now) and that it will continue. Then how can you get in on the action while the bull still reigns?

First and foremost: Buy and Hold on. A bull market will rise over time. Should your timing be off and you buy at an interim high, the bull will bail you out eventually. You can safely take the plunge at any item before the bull exhausts itself. Remember the adage of Dollar Cost Averaging in the stock market? Well, the same applies to any bull market. Invest a set portion of your funds on a regular basis and eventually your average buy-in price will be lower than the market price in a rising market.

Try to time the market. You know it's a bull market and that it is going to rise. Two steps forward and one step back. There are plenty of subscription services and free commentary on the Web to assist you with your timing in buying and selling.

Be the middle man. Since buying and selling activity is increasing as the bull market progresses, you can take your cut of the increased action, whether at gold jewelry 'parties' or the buying and selling of coins. There is always a spread or premium in every transaction.

Buy precious metal mining stocks or Exchange Traded funds (ETFs) that invest in and hold the metals. This option should only be pursued with expert guidance and knowledge. Mining issues are very volatile in both directions.

Work for a mining company, bullion supplier, or coin shop. Remember, it was the suppliers who got rich during the California and Alaska Gold Rushes for the most part. Those who sold the implements for mining often acquired greater riches than those who did the actual prospecting.

Mine it yourself. Small scale prospecting has really taken off the last couple of years with rising prices. While most gold and silver is mined in the Western United States, there are minable deposits in certain areas of the East. Browse the Gold Prospectors Association of America (GPAA) website at goldprospectors.org to find out more. At the website, surf over to the Lost Dutchman's Mining Association page. The LDMA members have rights to prospect certain claims.

Educate yourself and others. The more educated you become about the gold market, the more ideas you'll have on how to profit. By educating others, you'll become the go-to person for queries from friends, relatives, and acquaintances. You'll then act as an intermediary, for a profit, to help them with their own research and purchases.

Chapter 2
Gold

"Gold is money and nothing else."

J.P. Morgan

Why Gold Retains its Value over Time

Gold retains its value because of its inherent scarcity, whereas dollars can be created in unlimited supply. Gold retains its stability of value over time due to its occurrence, or supply, in nature and the rate at which it can be mined. Both the annual rate at which gold is mined in relation to existing supply, and the rate of increase in world population, regularly fall within the 1% to 2% range. Go back a half century and you will find that there was then, as there is today, approximately ¾ ounce of above ground (mined) gold in existence for each human on earth. This ratio remains quite constant over time because of the similarity in the two rates of increase.

Gold Attributes

What are some of the attributes that makes gold so special? After all, it's just number 79 on the periodic table of elements – only one of over a hundred known elements. Why gold?

I used to think that an element, mineral, or commodity had to be useful or beneficial in some other way to be prized as an asset to hold. After all, if it has no use then why hoard it? For example, water is needed (for all life), hoarded (think dams and reservoirs), and coveted (ask any farmer who irrigates or beachfront property owner).

There's a concept in urban planning called 'best use' of a property. For instance, a steeply sloping property with swampland and a river flowing through it may be best suited to be parkland. Sure, you could build houses on it with great effort and expense but there's cheaper and better suited land nearby for that purpose. It could be turned into a garbage dump but undesirable chemicals would leach into the wetlands and river and perhaps into the drinking water. You get the idea. Each parcel of real estate has a best or better user for it. Not that the best use always happens but most would agree that one use would be better than another.

It's the same with metals, only sort of backwards. Most elements and metals are used in many and various applications. However, each need for material has a particular element, metal, or commodity that works best. Why are aircraft bodies made primarily of aluminum? It's because aluminum is the best suited for that use. It's the strongest, cheapest, and safest material to use. Can substitutes be used? Sure. Fighter jets are made of titanium instead of aluminum because it's more rugged and can survive the G-forces better and enemy fire too. Could 747's be made from titanium? Sure they could, but at much greater and prohibitively expensive cost. Palladium is used in automobile catalytic converters. Silver is used for most mirrors. There are substitutes for both but these have been found to best suited for that purpose over time.

Now I ask you, what's the best material or substance to be used as money? Why it just so happens to be gold. Yes, gold is used for jewelry, dentistry, gold leaf, electronics, and other purposes but its best use is as money. Each of the above uses has one or more substitutes anyhow.

Why is gold's best use as money? Well, partly because it's Durable, Divisible, Easily Recognizable, Highly Liquid (financially), Hard to Counterfeit, Easily Portable, Relatively Rare, Non-Toxic, Beautiful, Compact, Unchanging, An Honest Measure, Won't Rust, Decay, or Burn, Convenient, Fungible, Holds its Value over Time, and Is Anonymous. Oh, and it's hard to come by, is extracted from the earth at great expense and hardship, and historically increases in supply at about the same rate as population expands.

But you know what? None of that really matters in the end. What does matter is that it is Desired and Coveted by others. Other people want it and are willing to trade goods and services for it. It doesn't really matter why they want it – just that they do and always have. As long as human nature does not change (and it never has), gold will always have value to people and thus will always be money.

Here are some other attributes that make gold special.

Gold is the only major asset class that is negatively correlated to all others (i.e. Bonds, Equities, Real Estate, Cash). *(Ibbotson Associates, 2005)*. When the stock markets are on a bull run and housing is booming you may not want to be all in gold. But when most of the other markets are down or sideways (since the turn of the last century), gold is normally increasing in price.

Gold does well in both Inflationary and Deflationary environments. (*The Golden Constant; Jastram, 1977)* The 1930's was a time of deflation and the 1970's was a time of inflation. Gold did well throughout both those decades.

Gold is **the most Conservative investment** one can make – more conservative than cash or bonds. This fact isn't widely known. Author and investor Stewart Thompson calls it the "World's Lowest Risk Investment." When I say conservative I'm not saying that it always makes you the maximum dollar gain. Not so. What I'm saying is that its value can never fall to zero. There's always a demand for it in bad times and in good. Your dollars can lose value over time and even become worthless. They can burn in a fire resulting in their value going to zero. Your bank can go bankrupt and perhaps you'll get something eventually but your dollar denominated account could go to zero. As I keep pounding the table about, gold is always in demand. There is always someone willing to take it off your hands, either honestly or dishonestly. That has always been the case through recorded history. Why would it change now? While your gold can decrease in dollar price over time, its value remains constant. It is a lump of metal. Its value and utility do not change over time. Just like the value of water or air doesn't change. Spanish gold coins taken from the bottom of the ocean after hundreds of years remain unchanged. They do not rust and still weight the same. If you have a house fire your gold may melt but it will weigh the same and retain its value (and dollar price). Someone will pay you just as much for that melted lump as for that shiny coin. It's the metal that has value, not what's stamped on it. And finally, as long as you don't have it stored at your bank, the bank's closure will not affect you if you hold gold. That is, if you hold it in your hands outside of the banking system.

In summation, gold is the one universal monetary means of settlement. It's always accepted where other forms of payment are not. Got Gold?

Gold Caveats

Although I'm a complete unapologetic gold bull, one must always we cautious with one's wealth and investments. No one can see the future or account for all potential factors that can influence one's investments. And there's that old saying: Don't put all your eggs in one basket. Let's look at some potential pitfalls and issues that warrant caution with our investment in gold.

Nobody knows the future.
Yes, I've been wrong in the past. Some of the best forecasters may only be right little more than 50% of the time. Having said that, I do see an almost limitless amount of anecdotal evidence and history rhyming going on today. That convinces me that gold is only going higher long term. However, anything can happen and it would be folly to place all of your investment eggs in one basket. Always consider alternative possibilities.

The return of your money versus the return on your money
At this point you should be buying precious metals to hold onto what you have in uncertain times – not necessarily to get rich. Gold is a preserver of wealth. Its value remains constant. Only its price changes. It's the (re)discovery by the masses of gold's true nature that makes it a bull market. Gold may only keep up with inflation from this point on or it may exceed the rate of inflation as people wake to our economic realities. There is no better protector of accumulated wealth than gold. Many of the wealthiest individuals in this world will speculate in the markets but will save in gold. You should too. Think of your precious metals as protection more than an investment.

Keep it simple

Don't get cute with exotic investments in paper gold or leverage. You could lose it all. Think conservative with gold. You will do well holding just plain, boring, metal. You don't need to try to beat the returns on gold or silver. They will do just fine for years to come. If you try playing the intermediate price swings you could get stopped out when the price really takes off, or worst, you could lose it all on margin calls. Then you'd miss out on the rest of this once-in-a-lifetime multi-generations bull market. That would be the worst outcome – knowing you were in the correct market, where it is going and why, buy watching from the sidelines. You'd never forgive yourself. Don't let it happen to you.

Buy and Hold
Like any market, and perhaps more so, the gold and silver markets can be highly volatile. Especially the silver market. Markets can go counter-trend for months or even years in a primary bull or bear market. Everything you heard about equities for all those years is now true for the precious metals. These are the assets that are now buy and hold for the long haul. This is the market that you should dollar cost average into. Always think long term with precious metals. Think retirement. Think multi-generation. Buy, sell, and trade in the stock markets if you must buy preserve wealth into the future with precious metals.

Know what it is you are buying
I shouldn't even need to write the obvious but it can be tricky. See the chapter on Gold versus Paper Gold and the section on ETFs. You're not always buying what it is you think you're buying. Make sure you do know. Your financial future could depend on it. A promise for future delivery of metal is a lot different than a known, assayed, quantity of metal in your hand. At some point there will be many sad individuals wishing they had purchased physical bullion instead of a promise. Don't be misled.

Anonymity in loss or theft
Can you prove it's yours? It's probably easier to prove your claim on a share of stock than on a lump of metal unless your bars have serial numbers. Even then, those bars can be melted and – poof – no serial numbers. Even dollar bills have unique identifying numbers printed on them. All metal is anonymous. That's mostly a good thing from my perspective but can be a liability when proof of ownership is required. Just something to keep in mind.

Taxes

Keep in mind that physical precious metals are treated as Collectibles for tax purposes. That means a much higher tax rate than profits on stock or mutual fund shares. See the section on taxes for further explanation.

Why Own It?   The Bull Case

Own it as an inflation hedge to protect against inflation of the money supply. Gold and the dollar have historically been almost exactly negatively correlated. This means that when one goes up the other goes down and vice versa. Since about the turn of the century gold has gone up every year and the dollar is about a third off of its highs. As there are more dollars being created every day in excess of productivity or population gains, and the amount of mined gold rises much slower, the dollar price of gold must increase to find equilibrium with the supply of gold.
Own it because it is outside the banking system. There should be no third party between you and your asset. You don't have to find an ATM to get at it. You don't have to deal with banker's hours to get at it. You don't have to pay interest for someone else to store it. Your gold will never go bankrupt and shut its doors. Your gold will never make you an unsecured creditor. Your gold will not make you hire a lawyer to get at it. Fully paid for physical bullion in your sweaty little paws will be forfeited to another at great expense. Possession is nine-tenths of the law and is how the world and people operate. You can always convert it on your terms to put into the banking system. Why leave it there when there's so much that can go wrong?
Own it because it's highly liquid. There will always be a buyer or barterer willing to accept it. It is actually the most liquid form of money. True, you couldn't spent it at Walmart (unless you care to spend time educating the cashier that that silver eagle is legal tender) but you can't spend federal reserve notes outside the U.S. You have to convert to another currency. Gold is universally accepted. It is, to paraphrase Charles DeGaul, money "par excellence". None better.

Own it because there is no third-party risk. Again, if it's in your hands or possession, there is little risk others can abscond with it. It is easier for a thief to steal what is yours if he first has access to it than if you do. In addition to our bank example above, think about contract risk, collecting on insurance policies, your retirement account safely, and the solvency of social security. What do they all have in common you ask? Promises! They are all promises by someone else or some entity to pay you in full at some future date. Will they do so? In today's dollars or tomorrows depreciated ones? Think of how many times others have failed to deliver in your life. Take control of your finances.

Own it now because surely there will not be any available, at any price, in a panic. People always want more of what they can't have or what has become scarce. If everyone on the planet wanted to acquire one ounce of gold today, there would not be enough to go around.

Normally when the price of something rises, demand falls. It works the opposite with precious metals. When people see the price of metals rise, they want more of them. They want o get some before the price goes even higher and perhaps, they won't be able to get any.

Own it as catastrophe insurance. You buy home, car, and life insurance to guard against catastrophe. What happens when you can't collect on those policies? Where do you turn then? Who insures the insurers? Is there insurance available to protect against the dollar losing its value? Yes there is. It's called gold.

Own it to guard against dollar repudiation or loss of confidence in the economy. If no one, domestic or foreign, will accept your dollars, they will still accept your silver or gold. If the economy goes sour and the banking system seizes, you still have money to barter with for what it is you require. If unemployment reaches depression levels or worse and money again becomes scarce, you'll still have a supply and it will likely buy you more than in good times.

Own it so that your wealth is mobile. If things get really bad, you may be able to use it to cross borders. It may become your exit visa. Gold has allowed people to cross borders in times of war when nothing else could. There are numerous accounts of people leaving Germany before and during WWII by bribing border guards. There are also numerous instances of people being able to leave former Soviet satellite states behind the Iron Curtain during the Cold War. Let's hope it doesn't get that bad.

What Good is It Anyhow?   The Bear Case

In this chapter I'd like to address and refute some of the common arguments against gold that I often read about or hear in my classes. I love this first one.

You can't eat it.
No kidding. How do those Federal Reserve Notes taste? Filling are they? Nourishing? I hear they have more toxic chemicals in them than cigarettes. The ink on each one contains arsenic, cadmium, mercury, thallium, and cyanide. What a dumb argument. Do you choke down your stock certificates too? Yummy. Careful, all that papers gonna make you constipated! In the world we live in we all have to convert whatever it is into dollars. My electric company will only take dollars in payment. Wal-mart doesn't accept oil futures contracts at the checkout the last time I checked. It's a total non-argument. If you're of a survivalist mentality, then just store food instead.

You can't use it at Wal-mart.
See above.

It offers no dividends/yield/returns.
Which would you rather have – a) 2% stock dividends and a sideways stock market for the last ten years or b) an average annual return of 16% on your gold for the last decade? If you said a) just give up now. I can't help you. No one can.

What if we get another downturn in the metals like in 2008?
Gold fell less in percentage terms than did the stock markets during the financial panic, rebounded quicker, and reached new highs before the stock indexes. What more needs to be said.

It's in a bubble.

George Soros famously called gold the 'ultimate bubble' in early 2010. His comment was widely reported in the mainstream media. Know what he was doing while the networks were reporting what he said? Buying Gold! I believe he almost doubled the amount of his gold holdings during the financial quarter his gold statement came out. Bubble indeed! I haven't seen the mania. I don't see people lined up around the block to buy gold like they were in 1979 and 1980. Tell me which gold stock has appreciated 10,000% recently. Some did better than that during the 1970s. Bubble indeed! The real bubbles are the dollar and bond markets. A 2010 study by Commodity Online of some 21,000 persons reveals that 93% were bearish on gold. 93%! When the numbers reverse and only 7% are bearish gold, that'll be the time to sell.

It's too 'risky'.
The only risk I see is having none. If the dollar does collapse, you'll be glad you had some, and if it doesn't, we're still in a bull market and you can exchange your metal for dollars at some point in the future. Like insurance, better to have it and not need it than the other way round.

The government will just confiscate it again.
If things get so bad that the government confiscates gold again, think of what the black market price would be. The last time they revalued the price of gold up 70% within a year of confiscating it. Most people did not turn in their gold and were allowed to keep up to 5 ounces per person. Those who turned it in got the prevailing price at the time. If you chose to turn yours in this time you would likely get the prevailing price. So you wouldn't actually lose anything in dollar terms. Look, the government can confiscate anything at any time. Real Estate is confiscated through Eminent Domain. Think about it. No property is safe from one form of government confiscation or another. Aren't taxes a form of confiscation of your time and labor?

What if we get deflation not inflation?
See the section on gold and deflation elsewhere in this book. That's the beauty of gold. It will protect you equally well in times of inflation and in times of deflation.

If it gets lost or stolen, you can't prove it's yours.

Can you prove that the ten dollar bill lying on the ground over there is yours? How so? I say it's mine. I'll fight you for it. The only signature I see on it is from the U.S. Treasurer. Maybe it's his. You say it fell out of your pocket. I say it fell out of mine. Just like you should be very careful with your paper money, you should be very careful with your gold. Don't flaunt it or brag about it or tell others where it is or how much you have. Remember not to discuss religion, politics, or money.

Who's going to buy it from you?
Anyone and everyone – especially when it's not readily available. There always has been a market for gold – in good times and bad – throughout history. Why would over 5000 years of recorded history change in our time? See above about gold being real money, highly recognizable, highly liquid, desired, etc. Could you imagine someone not wanting it? Could you imagine someone walking by a gold coin on the sidewalk? I couldn't. There will always be someone willing to take it off your hands.

What Gold Is. What Gold is Not. What Gold is Good for.

Gold is a currency. It is a store of value. That is its best and highest use. No other commodity shares this trait. Gold is the ultimate currency when all others fail. Gold is the measuring stick against which all else is valued. Gold is the currency of choice when given one. It is chosen by Central Bankers to store in their vaults. It is chosen by the wealthy to save in and store that wealth. Should you act any different?

Gold is not a commodity like oil or pork bellies. It is not consumed. It is hoarded and guarded. Gold is not to be traded easily for any other asset. It is not for trading purposes. It is not meant to turn a profit. It is not meant to provide a dividend. Its best and highest use is not for jewelry, chalices, or artwork. It is not just a lump of metal. It is not just money but the ultimate form of money.

Gold is becoming the reserve asset of choice by Central Banks once again. Ownership of gold means you are your own central bank. Holding gold means you have no counterparty risk. Gold is to be used for wealth preservation, insurance, and during catastrophe when all else fails. Gold never fails.

A Golden Timeline: The U.S. and the Gold Standard

The following is a rough outline of the role gold has played in the United States monetary system. Notice how the country has cycled from a metallic standard to a fiat system and back numerous times. This tells me we are on our way back to some form or metal backing for the dollar.

- 1792 – 1933 Gold backing of currency. Prices stable or falling (deflation) except in wartime.

- 1812   Some banks issue paper money. New England banks don't.

- 1862 – 1879   First U.S. paper Greenbacks (prices rise 2x)

- 1873 'Crime of 1873' Silver Demonetized.

- 1880 – 1914   Fixed Gold Standard.

- 1900   Gold Standard Act. 'Pure Gold Standard'

- 1913   Establishment of the Federal Reserve Central Bank. Dollar loses over 95% of its original value since then.

- 1915 –1925   Floating Fiat Currency.

- 1926 - 1931   Gold Exchange Standard.

- 1931 – 1945   Floating Fiat Currency.

- 1933   Emergency Banking Bill of March 9, 1933. Roosevelt Confiscates Gold and Re-values an ounce from $20.67 to $35. Gold Reserve Act of 1934 devalues the dollar by 41% (i.e. increases gold price by 69%). Gold Certificates become Irredeemable. Gold Possession is Illegal.

- 1944   Bretton Woods Treaty makes the U.S. Dollar the World Reserve Currency. Other nations can redeem dollars for gold.

- 1945 – 1971   Gold Standard.

- 1960 – 1968   London Gold Pool. World Central Banks work to depress dollar price of gold.

- 1963   New Federal Reserve notes with no promise to pay in "lawful money" released.

- 1963   Executive Order 11110 signed enabling United States Notes to compete with Federal Reserve Notes. Revoked the same year.

- 1965   Coinage Act of 1965: Coins no longer have any silver content. (Except 40% half dollar coins until 1969).

- 1968   The U.S. Government no longer redeems Silver Certificate Notes for actual government Silver Bullion. 25% Gold backing removed from currency.

- 1969   Bank for International Settlement creates Special Drawing Right (SDR) 'currency'.

- 1971   The U.S. 'Closes the Gold Window' by refusing to sell gold for dollars internationally. Back to a Floating Fiat Currency.

- 1971 – 1973   Fixed Dollar Standard: The Smithsonian Agreement was passed pegging world currencies to the dollar rather than gold at a fixed exchange rate.

- 1973 – today   The Basel Accord established the current floating exchange of currency rates we are operating under today.

- 1974   NY Commodities Exchange (COMEX) opens. Paper gold trading begins.

- 1975   Once again Legal for U.S. Citizens to own gold.

- 1976 – 1980   IMF sells 1555 tonnes of gold in bid to depress gold price.

- 1978   U.S. Treasury Gold Auctions gold in bid to depress gold price.

- 1985   Gold Bullion Coin Act mandates Gold Eagle Coin production.

- 1999 – 2014 Washington Agreement, Central Bank Gold Agreement, and CBGAII implemented in bid to depress gold price.

United States Gold Reserves

Are they there or aren't they? That is the question.
Supposedly, the United States has some 8134 Tons (261 Million ounces) of gold.
It once held over 20,000 Tons in the late 1940s.
I say supposedly because no independent third party audit of physical gold reserves has been conducted since 1953.
The gold is reportedly held at Fort Knox in Kentucky, at West Point in New York, at The Denver Mint in Denver, Colorado, and at The New York Federal Reserve in New York City.
The following is taken from an article by Christopher Weber titled *Fort Knox Gold.*
The Great American Disaster: How Much Gold Remains In Fort Knox?

- The only audit that has ever been done of the gold inside Ft. Knox was done days after Dwight Eisenhower became President in January of 1953.
- Representatives of the audit group were allowed to make the rules governing the audit. No outside private experts were allowed.
- Those government bureaucrats involved were inexperienced in their tasks, by their own admission.
- The entire audit of the largest gold hoard ever concentrated in history lasted only seven days.
- Only a fraction of the gold was actually tested. Later, the officials put this fraction at just 5%.
- Based on that fraction, the official committee reported that, in their opinion, all the holdings would have matched their records if they'd all been tested.
- If the audit was accurate, the fact remains that almost 80% of it went overseas in the coming years. If the audit was not accurate, the amount of gold lost could have been even more.

The only other time anything remotely approaching an audit was performed was in 1974 when six congressmen and one senator 'toured' Ft. Knox. The Press tagged along. They were shown an open vault door and what appeared to be gold bars stacked to the ceiling in front of the door. That's it. Conclusion of tour. No independent certified third-part audit of all the gold was conducted. No bars were weighed, assayed, or otherwise verified for authenticity. Only one vault was opened. Fort Knox has dozens of vaults. They did not peer behind this wall of gold in the only vault shown. Essentially, the whole episode was a for-public-consumption horse and pony show, not an audit.

A true 'audit' was to have taken place within 30 days of the 'tour'. Reportedly, some sort of audit was performed by the Treasury in conjunction with the GAO. The results were released in 1975. This self-conducted audit found that less than 10% of the gold held at Ft. Knox was of 'good delivery' gold. Good delivery gold is relatively pure gold of .995 fineness or better. The entire hoard was not audited.

You must remember that the world of gold is completely opaque. No one volunteers information as it's not in anyone's selfish interest to do so. So we're left with making educated guesses and inferences. One thing we can be certain of, since there is not, and has not been, any transparency with regard to U. S. Government controlled gold, that there is a reason for this. The reason is that not all of the gold they say is there is indeed there. If there was, the government would be advertising the fact and releasing annual audits to show what a bastion of stability the U.S. was. The truth is hidden for cause. We don't know what the truth is. We can only make an educated guess that there is less, perhaps much less, gold in U.S. custody than we have been led to believe. Should this fact ever become widely known and accepted, the dollar price of gold should spike quite sharply.

Who owns the United States gold?

Supposedly the people but, as usual in the gold arena, we don't have a clear answer. Both the Treasury and Federal Reserve keep U.S. gold on their books. We're left to conjecture or speculate as to the real state of our gold. We don't know for certain who owns it, how much of it there is, where exactly it is kept, or in what state of refinement it exists, and no one is telling.

Fractional Reserve Gold

A history lesson.

Since forever, Goldsmiths stored or hid their gold in a secure place. Over time, because of this security function, they began to store other person's gold. They then issued receipts for the gold they held on deposit for others.

These receipts were well known and became accepted by others for goods or services because they were "as good as gold" and could be converted to gold at any time when presented to the Goldsmith. These receipts became a form of currency.

Next, the Goldsmiths realized that they could make loans on their gold holdings.

They noticed that only a small fraction of the gold held in their care was being demanded by the receipt holders. It was much more convenient for these gold owners to simply exchange pieces of paper than to take the additional step of getting their gold and using that for their purchases. So the Goldsmiths increased the number of receipts in circulation relative to the gold that they stored.

Everything ran smoothly as long as they had enough gold to hand over to those with receipts. The receipt (gold) owners were none the wiser that there were more claims on their gold than gold available should everyone want theirs. This was free money to the Goldsmiths (Bankers).

This, by the way, is exactly how our modern banking system runs, on a fractional reserve basis. Not all depositors want their money at any given time, so the bankers can use those funds to make additional loans. The depositors are none the wiser.

Today, the Comex (New York Commodities Exchange) and the LME (London Metals Exchange) operate on a fractional gold reserve basis. It is thought that they have only 1 ounce of gold available for every 100 claims on it.

In 2007 Morgan Stanley settled out of court a class-action suit by precious metals investors. The suit alleged that Morgan Stanley told clients it was selling them precious metals that they would own and the company would store. But Morgan Stanley either made no purchase or investment specifically on behalf of those clients or it made entirely different investments of lesser value. It operated on a fractional reserve basis or no fraction at all.

The lesson is: An ounce in the hand is worth 100 at the exchange.

Chapter 3
Money

"Gold is no one's debt; it is no one's obligation, it carries no risk. Gold has been accepted by man as payment of debt since time immemorial, as gold cannot be controlled and printed or spoken into existence, as can paper money."

Doug Gnazzo

What has Historically been Used as Money

Basically, anything that 2 parties agree to use as a medium of exchange can be money. People have used Cows, Seashells, Tobacco, Liquor, Gold, Silver, Paper, Francs, Yen, Marks, Dollars... For over 5000 years of recorded history there have only been two things that people have consistently and continuously used as money: Gold and Silver. Greek Drachmas and Roman Denarius were both fashioned from precious metals. For thousands of years people intuitively knew what money was. Gold and silver rose to prominence over that time as the best solution.

There was no need for government decree nor legal tender law. The Free Market decided all on its own.

In many languages, the word for money and silver is one and the same. For example, the French word l' argent means both silver and money, ditto the Spanish plata. In Chinese, the word for bank means 'silver movement'.

Are Precious Metals Used as Money Today?

The short answer is no, even though they are still money. No nation today uses gold or silver coinage in daily transactions.

However, The ISO (International Organization for Standardization) has set the standards for international currencies. Silver and gold are listed by the ISO as currencies. They trade as currencies on the Forex (Foreign Currency Exchange) market. And most telling of all, every major central bank keeps gold in their vaults and as part of their foreign exchange reserves.

Think about that. They don't keep logs or rocks or bales of hay in those vaults. They don't even keep diamonds in them. They keep gold. So, the most powerful, elite, richest, most well-connected countries and organizations keep gold in their vaults. Maybe they know something. Maybe you should do as they do.

In addition, as of December 2008, when gold backwardation at the Comex (Commodities Exchange) first appeared, the market is now uniformly valuing all standard gold coins. As Assenov and Petrov put it in "A New Stage in Gold's Return to Money":

"Both the ugliest and the most beautiful gold coins are traded in indirect exchange strictly by the quantity and quality of metal content, completely disregarding the outward appearance of the coin."

What this means is that all forms of gold are now trading equally and are becoming recognized as money once again.

The Characteristics of Sound Money

When we speak of Sound Money, we can substitute Honest, Constitutional, Hard, or Real for Sound. The idea being conveyed is that there is a difference between just plain money and money that is backed by, or is itself, a tangible asset.

"The main uses of money are as a medium of exchange, a unit of account, and a store of value." Wikipedia

Indeed, Sound Money has the three characteristics mentioned by Wikipedia. I've added two more.

Sound Money must be a **Medium of Exchange**.

It must be liquid (in an economic sense), easily tradable, easily recognizable, and convenient to use. Three Characteristics of a Liquid Asset are:

1. Others will exchange goods or services for this asset instantaneously. No conversion or validation of the asset is needed. It is convenient to use.

2. The exchange can be made without offering a discount for accepting the asset. It will exchange at 'face value'.

3. One need not advertise or persuade another to accept the asset. It's already highly recognizable. There is no need to educate the other party as to its value. In other words, its value is easily recognized.

To be a medium of exchange, a sound money candidate must also be transportable. In other words it must have a high value to weight ratio. Nobody wants to lug around cases of beer as a medium of exchange. You'd need quite a few to buy that new car. However, you could carry the equivalent value of that car in gold in your pocket.

Gold and silver fulfill the medium of exchange function. Houses or barrels of oil, among others, do not. They may fulfill some of the characteristics such as having recognized value, but they are not liquid or convenient or transportable. Gold is highly recognizable in any form, at any time, anywhere on the planet. Dollars are only accepted in U.S. for the most part and are not legal tender in other locales.

Sound money must be a **Store of Value.**

It must be durable and can't easily decay. Wheat rots. Gold doesn't even rust. Paper burns and is consumed. Gold melts but is not destroyed. A lump of melted gold retains the same value as that nice shiny coin.

To be a store of value, money must be stable. It must retain a constant value over time. It must be difficult to counterfeit. It must be relatively scarce. After all, if it's ubiquitous, it will not have much value.

Finally, its best use should be as money. There should be no higher use for it than for money. If there were, it would not retain its store of value. Its value would increase to be used for that higher purpose. I used to think that sound money should be valuable in many ways but I was wrong. It only needs to be valuable in one way. No, it can only be most valuable in one way and that is for money. While gold is used for other purposes such as dentistry, electronics, and jewelry, other substances can be substituted for those purposes. Gold's best use is as money. To put it another way, there is no other asset that has superior properties for use as money than gold.

Sound money must be a **Unit of Account.**

It must be divisible without destroying its value. When you split a gold coin, each half retains its value. A dollar bill does not. Each half is not now worth fifty cents. Each half is now worthless. You can't divide the Mona Lisa either. The sum of the halves would not equal the sum of the whole.

It must be fungible (One unit is equivalent to another) and consistent (diamonds have different grades so they don't make good money). 24kt gold is 24kt gold is 24kt gold. It is homogenous. Dollars do actually meet this requirement.

We must be able to weigh or otherwise measure a unit. Some standard needs to be in place to, in some way, measure a unit of money. Sure, one hundred pennies equal a dollar but what is the measure of a dollar? We can weigh an ounce of gold and divide it into one hundred equal parts and know what we have. Pennies are even made of a different substance than a dollar. It's like comparing apples to oranges. They have a relationship but are not of the same stuff.

Just as an inch is a known length, and a gallon is a known volume, and a pound is a known weight, money needs to have a reference point to what its value is. That value needs to be fixed and unchanging. If it takes more dollars to purchase the exact same good over time, and the abundance, demand, or availability of the good has not changed, then it's the monetary unit which has. If something costs more than it used to, it is not necessarily more valuable. It still has the same utility or usefulness. Chances are that it's the monetary unit that has lost value and you now need more of them to procure that item. Money should not be an elastic unit that expands or contracts. It needs to be fixed. It's the only way that consumers can make correct and proper economic decisions.

Money must be **Anonymous.**

Money must not be subject to tracking or confiscation. After all, it is yours. You worked very hard for it. Why should anyone else know what you have or how you spend it? If it can be tracked it can be stolen or confiscated (That's redundant. Confiscation is stealing.). It should not require equipment, machines, or electricity to use. You need these to get dollars from an ATM. It should not have an image, seal, or mark to have value. By simply placing a mark on something does not increase its value. If I get an ink stamp that has a picture of a diamond and stamp a rock in my yard it does not increase the value of that rock just because it has a diamond mark on it. It is not a diamond. If I write my name on an object it doesn't make it mine. Why should it be any different with paper 'money'?. Why should a one dollar bill and a one hundred dollar bill have such different values just because of the number of zeros stamped upon them? It makes no sense. By having anonymity, it increases the honesty of the system. No one can manipulate the system at will. Yeah, it's good if you have the monopoly over the money but bad if you don't. The system we have today is dishonest and unfair.

There must be **No Third Party Risk** between you and your money.

It should be unencumbered. You should not have to depend on others either to get at your money or for the safety of your money. If you are using an ATM, a bank, a broker, or a credit card, there is a third party in the transaction and that party could fail in some way. There need only be two parties to any economic exchange: the two involved. ATM cards fail. Banks fail. People lie, cheat, and mislead. They do what is in their own selfish best interest. Why trust another person or corporation to perform in your best interest? They won't – especially when you most need them too. You can take that to the bank.

Now, does the current rendition of the dollar meet all of these criteria? The only one that it fully meets is that of Medium of Exchange. It is not a Store of Value, nor a Unit of Account, nor is it Anonymous, and yes, there is considerable third-party risk involved in holding dollars. Gold meets all of these requirements for use as Sound Money.

What is Money and Why is Gold so Important?

"Money is anything that is generally accepted as payment for goods and services and repayment of debts. The main uses of money are as a medium of exchange, a unit of account, and a store of value."
Wikipedia
Money, simply, is used as a measuring stick that enables people to communicate value.
Here's the definition of a currency.
"A currency is a unit of exchange, facilitating the transfer of goods and/or services. It is coins and paper bills used as money. It is one form of money, where money is anything that serves as a medium of exchange, a store of value, and a standard of value. Currencies are the dominant medium of exchange. Coins and paper money are both forms of currency." *Wikipedia*

Paper money, coins, checks and credit cards are several common types of currency but are not necessarily money. While both money and currency are used as a means of payment or exchange, there are subtle differences. Money retains its value. Currency may not, and normally does not. Money is stored wealth. Currency transfers wealth. Money can be used as currency but currency is not money unless it retains value over time. In that, I disagree with Wikipedia that a currency is a store of value. It may be, but only for a very short period of time. A gold or silver coin is money because it retains its value over time whereas paper money does not. An old silver dime is worth about a dollar today. A dollar will not purchase the same amount of goods it did ten years ago, one year ago, or even yesterday. Gold is so important to a monetary system because it retains its value over time. Today's dollar is currency, not money. It is used as a medium of exchange and nothing more. (ok, it is a means of confiscation too as Mr. Greenspan wrote) One should not save or hold wealth in dollars as they are guaranteed to lose in the end. Tangible items hold value through time and are measuring devices of relative value. Though many items have been tried, throughout recorded history only 2 items have continually and consistently been chosen by the free market as money: Gold and Silver. That is such an important fact that it was seen fit to include mention of it in the U.S. Constitution.

The United States has gone from a Silver Standard, to a Bi-metallic (Silver and Gold) Standard, then to a Gold Standard, and now a 'Floating Currency' Standard.

What is a Gold Standard?

'A monetary system in which a country's government allows its currency unit to be freely converted into fixed amounts of gold and vice versa. The exchange rate under the gold standard monetary system is determined by the economic difference for an ounce of gold between two currencies.' *Investopedia*

The U.S. was on a Silver Standard for over 100 years with no inflation and moderate deflation during that time period. A metal standard means price stability.

I can hear some saying 'I can just take my dollars and buy metal. What's the big deal?'

Here's the big deal.

Gold and silver are now demonetized and not legal tender except for gold and silver eagles and those have dollar values assigned to them. This is wrong. Unless the dollar is defined in weight of metal, a value cannot be assigned. Gold clauses in contracts have been deemed unenforceable by the courts. Dollars are not directly exchangeable for metal at a fixed price. The dollar price of gold is a moving scale and it moves continuously. You cannot go to your local Federal Reserve Bank branch and exchange your notes for metal at the gold window. Silver and gold certificates are no longer redeemable for metal. There are now premiums to make the conversion from currency to metal or vice versa. Money should not have a premium associated with it. It should be worth its face value.

Now, what happens if (when) the dollar is devalued? What happens when no amount of dollars will buy any amount of metal? What happens when all metal disappears from the market and you can't get any? How do you save? Your dollars will be worthless but not the metal.

What we use as money in the United States today is not Historically, Ethically, or Constitutionally Money.

Have Federal Reserve Notes been used as money historically?

Not in the U.S. until 1913 nor anywhere else in the world.

Is it ethically money?

Stealing is not and ethical act. Inflating the money supply is unethical.

Are we using constitutionally mandated money?

The Constitution has not been amended nor repealed concerning money. It mandates that our money be metal.

We'll explore what Federal Reserve Notes are and what the Constitution has to say in later chapters. But first let's look at what gold is good for and the characteristics of sound money.

What is a Dollar?

"The dollar is the unit of currency of the United States." Wikipedia

That sounds fair enough. That's what we've all been told. It seems logical. After all, we call those slips of linen, dollars, and use them every day. Again, notice the reference to currency, not money. Let's see what the U.S. Law has to say.

Section 9 of The Coinage Act of 1792 (which has not been repealed and is still in effect) defines a dollar as 371.25 grains of pure silver and gold in terms of silver at a 15:1 exchange ratio. Thus, $1 also equals 24.75 grains of pure gold and it takes $19.4 to equal 1 ounce of gold. (Hmmm. Gold just passed $1200 as I write this).

The dollar is supposed to be an **unchanging** unit of measure like a 'foot', a 'pound' or a 'gallon'. In this case a dollar is defined in grains. There are 480 grains in an ounce. The dollar is meant to be a **Unit of Account.**

Our current 'dollar' is, by definition, not a dollar. Actually, it is properly named a Federal Reserve Note which is what it actually is. The greenback is erroneously called a dollar when, in fact, it is not. Nowhere does the constitution or the Coinage Act of 1792 provide for paper or electronic currency or money.

In the Constitution, Article I, Section 10, Clause 1 states 'No State shall...coin money; emit bills of credit; make any thing but gold and silver coin a tender in payment of debt.'

So, nothing but silver and gold coin is legal tender in the United States. Furthermore, those functions not explicitly given to the Federal Government are reserved for the states. The Constitution does not give the Federal Government power to print paper currency and no state shall coin other than gold and silver. Therefore, a Federal Reserve Note is an illegal bill of credit.

Article I, Section 8, Clause 5 of the U.S. Constitution also states:

'The Congress shall have power... to coin money, regulate the value thereof, and of foreign coin, and fix the standard of weights and measures.'

How are we to fix the standard of weights and measures? As defined in the Coinage Act via a bi-metallic standard. A portion of gold is to be worth fifteen portions of silver and a portion of silver is to be worth one fifteenth a portion of gold. Congress was given power to **coin money**, not print currency.

Section 19 of the Coinage Act of 1792 provides, "That if any of the gold or silver coins which shall be struck or coined at the said mint shall be debased or made worse as to the proportion of fine gold or fine silver therein contained, or shall be of less weight or value than the same ought to be pursuant to the directions of this act, through the default or with the connivance of any of the officers or persons who shall be employed at the said mint, for the purpose of profit or gain, or otherwise with a fraudulent intent, and if any of the said officers or persons shall embezzle any of the metals which shall at any time be committed to their charge for the purpose of being coined, or any of the coins which shall be struck or coined at the said mint, every such officer or person who shall commit any or either of the said offences, shall be deemed guilty of felony, and shall suffer death."

Wow. The founding fathers must have felt very strongly about the error of currency debasement to provide for such a penalty. Even our fractional silver coins were debased in 1965. I don't believe anyone suffered the penalty above for the offense.

What is Fiat Money?

Fiat Money: Currency that a government has declared to be legal tender, despite the fact that it has no intrinsic value and is not backed by reserves. Historically, most currencies were based on physical commodities such as gold or silver, but fiat money is based solely on faith. Investopedia

Yup. That sums it nicely. The government declares by dictate or fiat what will be money. The people and the market have no say so. That's pure coercion. What happened to our supposed free market? I like the last part of the definition about it being based solely on faith. You have faith that it will retain its value long enough to pass it on to another for a like amount of goods or services. You only accept this stuff in payment because you believe there will be a demand for it from someone else. It's not the actual pieces of paper you want but the perceived purchasing power.

What is a Federal Reserve Note?

The cotton/linen 'paper' greenbacks in your wallet or purse are Federal Reserve Notes. It's printed right on top; front and center. There is also the word dollar at the bottom. As I explained in the preceding section – What is a Dollar? – this is misinformation. They are not truly dollars even though that's what we commonly refer to them as.

The U.S. Federal Reserve Note (dollar), as well as all world currencies, are not backed by any tangible good and not by gold. Until only a few years ago, the Swiss Franc was 40% backed by gold. At its inception, the Euro was 15% backed by gold. Since the Europeans have been selling off their gold since the Euro was created, and have continued to expand the supply of Euros, they are backed considerably less than 15% today.

There are two points I'd like to make. First, unless currencies are 100% backed by gold, they only retain a fraction of their supposed value. If a currency is only 20% backed by gold, then the currency is five times overvalued. Second, the backing of a currency and the convertibility of a currency are two separate things. Unless one can fully convert one's currency into gold on demand, the backing is useless. Ultimately, even conversion can be stopped, as it was internally in the U.S. in 1933, and externally to our foreign creditors in 1971.   By far the best alternative is to make your currency out of specie (gold or silver). Then no conversion or convertibility needs to be performed at all. It is what it's supposed to be already.

Until 1945, the Federal Reserve was required to hold Gold Reserves equal to 40% of its outstanding notes. This is no longer true.

The Federal Reserve Note is not backed by gold nor anything else but the 'full faith and credit' of the US Government. In other words, it is backed by you, or your taxes, or the belief that the government can somehow make good its promises. It's all a CONfidence game.

There is no definition of what a FRN is! It's certainly not mentioned in the Constitution anywhere. Try to define it. I bet you can't. It's a note. A note is a debt obligation, not unlike a mortgage. It's an I.O.U. What's it payable in? Why, it's payable in more I.O.U.s. You can not redeem it for specie. Try going down to your local friendly neighborhood Federal Reserve office to get an ounce of gold for $19.40. They don't want their own I.O.U.'s back and don't have the gold to buy them all back at yesterday's price or today's.

Federal Reserve notes are created out of thin air. Literally. Only a small portion are actually printed. The vast majority come into existence via ledger entries in an electronic spreadsheet.

In an oversimplification of the process, the Treasury sells bonds to the Fed and the Fed in return creates 'money' which it sends over to the Government. Both the bonds and the money did not exist before. Both were simply conjured up. Both are now seen as assets. Neat trick.

In 2008 the Fed paid 4.7 cents to print a $1 bill, and 12.5 cents to print a $100 Federal Reserve Note. That is a 99.875% gross profit margin. Most businesses are satisfied with 10% profit margins.

As of 2010, the metal in a nickel is worth about $.07, and the copper in pre-1982 cents is worth 2.5x the penny. Pre-1965 dimes, quarters, and half dollars, which contain 90% silver, are going for about ten times their 'face' value.

Let's review the Fed's game, shall we. Let's see, they (1) create 'money' out of thin air. Then they (2) lend it to us and charge us for using it. (3) The more money they create and lend, the more profit they make, and (4) the less spending power we have as a result of their over issuance of the currency. In sum, they lend us our money and charge us for the 'privilege' of doing so. Niiiiicccceeee…

The Federal Reserve

The Federal Reserve is not part of the Federal Government, even though it has a .gov at the end of its Web address. It is no more Federal than FedEx. It is a for-profit privately owned bank. It's hard to find reliable information on who owns the Fed exactly, but it appears to be owned by both domestic and foreign large banks. Indirectly, foreign entities are somewhat in control of U.S. monetary policy.

Although there is some debate about which entity actually owns or controls U.S. gold, the Fed supposedly has no bullion reserves to back any of its notes. Its 'reserves' are dominated by 'toxic assets' that, if sold on the open market, would command much less than what the Fed is currently valuing them at. If they did, they'd be shown to be insolvent.

The Fed is not accountable for its actions. That's a bold statement but true nonetheless. Yes, the Chairman goes before the Banking and Finance Committee a couple of times a year and politely does his horse and pony show for all to see. It's also true that the U.S. President picks the Chairman and the Congress confirms. However, the Federal Reserve does not receive congressional oversight. It does not make its books public. It has not been audited in over 50 years.

HR 1207, introduced by Dr. Ron Paul (R-Texas) with over 300 co-sponsors, would require an audit of the Federal Reserve. The bill is only 446 Words. The Senate is considering an identical bill, S 604 "Federal Reserve Sunshine Act of 2009". It has over 30 co-sponsors.

The Fed is an entity unto itself. It is accountable to no one and seeks permission from no one.

Dec. 12, 2008 (Bloomberg) – 'The Federal Reserve refused a request by Bloomberg News to disclose the recipients of more than $2 trillion of emergency loans from U.S. taxpayers and the assets the central bank is accepting as collateral.'

Bloomberg filed suit Nov. 7, 2008 under the U.S. Freedom of Information Act requesting details about the terms of 11 Fed lending programs. (i.e. which banks received bailout money).

On August 24, 2009, the judge ruled that the F.R. must make this info public by August 31.

On August 26 the F.R. asked the judge not to enforce the ruling until it can appeal.

On August 31 the judge gives the Fed till Sept. 30 to appeal.

On September 9, Fox News appealed the ruling above.

On March, 2010, Bloomberg won the appeal. The Fed vows to go to Supreme Court.

On and on it goes. They fight tooth and nail to hide their books. Nobody but them knows what it is that they really do. They are accountable to no one.

One of the Fed's mandates is to keep 'stable prices' (Low 'Inflation'). Since the founding of the Fed in 1913, by their own calculation, the dollar has lost more than 95% of its purchasing power. This is equivalent to a more-than 20-fold increase in inflation since then. Gasoline and milk have gone from 20 cents to $4 a gallon. A Coke has gone from a nickel to a dollar. Cars have gone from a thousand dollars to twenty thousand. Houses increased in price from five grand to one hundred grand. There are countless examples. The Fed has failed miserably in this mandate.

"...the Fed is not there to fight inflation or encourage full employment or any of the other laudable reasons given for its existence. The true and unmentioned reason is that the Fed has one mission. It is to make sure that the federal government obtains all the dollars it wants to spend." James Turk, commentator and founder of Goldmoney.com

This is *your* Central Bank folks.

Where do Dollars (Federal Reserve Notes) come from?

They are created out of thin air or simply printed as needed. Literally. No kidding.   Ever wonder where that TARP money for the banks came from in 2008? Ever wonder where the trillions of dollars come from to fund two simultaneous wars? They aren't tax dollars.
This is a gross oversimplification of the process but this is how new dollars come into existence for the most part. The Treasury sells bonds to the Federal Reserve and the Fed in return creates 'money' (that didn't exist before) which it sends over to the Government. It's all balance sheet accounting of course. Nothing physical actually changes hands. The Fed counts the bonds as assets on its books and the Government spends the money into the economy. That's it. The only thing stopping them from creating more is fear of rampant inflation of the money supply and facing the wrath of the people.

In 2008 the Fed paid 4.7 cents to print a $1 bill, and 12.5 cents to print a $100 Federal Reserve Note. That's a 99.875% gross profit margin. Most companies are satisfied with a 10-15% profit. I guarantee you it costs a lot more than 12.5 cents to mine $100 worth of gold. Most gold miners have been marginally profitable for decades and some have not been at all.

In 2010 the metal in a nickel is worth about $.07 and the copper in a pre-1982 penny is worth 2.5 times its face value.

Here's how the game is played.

They create 'money' out of thin air.

They lend it to us and charge us for using it.

The more money they create and lend, the more money they make in interest and the less spending power we have. Each dollar created dilutes the value of each existing dollar.

So, they lend us our money and charge us for the 'privilege' of doing so.

The Dollar's Relationship to Gold

The dollar and gold have historically been inversely correlated with a coefficient of correlation of something like .9 (point 9). This means that changes in one are reflected inversely in the other 90% of the time. Gold is the anti-dollar. When the dollar is up gold will most likely be down and vice versa. They tend to be mirror images of each other. However, that's been breaking down recently and gold is rising in all currencies as they float against each other and all sink in unison against gold. It is gold that is stable and the dollar that is changing.

Basically, U.S. debt monetization = dollar devaluation = higher gold prices.

Compare ounces of gold to barrels of oil or ounces of silver to gallons of gasoline and see that they are relatively fixed constants over time. The dollar is what's changing, not commodities.

Let's do the math.

In 1930, a $100 bill and 4.84 ounces of gold (at $20.67/oz.) were of the same value. They were indeed interchangeable as the currency was redeemable in gold.

In 2010, all that remains of the 1930 $100 bill is $8 of purchasing power per the official CPI. A 92% devaluation of the currency has taken place in the last 80 years.

4.84 ounces of gold are worth $6,050 at $1250/oz.

6050 : 8 is a difference of 756x.

Would you rather have that old $100 bill and 756 times less purchasing power or the one ounce of gold and 756 times more purchasing power?

$6,042 was stolen via inflation (money printing).

What Gives Money Value?

The value of money is derived from its strict limitation of supply. It's the old supply and demand equation. The more of something there is, the less valuable it is. The less of something there is, the more valuable it is. If there were only 100 dollars in the entire economy, each would have great purchasing power and awesome value.

The supply of gold is limited by nature. The supply of fiat money is limited by the tolerance of the people to put up with inflation of the money supply and rising prices.

Our dollars are no longer backed by gold. No other world currency is backed by gold, or anything else for that matter. It's all a confidence game or 'CON' Game. We have confidence that we can exchange our dollars for goods or services. Once we stop believing that others will accept them as payment, they become worthless. The confidence in the system is gone.

All currencies 'float' (or sink) against each other. They have the appearance of stability when viewed in opposition to each other. Think of two dissimilar objects being dropped from a tall building at the same time. One may have greater air resistance and fall slower. One may be pushed up or down by a gust of wind. However, both will fall to the ground eventually. Viewed from one of the objects, the other appears relatively stable or unmoving (like cars on a highway). But compare them to gold and that perception is lost. Gold sits separate and watches both fall (in value). This can be seen by the rise in the price of gold in all currencies.

And the price of gold has been rising in all world currencies. This is another way of saying that all currencies are being devalued against gold. It isn't gold that's changing, it's the currencies. Gold just is. It's element number 79 on the Periodic Table of elements. Gold is unchanging. Gold coins taken from Spanish Galleons sunk hundreds of years ago appear as new and are not degraded. Gold doesn't rust. If one should experience a house fire, paper money will burn. There is no restitution. Gold may melt but it retains the same value as before. It doesn't need to be pressed into pretty images or have fancy designs to be valuable. It has value just for what it is.

Currency Heaven

All currencies eventually attain their intrinsic value. In other words, they reach the value of what they are made of. There are hundreds of examples. The French Assignat (1790), U.S. Continentals during the Revolutionary War (Not worth a Continental), Confederate Scrip of the U.S. Civil War, the German Reichsmark (1923), and the Zimbabwe Dollar in the last couple of years are notable examples of currencies which lost all value. Zimbabwe's inflation rate reached 79,600,000,000% percent in Nov. 2008. History records some 3800 paper currencies have come and gone thus far.

The average age of all currencies in circulation today is 39 years. The U.S. Dollar is 218 years old. It's the third oldest currency in continuous use behind the Scottish Pound and the English Pound. The optimist would say, 'we beat the odds' or 'the dollar's been around so long, it will never fail'. The pessimist will see the glass as half empty and say, 'the dollar is way past its expiration date'. So who's correct? The reality is that the 'dollar', in name only, has been around for 218 years. But the dollar of two hundred years ago and the dollar of today couldn't be more different. They are not the same thing at all! The dollar of old was not only backed by, and redeemable in, gold and silver, it **was made of** gold and silver. Today's dollar has not been made of, redeemable for, or backed by gold or silver since at least 1971. 39 years ago! On August 15, 1971 President Nixon signed an Executive Order revoking the United States' promise to the world to exchange their excess dollars for gold as had been promised at Bretton Woods in 1944. In effect, the U.S. defaulted on its obligations (debt) at that time.

Chapter 4
Inflation

"In the absence of the gold standard, there is no way to protect savings from confiscation through inflation. There is no safe store of value."

Alan Greenspan

Monetary Inflation and its Effects

Monetary inflation causes rising prices just as rain causes wet sidewalks – not the other way round. Prices simply do not rise for no reason. They rise because additional money is added to the economy over and above that needed for normal expansion due to population or productivity gains. First comes monetary inflation (expansion) and then comes price inflation. If the monetary base is doubled, retail prices will, on average, double in due course, everything else being equal. Expanding the money supply does not increase productivity or the output of goods and services except in the very short term (i.e. the Cash 4 Clunkers program stealing sales from the future) or in targeted areas. Current estimates indicate we're getting $.80 of benefit for every dollar pushed into the economy. A negative benefit! Those who get the money first realize the greatest benefit as they can spend it at current value. Those who get it months or years later pay the inflation price.

Inflation is a hidden tax on every holder of dollars. The Federal Government gets to spend newly created money at its current value. Those 'dollars' have a lesser value once we earn and spend them. Thus, we need to earn more of them to maintain our standard of living. The Government gets the benefit and we pay the price (tax).

The historic record indicates that a surge in money growth has its peak effect on economic activity about 9 to 18 months later. Add another 12 months or so for the peak effect on consumer price inflation. *(Casey Research)*

Precious Metals are a near-ideal inflation hedge. *(Davidson, Faff and Hillier, 2003)*

Gold has the strongest correlation with inflation of any commodity, especially in periods of high inflation. From May 1978 to July 1982, during the last great inflation spike, the correlation ratio was a fairly strong 0.73. Since August 2007, the ratio has come even closer to its absolute maximum of 1, touching 0.85. *(Andrey Dashkov, Casey Research)*

What this means is that gold (and silver) can protect you from the ravages of inflation to a great extent.

The value of a Federal Reserve Note (dollar) is neither consistent nor stable. Here are some examples of how well it has held its purchasing power over almost a century. The prices were taken from the *Daily Record [Morristown NJ] in 1913.* At that time the paper cost one cent for the daily.

Boy's shoes for school, .98/pair

Women's shoes, 2.00-8.00/pair
Bread, .10/3 loaves

Butter, fancy, .30/lb
Cereal, Kellogg's Corn Flakes, .09/box

Eggs, Fresh Western, .27/dozen
Peanut butter, .09/jar

Toilet paper, .26/6 rolls

The CPI on January 1, 1914 was 10.0. The CPI on January 1, 2009 was 211.1. That's a 2111% increase in prices. In other words, prices have increased more than ten times in less than one hundred years by the U.S. Government's own calculations.

Silver holds its value just like gold.

In 1950 you could buy about 4 gallons of gasoline for one dollar: Silver dollar or paper dollar. At the time, they were interchangeable value-wise. An ounce of silver was valued at $1.29 and there were .77 ounces of silver in a silver dollar.

In 2010 a Silver Dollar will still buy you that same 4 gallons and get back change. A paper dollar will not. At $18 per ounce, that silver dollar is worth about 14.5 of today's dollars. You can get over five gallons of gas at $2.75 per gallon with a silver dollar. Silver not only held its value over that time but actually increased its purchasing power. This is why you hold precious metals for the long term.

Double Trouble

Picture a small tropical island. There is only one palm tree and only 5 coconuts. That's all there is. There is also only $5 available in the island economy for trade. That's it. Since the entire economy consists of only 5 coconuts, each one is worth one dollar. One day five additional dollars wash ashore. Instantly the economy doubles to ten dollars. But there are still only five coconuts. How much is each coconut now worth? Answer: $2. What happened is that the economy doubled but the productive capacity stayed the same. Even though prices doubled, the output of goods and services did not. Adding money to the economy does not necessarily increase production. What it will do is increase prices of goods and services over time.
Question: If, tomorrow, everyone had twice as many dollars, would we all be twice as wealthy?

Answer: No.

Prices would simply double to reflect the new reality. The value (purchasing power) of each dollar would now be halved. That's the Law of Supply and Demand. Prices go up because the value of the money goes down. Think of a dollar as one share of USA, Inc. Should the supply of money in the economy double but your share stay the same, your share would then be worth half of its former value. Nobody outright stole your money. You still have the same number of dollars. But they stole your purchasing power by diluting the value of the existing dollar supply. Half of your wealth was stolen.

This is what your government, in conjunction with the Federal Reserve, does over time. This dilution is what causes price inflation. The United States Monetary Base doubled in a few short weeks in late 2008. It has now (mid-2010) close to tripled since mid-2008. The monetary base consists of all currency in circulation (known as M0) plus reserve balances with the Federal Reserve banks. Much of this money has not yet entered circulation in the country, but if and when it does, expect prices to rise a corresponding amount within about 18 months. One way to protect yourself from this coming inflation is to purchase gold or silver bullion.

U.S. Government Liabilities

Depending on whose numbers you use, the United States Government has somewhere between $44 to over $100 trillion of unfunded obligations (Social Security, Medicare, Medicaid, Veterans Benefits, Civil Servant Pensions, etc.). That's more than all of the goods and services produced in all economies on the planet combined. Furthermore, the number is growing every day and is certain to increase as the Baby Boomer Generation ages. Sprott Asset Management calculates these liabilities to be some $118 trillion today. This number grows about $2 trillion per year currently.

The Gross Domestic Product (GDP) of all goods and services produced in the U.S. for an entire year is some $14 trillion. According to John Williams at Shadowstats.com, even if the government raised income taxes to 100%, these debts could not be paid down. Also, on a GAAP (Generally Accepted Accounting Principles) basis, the U.S. deficit was actually $5 trillion in 2008 and an estimated $8 trillion in 2009.

To help meet its funding needs, the U.S. takes in over $3 billion per day from other nations. The money is acquired in the form of U.S. Government Bond and Treasury sales. Some see a greater need. "According to our calculations, at least US$15 billion [of U.S. Gov. Bonds] may need to be issued every single business day until the end of the year." *Axel Merk, 6/16/09.*

The U.S. has borrowed 50% of the FY09 'budget'. The fact is they created the money through the creation and sale of U.S. Bonds and Treasuries. The profligate spending doesn't come from taxpayers. It is created to fill the need. The ones who get hurt the most are the holders of U.S. dollars and dollar denominated assets.

"The system is unstable and unsustainable." *(David Walker, former Comptroller of the Currency, OMB).* If anyone is in position to know what the real numbers are, it is the man who was the Comptroller of the Currency for the Office of Management and Budget for nearly a decade. Even the Commander in Chief admitted our national condition.

"We are out of money". *President Obama, May 2009.*

Here's more from some very reliable sources.

From 'GAAP Numbers' by
John Williams of Shadowstats.com:
"It's beyond control. The government does put out financial statements usually in December using generally accepted accounting principles, where unfunded liabilities like Medicare and Social Security are included in the same way as corporations account for their employee pension liabilities. And in 2008, for example, the one-year deficit was $5.1 trillion dollars. And that's instead of the $450 billion, plus or minus, that was officially reported."

"These numbers are beyond containment. Even the 2008 numbers, you can take 100 percent of people's income and corporate profit and you'd still be in deficit. There's no way you can raise enough money in taxes."

From the Congressional Budget Office's
The Long-Term Budget Outlook Report June 2009:
"Lenders may become concerned about the financial solvency of the government… and demand higher interest rates…"
"Both foreign and domestic lenders may not provide enough funds for the government to meet its obligations."
[This will lead to] "… causing the exchange value of the dollar to plunge, interest rates to climb, and consumer prices to shoot up."

From The Financial Times, July 2009:

"Neil Barofsky, special inspector-general for the troubled asset relief programme, [TARP] said that the various US schemes to shore up banks and restart lending exposed federal agencies to a risk of $23,700bn [$23.7 trillion]."

Bloomberg estimates the number to be $24 Trillion
http://www.bloomberg.com/apps/news?pid=20601087&sid=aY0tX8Uysl aM

The Greenspan-Guidotti Rule

The following was taken from an article by Porter Stansberry as published at
http://www.kitco.com/ind/stansberry/dec022009.html
"Alan Greenspan and Pablo Guidotti published the secret formula in a 1999 academic paper. The formula is called the Greenspan-Guidotti rule.
The rule states: To avoid a default, countries should maintain hard currency reserves equal to at least 100% of their short-term foreign debt maturities.
The principle behind the rule is simple. If you can't pay off all of your foreign debts in the next 12 months, you're a terrible credit risk.
Speculators are going to target your bonds and your currency, making it impossible to refinance your debts. A default is assured.
So how does America rank on the Greenspan-Guidotti scale?
It's a guaranteed default.
The U.S. holds gold, oil, and foreign currency in reserve. So altogether... that's around $500 billion of reserves. Our short-term foreign debts are far bigger.
According to the U.S. Treasury, $2 trillion worth of debt will mature in the next 12 months."

What all of this means is that 1) The United States is in debt more than it can ever hope to pay, and 2) It will be unable to resort to foreign buying of its debt at some point in the not-too-distant future, and 3) It will have to print the money necessary to pay the interest on its bills which 4) will lead to much greater inflation going forward. Gold and Silver can help protect you from these problems by retaining their purchasing power in an inflationary environment.

The Road to Ruin: Historic Inflations

Currency hyperinflations happen all the time. Usually it happens in a relatively small, obscure country and we either don't hear about it or it's on the news one time and that's it. It's far away and doesn't affect us so we forget about it. But they really do happen all the time. Here's a partial list of recent hyperinflationary events.

- Angola 1991 to 1995
- Austria 1921 and 1922
- Belarus 1994 to 2002
- Bolivia 1984 and 1986
- Bosnia-Herzegovina 1993
- Brazil 1986 to 1994
- Chile 1971 – 1973
- China 1948-1949
- Free City of Danzig 1923
- Georgia 1994
- Germany 1919-1923
- Greece 1944-1946
- Hungary 1945 -1946
- Israel 1971 - 1984
- Japan 1943-1951
- Madagascar 2004
- Mozambique 1975
- Nicaragua 1987 -1990
- Peru 1988 -1990
- Philippines during WWII
- Poland 1989 -1991
- Russian Federation 1921 - 1922; 1992 - 1994
- Turkey 1990's
- Ukraine 1993 -1995
- Yugoslavia 1989 - 1994
- Zaire (now Congo) 1989 - 1996
- Zimbabwe 2008

Some of these countries are large, modern nations like ours, not just small backwaters.

Don't make the mistake of thinking it can't happen here. It happened during the Revolutionary War and on both sides during the Civil War. It almost happened again in the 1970s and we're on that path again, only with greater imbalances this time.

The classic case of hyperinflation often referred to is that of the German Weimar Republic which reigned between the two world wars. It culminated in late 1923 when the devaluation of the German Mark went exponential. The problem was solved by the introduction of the Rentenmark which was just a new Mark with some zeros erased but it did stop the hyperinflation. During this German hyperinflation, the German stock market went up some 50 million times. That sounds like a lot but it did not keep pace with the devaluation. What did keep pace was gold which went up some 100 billion times, or about 2000 times more.

The Zimbabwe instance was much the same as the German one. In 1980, it took Z$1.47 to buy one US$. In 2008, it took Z$100,000,000,000,000 to buy one US$. During this inflation, prices in $Z increased some 231,000,000%.
During that same time, how much did gold increase? 100,000,000,000% (Source: Jim Puplava, FinancialSense.com)
That is, gold did 433x better than inflation. So, not only did gold hold its value, it actually increased faster than the rate of inflation, though I doubt that you could have found anyone willing to exchange their gold for Zimbabwe Dollars at that time.

There have also been a number of more recent currency devaluations. Devaluing a currency is just another way of inflating. Instead of issuing more currency which decreases the value of all existing currency in circulation, the existing currency is devalued by government edict all at once, which allows for more currency to be added to the money supply. It's just the flip side or mirror image of money printing and has the same effect.

- In 2008 the Icelandic Krona fell more than 50% in a matter of weeks against the U.S. Dollar and 70% against the Euro.

- On February 5, 2009, the Kazakhstan Tenge lost 11% of its value in 2 days against gold.

- On March 4, 2009, the Armenian Dram devalued by 30%.

- On April 15, 2009, the Fiji Dollar devalued 20%.

- On November 26, 2009, the Vietnamese Dong devalued 5%. It lost 50% against gold from the beginning of 2009 till then.

- On December 1, 2009, the North Korean currency was devalued by the government by 99%. In other words, it would take one hundred times more to purchase the same good or service on December 1 than it did on November 30.

- On January 8, 2010, the Venezuelan Bolivar was devalued by the government by 50%.

All it takes is a government proclamation for a person to lose their entire life savings if it is denominated in the local currency.

Often, an economy will experience a bout of deflation before the ensuing hyperinflation kicks in. This happened in Weimar Germany. Many think that we are currently in this calm before the storm.
"The ongoing decline in the purchasing power of the dollar has been masked by wealth destruction as over-priced assets like houses fall back to realistic levels." JamesTurk
Prices of goods and services are rising, but as it warns, the quantity of dollars in circulation is "shrinking, after taking into account inflation." James Turk quoting the Globe & Mail
"When prices are going up faster than the money supply, the people begin to experience a severe shortage of money, for they now face a shortage of cash balances relative to the much higher price levels. Total cash balances are no longer sufficient to carry transactions at the higher price." Murray Rothbard
"The Federal Reserve must 'print'...– to make sure the federal government gets all the dollars it wants to spend, which consequently has put the dollar on a hyperinflationary course." James Turk again

In his weekly broadcast from December 11, 2009, Jim Puplava (Financialsense.com) provided us with his four signs of an impending hyperinflation. They are:
- Negative Real Interest Rates
- Profligate Money Printing
- Commercial Price Inflation
- Un-Repayable Budget Deficits

We now have all four of these conditions in place.
What a hyperinflation actually is, is a currency collapse. I've come up with a number of warning signs of an imminent currency collapse.
- A strong increase in interest rates or Treasury yields.
- A failed Treasury auction or foreigners start dumping their U.S. Bonds or Treasuries.
- A U.S. debt rating downgrade. (anything less than AAA)
- A major nation(s) no longer accepts dollars for goods.
- A bank 'holiday'.
- Currency controls.
- A major bank nationalization.

- Gold or oil experience a price spike.
- Consumer shortages. Look to groceries first.
- A large scale terror attack or massive natural disaster.
- Don't look to the DOW. It will hyper inflate as the currency collapses just like in Germany and Zimbabwe.

Of these, we have seen foreigners shy away from U.S. debt purchases and begin modest selling. There are some currency controls being implemented, such as exorbitant taxes for moving money abroad. Consumer prices have been escalating lately. Wal-mart raised its prices an average of 6% in one month in the summer of 2010. The rest we have not seen yet but nobody will tell you when a bank nationalization, debt downgrade, or terror attack is going to occur. It will happen overnight or suddenly when few are paying attention. Those events, especially two or more in a short time span, may well set off the collapse.

Gold in Times of Deflation

Gold has a split personality. It performs best during both inflations and deflations. In short, these are times of uncertainty. It performs worst during 'dis-inflations'. By dis-inflation I mean times of modest inflation of 1-5% such as we had for most of the 1980s and 1990s. During that time gold and silver went mostly down in dollar denominated price. The 1970s and 2000s have been times of inflation. Officially reported (U.S. Government statistics) inflation topped out at over 14% in the late 1970s. As recently as 2008, Shadowstats.com (which calculates inflation the same way the government did in the 70s) was reporting inflation of over 13%, though officially, inflation never got as high as 6%. These two decades saw a generally rising gold price. In the 1930s, the velocity of money in circulation declined by 30% even though the government was spending money and running deficits to pay for its works programs. The 1930s are widely recognized as a time of deflation. You could purchase more at the end of the decade with your dollars than you could at the beginning. This is the definition of deflation. The 1930s saw gold rise from $20.67 an ounce to $35. It was revalued by government dictate but still linked to the dollar. Both dollars and gold were relatively scarce (people were hoarding and not spending due to uncertainty) and thus, purchased more.
Here is a key piece of information to remember.

Gold rises faster in price than dollar denominated assets in times of inflation and falls slower in price than dollar denominated assets in times of deflation.

Gold could conceivably fall (in $ price) in a deflationary depression but still purchase more goods or services. In a deflation, if gold fell in dollar terms, the price of goods and services would likely fall at a swifter rate. Thus, your gold would still purchase more even though its price fell. Think of it this way. Let's say that your ounce of gold at $1000 would purchase 50 restaurant meals of $20 each today. Let's say gold falls to $700. The meals will likely fall faster. They may cost $10 when gold is at $700 which would give you 70 meals. You would have more value for your money. You'd be 40% ahead. Don't think it could happen? The period from mid-2008 to mid-2009 was widely touted by the government and in the mainstream media as a deflationary period. Gold fell from about $1000 to about $700. The DOW fell from over 14,000 to under 7000. Even with the diminished price of gold, your ounce would have fetched a greater share of the DOW. You could have purchased 40% more shares.

This duality of gold has been confirmed in a famous study of the issue titled *The Golden Constant (Jastram, 1977).*

It was also recognized by respected gold pundit Aubie Baltin' who, in 2009, wrote: "…as far as investors in Gold are concerned, they need not worry about INFLATION OR DEFLATION since Gold does well in either an INFLATIONARY or DEFLATIONARY environment."

Unlike other products or commodities, precious metals are in greater demand as the price rises. Increases in demand are for reasons of both greed and fear. Greed because of wanting to get in on a sure thing that's rising in price, and fear of not wanting to miss out, fear of not being able to get any at any price, and fear because of the general economic turmoil and uncertainty. Fear is by far the greater motivator. This cycle of greed and fear will create a positive feedback loop once it gets going. The higher the price rises, the more people will want in. The more people who get in, the more the price will rise until we get to the final parabolic blow-off phase.

In any environment, precious metals never lose their value or go to zero in any currency. They have never and they can never. They have inherent, intrinsic value.

Chapter 5
It's Our Dollar but Your Problem

[The dollar] "is our currency, but your problem." John Connally,
Treasury Secretary under Nixon, speaking to a European delegation.

Bretton Woods and the World Reserve Currency

In 1944, in the waning days of WWII, the major Allied Powers met at
Bretton Woods, New Hampshire to hash out a post-war economic
arrangement. What came from the Bretton Woods Agreement was that
the U.S. Dollar would become the World Reserve Currency, usurping
that role from the British Pound. What this meant was that most
commerce worldwide would be conducted in dollars and those dollars
later sent back to the U.S. in exchange for a pre-determined amount of
gold (if in excess of what was needed to be bought from the U.S). This
also meant that should, say, Japan want to purchase oil from Saudi
Arabia, the means of settlement would not be Yen or Riyals or gold, but
Dollars. Those dollars had to first be earned by selling something of
value to the United States in return for those dollars. In effect, free
goods to the United States for promises of redemption later on.
Imagine an American firm making a purchase from a Canadian firm and
settling in Russian Rubles to get an idea of how others see it. Since the
U.S. then held about three quarters of all the gold bullion in existence,
the system could proceed. Charles DeGaul later called the role of the
Dollar as reserve currency and 'exorbitant privilege'. He was correct.
The Bretton Woods system more or less worked and was functioning
until August 15, 1971 when President Nixon closed the 'gold window' of
dollar redemption. During the preceding 27 years, about two thirds of
U.S. gold was sent overseas in settlement of dollar claims. The system
had to end. It was unsustainable. There were still outstanding dollars
promises in foreign hands when Nixon reneged on the Bretton Woods
Agreement it had entered into. What really happened was that the U.S.
defaulted on its commitments to pay its creditors.
Since that time, there has been an unprecedented increase in the
amount of currency of all national flavors in use globally.

Politicians and Economists call it a 'floating' currency system where one currency floats against another or a basket of others on the currency exchange markets. In reality they are all sinking (in value) at varying rates. Imagine two vehicles travelling side-by-side down a hill at nearly the same speed. In relation to each other they are nearly static. But they are both moving down the hill at great speed and will eventually make ti to the bottom. Perhaps a better analogy is of two objects being dropped from a skyscraper. Depending on their weight, shape, initial velocity, or size, they will fall at different velocities. Perhaps a gust of wind will levitate or even raise one or both momentarily. But in the end they will both reach the ground. All fiat currencies fall to zero eventually. The average life expectancy of any given currency, historically, has been 39 years. An optimist will say that the dollar has been around for over 200 years, therefore, it is unlikely to fail. A pessimist will say that it's long overdue.

In reality, the dollar has already failed. It failed in 1971. That was 39 years ago as of this writing in 2010. And before that it faltered as an internal currency 38 years before that when President Roosevelt stopped dollar redemption for gold by citizens in 1933. We kept the name of the dollar and the look of the paper dollar bill. That's all. The pre and post 1971 dollars actually have nothing in common. One was backed and redeemable in gold. In effect, it was then (almost) as good as gold. The dollar of today is backed by what? 'The full faith and credit of the United States'. What does that mean? Do you have faith in government to always do the right thing? If so, how did we get into this mess in the first place if they always do the right thing? Will foreign governments keep extending our credit by buying our bonds to support the dollar? They've already bought all that they could. Our credit is no good as a nation. There is nothing backing the U.S. 'dollar'.

If Everyone is Against Us, then Who is With Us?

The U.S. dollar is finally being recognized for what it is: A promise of payment by the U.S. Government. That's all it is. It's not actual payment for goods and services. It's not a settlement. It's an IOU. Until 1971 the world settled debts internationally in gold, but that is no longer the case. Now we settle in currencies, which is to say we don't settle at all. Each country keeps other countries currencies on its books as reserves. Heck, they're just ledger entries. China sends us goods for dollars. Japan sends us autos for dollars. OPEC sends us oil for dollars. Dollars are hot potatoes that have to be passed along before the holder gets burned. While many have always known this, they were in the minority and could not or would not do anything about it. But now the U.S. isn't the dominant force it once was. Its share of global commerce and importance on the world stage is on the decline. Other world powers do not want to play by the dollar exchange standard any longer. They want change and change is in the wind.

For example, Iran began trading its oil in currencies other than the dollar in 2009. Iraq did the same thing the year before it was invaded. Iran also announced in October of 2009 that they were switching their reserves out of dollars and into euros. The Gulf Co-operation Council (GCC) has been discussing a monetary union pact for a number of years and a common currency called the *Kaleeji* (Gulf in Arabic). Likewise, the Union of South American Nations are doing the same with their *Sucre* currency. Many nations are by-passing the U.S. dollar and setting up bi-lateral trade agreements or doing currency swaps with each other. This direct trade in their own currencies allows them to bypass use of the U.S. dollar, thus suppressing demand for dollars, thus suppressing the market for U.S. bonds. Good for them. Not good for the U.S. The bond market is what allows the United States and its people to live beyond its means and/or receive products from other nations in return for pieces of paper or electronic digits on a ledger. Partially because of this lack of demand for U.S. debt, as well as a lack of restraint in spending by the U.S., the major rating agencies are sending out warnings of a possible U.S. credit worthiness downgrade. In January of 2010 Fitch sent out an alert regarding the U.S. AAA credit rating. They haven't downgraded yet, and have not threatened to do so, but they wouldn't be sending out an alert (where there's smoke...) if there wasn't a strong possibility that they would do so sometime in the future (...there's fire). Also in January of 2010, Moody's Lead Analyst, Steven Hess, said "The AAA rating of the U.S. is not guaranteed." Again, why make a statement like that if you don't foresee a strong possibility of a downgrade coming. Foreshadowing anyone?

Russia has openly called for the return to an international gold standard. It wants to have up to 10% of reserves backed by gold. China has called for a basket of currencies - to include gold and SDRs Special Drawing Rights) - to replace U.S. Dollar as the world reserve currency. On June 16, 2009, the BRIC nations (Brazil, Russia, India, and China) held a meeting in Russia. The U.S. was not invited and was denied its request for observer status. A joint statement from the meeting read in part: "The emerging and developing economies must have a greater voice and representation in international financial institutions...." and "We also believe that there is a strong need for a stable, predictable and more diversified international [financial] system." This is a direct attack on the U.S. dominated dollar system and the U.S. controlled International Monetary Fund and World Bank. All four countries are buying IMF bonds in exchange for SDRs. This is a way to diversify out of U.S. Dollars.

Then there are the supra-national organizations. The Bank for International Settlement (BIS), which is the central bank for the Central Banks, based in Basel, Switzerland, has called for a replacement of the dollar as world reserve currency. The United Nations came out in favor of replacing the dollar with a new reserve currency with a September 2009 statement. It again reiterated its position in another statement in June 2010. It read in part:

UN calls for scrapping dollar
Wed, 30 Jun 2010 00:40:31 GMT
A UN report released on Tuesday calls for abandoning the US dollar as the main global reserve currency to achieve greater stability in the world financial system.

"The dollar has proved not to be a stable store of value, which is a requisite for a stable reserve currency," said the World Economic and Social Survey 2010.

The use of the dollar for international trade came under increasing scrutiny when the US economy fell into recession.

The report said a new global reserve system should be created, which "must not be based on a single currency or even multiple national currencies." Instead, the report advocates using assistance from the International Monetary Fund to create a standardized international system for liquidity transfer.

The report added that developing countries have been hit hard by the US dollar's loss of value in recent years. Presstv.com

And finally, in a September 27, 2009 dispatch, Reuters quoted World Bank President Robert Zoellick as saying the United States should not take the dollar's status as the world's key reserve currency for granted because other options are emerging. "The United States would be mistaken to take for granted the dollar's place as the world's predominant reserve currency," he said. "Looking forward, there will increasingly be other options." Hmmm. What does Robert know that we don't?

Even Tim Geithner said, in September 2009, that the U.S. would back a new world reserve currency. Now I ask you, if even our own Treasury Secretary is against the U.S. dollar, who then, is for it?

What Happens should the Dollar Fail?

The U.S. dollar really is everyone's problem. There are more dollars in circulation worldwide than any other currency; perhaps more than all other currencies. A full two-thirds of the rest of the world's foreign reserves are denominated in U.S. dollars. It's also true that two-thirds of all dollars circulate outside of the United States. They have long been the choice of exchange on the world's black markets. The reason is because they are so recognizable and accepted everywhere else; in other words, liquid and fungible. They have also tended to keep their purchasing power value relatively constant till recently. But there are too many of them anymore and the law of supply and demand states that the more of something there is, the less value it has and the less demand there is for it. The world is becoming saturated with dollars and many are looking for alternatives. I believe that it is only a matter of time before the dollar does fail. When, how, and at what speed are the only things left for debate.

What are some of the possible triggers and what will happen once they are pulled?

The Chinese could start selling their U.S. Bonds and Treasuries. This would make interest rates rise, collapse demand for new offerings, and make dollars return to the U.S., thus stoking domestic inflation.

The dollar could suddenly or gradually stop being the world reserve currency. This would cause the value of the dollar on the Forex (currency market) to fall against other currencies, possibly setting off a self-fulfilling hyper inflationary event.

Another currency could become backed by gold before the dollar, setting off a scramble to convert dollars into that currency and causing the dollar to fail.

There are any number of scenarios one can come up with that precipitates the failure of the dollar. The important point is that this failure is not only possible but likely, and likely to happen sooner rather than later.

What are the options available to circumvent this event?

The United States could collectively (we) start living within our means and stop debasing the currency.

I believe this to be politically and socially unacceptable to both the government and the people.

Implement a new currency (Nuevo Dollar, Amero, etc.).

The problem is that the problem doesn't go away by simply erasing zeros on the currency. The inflation dynamic is still present if no other action is taken in conjunction.

Hyper-inflate.

This is only a temporary solution and not a cure. The U.S. Government has already caused a bubble in the Dollar, Bond, and Treasury markets. The bailout schemes of the last few years necessitated trillions of new dollars be created. I believe this is the path we have been on for some time and it has masked the problem to a certain extent but this 'solution' is by no means a cure.

Default.

Heck, the U.S. already defaulted on its internal obligations in 1933 and to its external creditors in 1971. The U.S. continues in default every day by issuing more dollars than can ever be redeemed honestly. It is the chosen path, the inflation path. The question is, will the U.S. default en-masse on all of its remaining obligations all at one time? If so, it's a moon shot for gold, silver and all commodities immediately following the default. This would likely be done at the most advantageous time (night, holiday) for the government and the worst time for you, leaving you without time to prepare or protect yourself.

Revalue the U.S. dollar in terms of gold.

This is already happening gradually and goes hand-in-hand with the previous two scenarios. In this scenario, instead of the U.S. defaulting on its obligations or re-valuing the currency, it re-values the price of gold in dollars. It could do this by announcing that it would pay (buy) a certain (higher) price for gold on the open market. This would have the effect of immediately re-valuing every ounce of gold on the planet. It would then be possible to cover our outstanding debt with our gold reserves, leading to a de-facto gold standard. I lean towards this scenario.

Return to a Gold Standard.
I believe this to be inevitable at some point. How we get there and the ultimate price are up for debate. In all likelihood, plans are already afoot and this will be a 'surprising' event for most when it does happen.

A combination of the above.
This is also very likely.

What *May* Happen.
The dollar failed in 1933 internally and in 1971 externally because there were too many dollar claims against available gold.
Today there are too many paper claims (100:1?) against available gold bullion.
What if a 'new dollar' (N$) was introduced at one new for 100 old (O$)?
What if the N$ was fully backed by physical bullion but not the old?
Claimants to gold would be paid in O$s convertible to N$s.
The price of bullion in N$ would be the same as it was with O$ but you could no longer use those O$s to purchase gold but only to pay off debt.
Holders of gold (N$) would see their wealth preserved and holders of debt (O$) would suffer a 99% loss.
OR
The price may simply be allowed to rise to clear the market.

Someone(s) somewhere in the U.S. power structure knows what the plan is but isn't telling us. Rest assured, there is a plan. There is always a plan. To paraphrase Franklin Roosevelt, nothing happens by chance in government. Don't be caught in the 'surprise' whatever it may be. Holding physical gold is your lifeline in any of the above scenarios.

"May you live in interesting times."
Chinese Proverb

"The times they are a-changing."
Bob Dylan

Current Developments and Anecdotal Evidence

This section is a hodge-podge of seemingly disparate events and occurrences presented in support of the ongoing bull market in precious metals.

United States Mint Eagle Coin Scarcity
August 2008: The U.S. Mint stopped accepting orders for both its Silver Eagle and Gold Eagle coins. This is the first time this has happened since the inception of the programs in 1986.
March 2009: The U.S. Mint suspended or delayed production of nearly all gold and silver products except for the 1-ounce gold and silver eagles, which are being rationed.
There have been numerous stops and starts to both Eagle coin's production the last couple years. It's getting so I've lost track. They keep blaming suppliers for not having enough blanks in stock. I think that's an excuse for a shortage of bullion. No matter, these stoppages are in direct defiance of Public Law 99-185 and Public Law 99-61 which provide under <u>31 United States Code 5,112</u> that "... the Secretary shall mint and issue, in **quantities sufficient to meet public demand**,..."
The U.S. Mint has been breaking the law. The demand is there and the product is snapped up in short order every time they do release more coins. The last time this happened earlier this year, all Eagles were spoken for by buyers in less than one day.

Global Metal Shortages

There has been irrefutable evidence of physical gold and silver bullion and coin shortages. Many bullion suppliers are reporting scarcity, shortage, and delay in acquiring additional supplies. Those seeking to obtain bullion in size are being thwarted in their efforts. For example, The Central Fund of Canada (CEF) was informed that it had to wait 5-6 months for its metal to be delivered for its May 2010 stock offering. If there is an excessively long delivery wait for an item you purchase, that is a shortage. The item is not on hand to be shipped. Mints rationing supply is a shortage. There is more demand than supply. That is a shortage. When Dealers or E-bay are selling bullion at an excessive premium over the 'spot' price, that is a shortage. Price increases when there is not enough product to meet demand. Canadian Banks stopped redeeming Silver Certificates in July of 2009. Could it be that they were having difficulty sourcing metal? It's called a shortage.

State Honest Money Bills
There are a number of Bills in various State legislatures requiring the use of metal in settling debts owed to the State. Among them are:

New Hampshire Sound Money Bill (2005)
The Indiana Honest Money Act (2008)
Colorado Honest Money Act (2009)
Missouri House Bill No. 561 (2009)
Maryland House Joint Resolution 5 (2009)
Montana H.B. 639 (2009)
Georgia Bill HB-430 (2009)

Georgia Bill HB-430 a.k.a. Constitutional Tender Act
http://www.legis.state.ga.us/legis/2009_10/versions/hb430_LC_21_029 7_a_2.htm
"An act which states as of Jan. 1, 2010, Georgia will only accept gold and silver eagles and pre 1965 silver U.S. mint coins for payments to and from the state."
State chartered banks would be required to provide metal denominated accounts and pay out with same. This would make it illegal to settle debts with Federal Reserve Notes in the Georgia.
"The General Assembly finds and declares that sound, constitutionally based money is essential to the livelihood of the people of this state, to the stability and growth of the economy of this state and region, and vitally affects the public interest. The General Assembly further finds that Article I, Section 10 of the United States Constitution provides that no state shall make anything but gold and silver coin a tender in payment of debts."

"Banks and lending institutions chartered by the state pursuant to this title, and any bank or lending institution serving as a depository for the state or any department or agency of the state, shall offer gold and silver coins minted by the United States to, and shall accept them for deposit from, the state and other customers.

(a) Banks and lending institutions designated in Code Section 7-9-3 shall offer accounts denominated in:
(1) Federal Reserve Accounting Unit Dollar accounts;
(2) Pre-1965 silver accounts;
(3) Silver eagle accounts; and
(4) Gold eagle accounts.

The General Assembly finds that, as mandated by Article I, Section 10 of the United States Constitution, the state shall not make anything but gold and silver coins as tender in payment of debts. Federal Reserve Accounting Unit Dollars, having no redeeming value in gold or silver coin, shall not be made a tender in payment of debts by the state."

South Carolina Representative Mike Pitts has introduced legislation that would mandate that gold and silver coins replace Federal currency as legal tender in his state. It would ban *"the unconstitutional substitution of Federal Reserve Notes for silver and gold coin"* in South Carolina.

H.R. 4248
Also known as the Free Competition in Currency Act of 2009.
It would:
Repeal federal law which currently decrees unconstitutional forms of currency legal tender.
Prohibit federal taxes on gold, silver, platinum, palladium or rhodium bullion.
Prohibit States from assessing tax or fees on any currency or monetary instrument used in interstate or foreign commerce that has legal tender status under the United States Constitution.
Repeal federal criminal code pertaining to gold, silver or other metal coins and nullify any previous convictions under those codes.

March 18, 2009

The Federal Reserve announced that they would purchase some $1.25 trillion of U.S. Bonds on this date. This is highly inflationary and a direct monetization of U.S. debt.

The Comex Gold Market responded by a price increase of some $70 in minutes. This was the largest one day increase in the price of gold ever. Gold was responding as it should to this currency debasement event.

The Federal Reserve has been reported (by Bob Chapman, International Forecaster) to be buying 50 to 80% of Treasury offerings in 2009. According to Zerohedge.com, 91% of recent Treasuries have been bought by the Federal Reserve.

This is exactly what Argentina did earlier this decade and Zimbabwe did during their currency collapses. Gold has been the thermometer or 'canary in the coalmine' in reacting to these events.

LBMA Problems

The Bank of England and the International Monetary Fund (IMF) have been rescuing the London Bullion Market Association (LBMA) with 'less than London Good Delivery bars' to avert an exchange default. This corresponds to the appearance in world markets of U.S. gold melt bars. These bars are from the gold coins confiscated in the U.S. in the 1930s. They were less than .995 fine and thus are highly recognizable and not acceptable for LBMA contract settlement. Buyers have also been offered and are sometimes refusing to settle their contracts in cash at a 25% premium. This has been ongoing since October of 2009.

The Shunning of the Dollar

Many countries have been signing trade agreements and performing currency swaps in anticipation of a collapse in the value of the U.S. Dollar. They no longer want to hold them or have the dollar be the world reserve currency. They want to conduct trade in their own currencies.

Iran has begun an oil trading bourse in currencies other than dollars and has announced it is switching all currency reserves from Dollars to Euros as of October 2009.

Saudi Arabia has stopped using West Texas Intermediate to price its oil as of mid 2009. WTI has been the benchmark crude for decades. This shows the level of Saudi confidence in the U.S.

Russia has openly called for the return to an international gold standard. It wants to have up to 10% of its reserves in gold.

China has called for a basket of currencies to include gold and Special Drawing Rights (SDRs) to replace the U.S. Dollar as the world reserve currency.

The Bank for International Settlement (BIS) has also called for a replacement to the U.S. Dollar.

The Gulf Co-operation Council (GCC) has signed a Monetary Union Pact as of December 2009 but has taken no action to consolidate currencies yet. It is to be named the Kaleeji ('Gulf' in Arabic).

The Union of South American Nations is planning to introduce the Sucre regional currency at some point. Discussions are ongoing.

The province of Kelantan in Malaysia implemented the Gold Dinar and Silver Durham as currency units in July of 2010.

There are also persistent rumors of a North American currency union with the introduction of the Amero.

AAA

March 15, 2010 (Bloomberg) — The U.S. and the U.K. have moved "substantially" closer to losing their AAA credit ratings as the cost of servicing their debt rose, according to Moody's Investors Service.

Fitch rating service placed an Alert on the U.S. AAA Credit Rating in January of 2010.

Moody's Lead Analyst, Steven Hess, in January of 2010 said:

"The AAA rating of the U.S. is not guaranteed."

China's Dagong Credit Agency downgraded U.S. debt to AA in July of 2010.

The China Factor

China is a major support factor for the price of gold. Both the government and the people of China, by and large, recognize the value and importance of gold. Because China is becoming the 800 pound economic gorilla in the world economic room, and has been procuring commodities at an almost insatiable rate, they are the most important wildcard for the gold market going forward. While India consumes as much, if not more, gold than China, Indian demand is relatively static. Also, India is not industrializing to the extent that China is. I see China being a very supportive force in the gold market from here on out. This is why.

China:

- Has legalized and encouraged precious metal ownership by its people. This was not true until recently. It has set up silver and gold exchanges and allowed many more banks to import gold for internal consumption. It has an advertising campaign in place to encourage citizens to purchase physical gold and silver. It is buying all of the gold produced in the country as well as on the open market to fill the Central Bank vaults.

- Has been consistently dumping dollars for commodities. It has entered into many long term contracts with many countries, especially African ones, for its long term natural resource and commodity needs.

- Has allowed coastal cities to exchange exports for Yuan instead of U.S. Dollars. This lessens the demand for dollars internationally and weakens the position of the dollar, thus supporting the price of gold in dollars.

- Has been conducting foreign currency exchanges and signing contracts with other nations in Yuan instead of U.S. Dollars; Argentina, Brazil, Malaysia, and Hong Kong, among many others. This lessens the demand for dollars internationally and weakens the position of the dollar, thus supporting the price of gold in dollars.

- Has announced its intention to renege on commodities derivative contracts with Western Banks. They were entered into fraudulently. This action highlights the fraud and corruption rampant in the West, thus confidence in Western Banking Centers. Banks depend on interest from fiat currency to survive. Weaker banks equals stronger gold.

- Has banned silver exports. China refines more scrap silver and silver ore concentrate than any other nation. This has the effect of China vacuuming up the world's silver and holding on to it. No silver for the markets mean higher long term prices.

- Has established a modern, world-class metals repository in Hong Kong and is moving its metal formerly stored overseas. In addition, it is vying for world precious metals storage with the long established industry leaders in London, New York, and Switzerland. With less metal for delivery on the LBMA and Comex exchanges, world supplies dry up and the price rises.

- Has surpassed India in gold consumption for the first time during the first half of 2009.

- Has had its Central Bank clandestinely buying gold for years.

- Says it is going to up its gold holdings to 3% of foreign exchange reserves. It currently has about half that amount (1.6%) in gold. The increase would be approximately $80 billion in gold at today's price. Because China has more reserves than any other nation, even a small increase can have an outsize effect.

- Is now offering Yuan denominated bonds. This bond is in direct competition with U.S. Bonds. This lessens the demand for U.S. Bonds internationally and weakens the fiscal position of the U.S., thus supporting the price of gold in dollars.

- Has stated its intent to buy 10,000 Tonnes of gold in the next 10 years.

- Had its sovereign wealth fund, The China Investment Corp., invest $155M in the GLD ETF in February of 2010.

- Was part of a recent survey by ING that found 45% of Asians picked gold as the best inflation hedge.

What is China thinking internally? Here are some recent statements by Chinese officials.

"China's Gold Reserves should reach 6000 tonnes in the next 3-5 years and perhaps 10,000 tonnes in 8-10 years." *State Council Advisor and Task Force Leader Ji Xiaonan*

"...We will diversify Reserves...Gold is definitely an alternative." *Cheng Siwei, former vice chairman of the Standing Committee of the Chinese Communist Party.*

Chapter 6
The Precious Metals Markets

"Gold is no longer an investment. Gold is no longer a portfolio item. Gold is certainly not a trading vehicle. Gold is your lifeline and I mean that literally."
Jim Sinclair

Do as They Do. Who's Buying Now?

A (2009) survey of US hedge fund managers by London-based Moonraker Fund Management found that 90 percent (20 of the 22) of the hedge fund managers surveyed admitted they had bought physical gold for personal investment. They weren't necessarily *gold* fund managers. Are you smarter than those 20 managers? I'm not.
In the preface to this book I mentioned giants whose shoulders I stand on. Let's meet some of them and hear what they have to say.
Are you smarter than this guy?
"By one estimate, if the world's pension funds and hedge funds moved only five percent of their assets into gold, which these days seems quite conservative, gold would trade above $5,000.
Right now the Chinese and Indian public, the non-Western central banks, the sovereign wealth funds, the pension funds and the hedge funds of the world are all looking for ways to increase their long-term gold holdings." Nick Barisheff, President and CEO of Bullion Management Group Inc.
Mr. Barisheff is one of the old hands in the business and by my reckoning, one of the smartest. It would be foolhardy to bet against him.
Richard Russell is a well respected octogenarian who has been publishing the *Dow Theory Letters* for over half a century. What does Mr. Russell have to say?

"If the current monetary system collapses, nobody will know what any currency is worth. In that event, I'd want to be 100% in gold. The reason is - as the monetary system moves ever-closer to collapse (distrust), people will turn to the one currency that has been trusted and hoarded since Biblical times, and, of course, I'm referring to gold."

"If your nation's currency is losing purchasing power and is being devalued, how much is gold worth in terms of your currency? The answer is, in that case, the price of gold is open-ended in your currency, since you will pay any amount in your fading currency to obtain money of unchallenged value. What's a life-saver worth to a drowning man? Answer - It's worth everything he owns." Richard Russell - 1/20/10 Publisher of the Dow Theory Letters since 1959

Casey Research has a great team of economists, geologists, and researchers mainly focused on the natural resource sector at this time and primarily on the precious metals sector. They're a leader in their field. Here's what they have to say.

- The privately owned hedge fund sponsor Paulson & Co. added over $3.7 billion in new gold positions during the first quarter of 2009, increasing its total investment to $4.3 billion. About 46% of the equity portfolio is now allocated towards gold and gold stocks.
- Paulson's bet on the subprime mortgage debacle *earned $3.7 billion* in 2007.
- The company made an estimated £606 *million profit* selling short British bank stocks in September 2008.
- John Paulson ranked #2 *on Alpha's Highest-Earning Hedge Fund Managers of 2008.*
- Two of Paulson & Co.'s funds ranked #1 and #4 *on Barron's Top 100 Hedge Funds 2009* list.
- ...AND NOW THEY'RE BUYING GOLD! *(Casey Research 6/4/09)*

Paulson & Co. have over $4.3B invested in gold and precious metals mining stocks. They've also recently started their own precious metals fund as well. John Paulson himself invested $250M of his own money to start the fund.

Why Should You Care?

Often we hear that bull markets are characterized by three phases; The Stealth Phase, The Institutional Phase, and the Mania Phase. When people like those above are investing, we're in the institutional phase. We've been in this phase since late 2008 by my reckoning. I'd say we're in the fifth inning of the nine inning bull market time-wise but only the second inning price-wise. By far the largest gains are made in the mania phase and specifically towards the end of the mania phase. Again, think back to the stock bull of the eighties and nineties and the Nasdaq of late 1999 and early 2000. These guys are buying and holding when others are still clueless. They're in it for the big payoff and will unload on late-comers toward the end of the mania phase. So who else is investing in gold at this time? This guy is.

Gross Says Diversify From Dollar as Deficits Surge
June 3 (2009) (Bloomberg) -- Bill Gross, founder of Pacific Investment Management Co., advised holders of U.S. dollars to diversify before central banks and sovereign wealth funds ultimately do the same amid concern about surging deficits.
Ok. He didn't exactly say 'buy gold' but what else is there? When the manager of the world's largest bond fund tells you to diversify out of dollars what does that tell you? Bonds are denominated in dollars. Gold is the anti-dollar. Enough said.

Northwestern Mutual Makes First Gold Buy in 152 Years
June 1 (2009) (Bloomberg) -- Northwestern Mutual Life Insurance Co., the third-largest U.S. life insurer by 2008 sales, has bought gold for the first time the company's 152-year history to hedge against further asset declines.
"Gold just seems to make sense; it's a store of value," Chief Executive Officer Edward Zore said in an interview following his comments at a conference hosted by Standard & Poor's in Brooklyn. "In the Depression, gold did very, very well." Northwestern Mutual has accumulated about $400 million in gold, and Zore said the price could double or even rise fivefold if the economy continues to weaken.
Mr. Zore knows his history. First time in 152 years. Wow. He must know something's up.
How about another...
David Einhorn, a hedge fund manager who correctly predicted the downfall of Lehman Brothers recently bought gold for the first time.

July 14 (2009) (Bloomberg) — Greenlight Capital Inc., the $5 billion hedge-fund firm run by David Einhorn, told investors it switched all of its holdings in a gold exchange-traded fund into bullion during the second quarter."

So, he wanted the real stuff instead of paper gold. Smart man.

Anyone else?

Bloomberg: "Steven Lehman, the Federated Investors Inc. fund manager who beat 99 percent of his peers last year, is betting on bullion with Toronto-based Yamana Gold Inc. and Goldcorp Inc."

What about this company?

Blackrock Capital has invested $4.655B in the Precious Metals Sector.

What about this fellow?

"Precious metals exposure has been increasing and is currently the largest commodity exposure. As a result we have included, for this quarter, a separate discussion on gold as an appendix. I have never been a gold bug. It is just an asset that, like everything else in life, has its time and place. And now is that time." Legendary Commodities Trader Paul Tudor Jones who controls an $11 billion fund.

He's not a gold bug but now is the time.

One more?

How about Shane McGuire, Director of Global Strategy at the Teachers Retirement System of Texas, the 7th largest pension fund, who has put $250 million of the fund's $95 billion in assets into Precious Metals Sector.

These are all people who manage billion of dollars of assets. And each of these people listed below has advocated owning some gold at some time. George Soros (Owns $663M as of EOY 2009), Jim Rogers, David Tice (Prudent Bear), Kyle Bass (Hayman Capital), Donald Coxe (Coxe Advisors), and Frank Holmes (U.S. Global Investors).

Finally, I'll conclude with a few recent quotes from Mike Maloney, author of *Rich Dad's Guide to Investing in Gold and Silver.*

"The tipping point is upon us!

A "tipping point" in sociological theory is defined as "the level at which the momentum for change becomes unstoppable." An idea or a movement has reached "critical mass."

This tipping point corresponds to the beginning of the second phase of the current bull market in gold and silver. In almost any bull market throughout history, the second phase of the cycle, when the public really becomes aware a bull market is occurring, is the longest phase in duration and also the phase when the greatest gains are made."

Sounds like Mike believes that phase two has started too.

And…

"So, in a nutshell, in the gold and silver bull market of the 2000s compared to the metals bull market of the 70s, you have 10 times more people able to invest, of whom 10 to 100 times more possess an investment mentality and ready to pile onto the next big thing, and there's 10 times the money (currency) in existence."

I'd say he's a wee bit bullish on the metals, no?

Do as they say and do as they do.

Phases of a Bull Market

It is often said that there are three phases or stages to a bull market in anything; The Stealth Stage, The Institutional Stage, and the Mania Stage. The Stealth Stage is so named because it is recognized by only those very bright early adopters who can see the changes taking place and position themselves accordingly. The institutional Stage is so named because this is the time during which Institutional Money begins accumulating the asset. The smart money managers such as pension fund and hedge fund managers get on board for the coming parabolic rise in price. The Mania Stage is so named because it is when the General Public becomes aware that the asset's price has been rising uninterrupted for years and doesn't want to miss out on a piece of the action. By virtue of the size of the funds coming from the public, the market becomes self-fulfilling in that the public makes the market rise and the more it rises, the more funds people throw at it until all investable funds are exhausted.

Lorimer Wilson, in his July 7, 2010 piece titled 'Historical Silver: Gold Ratio Suggests Parabolic Top for Silver of Over $100 per Ounce!' explains these stages this way:

"The collective demand trends of gold/silver investors effectively divide precious metals bulls into 3 distinct demand-driven stages, namely:

1. Stage One which occurs when a devaluation of the dominant currency in which gold is priced, i.e. the USD, leads to a moderate increase in the price of gold. Stage One for gold began on February 15th, 2001 when it reached a 22-year secular low of just $255.10.

2. Stage Two which occurs when the decoupling of gold from local-currency devaluation begins to outpace the dollar's losses and gold starts rising significantly in virtually all currencies worldwide. Stage Two began on June 5th, 2005 when gold (at $417.67US) first surpassed 350 Euros for the first time.

3. Stage Three which occurs when the general public around the world starts investing in gold and this deluge of capital into gold causes it to escalate dramatically (i.e. to go parabolic) in price. We are approaching Stage Three and it will become clearly evident when the price for gold begins its daily record ascents to dramatically higher prices."

James Turk of GoldMoney.com says that "…when gold climbed above $1,000, it only entered its second stage." Gold first climbed above $1000 in early 2008.

Casey Research reported in June 2010 that it believed that we are at the same spot, when we decisively moved above $1250 gold, that we were in the 1970s when gold took off and went parabolic. Gold has briefly touched $1250 in 2010, pulled back, and has not yet cleared that number as of mid-2010 but should shortly (by the end of 2010).

John Hathaway of The Tocqueville Gold Fund sees things a bit differently. He speaks of the 4 Phases of the Gold Bull Market and defines them thusly:

- The Beginning.
- The End of the Beginning.
- The Beginning of the End.
- The End.

He believes that when we passed $1000 gold, that we entered the Beginning of the End phase.

What all of these forecasts have in common is that we have definitely passed the Stealth Stage and are approaching widespread recognition of the Gold Bull Market, similar to about 1995 when the general public began heavily investing in the stock markets a couple of years before the final parabolic 'blow off' phase of late 1999 and early 2000. What this means is that a wave of money is about to enter the gold market and should continue and propel the price of gold and gold equities northward for the next couple of years.

Let's look a little closer at the parallels between today's gold bull market and the last one of 30 years ago.

In the 1979/1980 gold bull mania phase, the price of gold rose 34.1% in the final 10 days before the ultimate top in price on January 21, 1980. In the final 20 days before the top, the gold price surged 80.3%, and in the final 30 days the gain was 95.9%. Gold nearly doubled in price from mid December 1979 to the third week of January 1980 after almost a decade long bull market. This is why I say that we're maybe in the sixth or seventh inning time-wise but only maybe the second or third inning price-wise of this gold bull market. The greatest percentage gains come at the end of the Mania Stage. The 1970s gold bull market had to transition through the three stages and it took about 8.5 years from the time gold was detached from the monetary system on August 15, 1971. According to the writings of Jordan Roy-Byrne of February 8, 2010:

"In the 1970s, Gold began to go parabolic in the middle of 1979, almost 10 years into the bull market. The important breakout occurred in 1978, and then corrected 20% back just below the breakout point. This time around, the important breakout occurred at the end of 2007 and then in 2008 we had the snapback to support, though the snapback was a large 34%. Note that in the last bull market the process of breakout, snapback and parabolic move took a year to develop, while this time it is taking about two years. That means this parabolic move will last longer."

and

"There are some distinct similarities with other bull markets. Look at Oil. Its major breakout occurred in 2004 and its parabolic move began about two and a half years later. The difference is Oil's snapback to support didn't occur right away. Its parabolic move began in the ninth year of that bull market."

So we have some similarities with other bull moves for comparison. This all points to a similar move in gold in the not-too-distant future.

Lastly, in mid 2010, writer and analyst Dudley Baker has done some research on other bull market moves to determine the multiple of the final market move from the final pullback. He first looked at the Nasdaq index from the 1990s. He found that the beginning of the final move started at about 1500 and when the Nasdaq ultimately reached its pinnacle of about 5200, he saw that the final move was a multiple of 3.5 (5200 divided by 1500). Then he looked at the Japanese Nikkei index of the 1980s and found the multiple to be 5.6. Using Toll Brothers as a proxy for the housing market bubble of the early 2000s, he came up with a multiple of 3.6. Next, he looked at the late 2000s surge in the price of crude oil. That multiple came in at 3.7. The final move he investigated was the move in the price of Homestake Mining in the 1930s. Homestake was the largest gold miner in the United States at the time. The move in that gold stock was a multiple of 3.6.

Mr. Baker sums his research as follows: "Taking the minimum multiple of 3.5 from the above table and a conservative starting point of 700 for gold, we have the possibility of a peak of at least $2450. We personally believe there is a strong argument for using $1000 as our beginning point and this projects a target of at least $3500."

No arguments with Mr. Baker here. I think he's being very conservative. Since we have an arguably longer and stronger bull market than either the 1930s or 1970s, I believe that the ultimate multiple will be much greater, perhaps double or more the multiple he uses, thus a double of his ultimate price figures.

When's a Good Time to Buy Gold?

The short answer is that anytime is a good time to buy in a bull market. The beauty of a secular bull market is that it will make up for any losses suffered if you wait long enough, as long as the bull market continues. If you bought at an interim high, you may have to wait a number of months (or a year or more) for the price to return to your entry price. But as long as the bull reigns, it will bail you out. Basically, if you dollar-cost-average into the market you'll be fine as long as you get out once the market tops and turns. Just make sure you have the trend right and get out near the top. If gold makes it to $10,000 an ounce, you won't care if you bought at $1000 or $1200.

The best time to have bought was the day the market hit its low and turned into what would be the current bull market. That was years ago and we can't go back. But when you think about all of the money creation that has occurred since the turn of the century, today's price doesn't seem all that far off the lows. For example, as of the day I'm writing this, gold is just about five times what it was at its low. However, if the nation's money supply has doubled in that time, then the price rise has only risen about two and a half fold off the low.

If you have no portfolio exposure to the precious metals right now, you may want to use a *portion* of your available investment funds to purchase some metal soon. Then scale in at the appropriate time and in as great a size as you feel comfortable. Do this so that you do not miss the parabolic 'blow-off' phase. No one knows when it will start. It could at any time, though probably not tomorrow.

You should always be asking yourself the question: Do I own enough gold? Enough to protect myself from another stock market crash? From inflation? From deflation? From war? From an ever value-less dollar? When the answer is no, it's time to buy. When the answer is yes, it's time to sit tight. Many portfolio managers, even in good times, will recommend a 10% gold holding in your portfolio. These are not good economic times.

For those so inclined, watch the market 'technicals'. All markets, whether bull or bear, become overbought or oversold at times. There are any number of signals or indicators to watch for. Buy a good book on technical analysis (Edwards and Magee wrote a well respected one). Follow the moving averages. During this entire bull market the 350 day moving average has proved to be a reliable indicator of when to sell at interim highs. Gold got 40% above its 350 day moving average on May 15, 2006 and then it fell from $720 to $542 in one month. Gold also got 40% above this key moving average on March 17, 2008. It then declined from $1032 to $682 by October 24, 2008. Once gold gets below this average, it becomes a good time to begin to scale back in to position.

Another good tactic in a bull market is to wait for a 'scare' to come along. It always seems to happen at some point. The gold market had its scare in 2008 when the baby was thrown out with the bathwater and most assets were sold off to raise cash. The dollar price of gold dropped by about a third in the second half of 2008. That bottom would have been a most excellent time to load the cart. It was the best opportunity to get on the bull since it started. There may be more such opportunities ahead.

Subscribe to a service that specializes in precious metals and/or their associated stocks (See appendix K for a list). Any service worth its salt should be able to get you in and out of the market at the appropriate times and should be able to identify the solid companies in the sector for you.

Aubie Baltin and Alf Field are two well-respected old-time gold market analysts. Each has come out with his own prediction of the major moves for the gold market from its inception to its end. So part of their predictions are looking in the rearview mirror and part are future predictions. They've both posted their 5 wave Elliot Wave analysis for public consumption.

Here's Aubie Baltin's view of the likely gold market waves.

Wave I $255 - $1030
Wave II $1030 - $735
Wave III $1975, $2285, or $2545
Wave IV   ? (he provides none)
Wave V $6193 (ultimate top)

And here's how Alf Field sees the market developing.

Wave I $256 - $1015
Wave II $1015 - $699
Wave III $699 - $3500
Wave IV $3500 - $2500
Wave V $2500 - $10,000 (ultimate top)

In either perspective, we are currently climbing wave 3 as of this writing.

Whatever you decide to do during the remainder of this bull market in gold and the precious metals, never sell all of your position (gold) so that you won't be caught outside looking in if we do get a 'once-in-a-lifetime' event which moves the metals by orders of magnitude over night. It could happen. What will matter in the end is not how many dollars you have but how many ounces you've managed to accumulate. Have a portion of your gold tucked away and never trade it. Only then use a portion that you can trade to try and increase the number of ounces that you own.

Also, never use leverage or borrowed funds. Leverage can wipe out your entire position. Just buy what you can afford and wait for the top. See my hub on what signs to look for to know when the gold bull market top is in.

Gold Market Seasonal Factors

There is a very distinct seasonal buying (demand) pattern in the gold market. It is less apparent in the silver market but still present. Go back as far as you like and these patterns are consistent. During this past ten year bull market in gold, the average annual appreciation of the metal has been close to 16%. But the gains have not been consistent on an annual basis or on a seasonal basis. There are fluctuations depending on the time of year. Since the gold market is a global market and gold is completely fungible, the seasonality is also a global phenomena, though it is dependent upon events transpiring (or not) in certain parts of the world.

The two largest markets for gold are India and China. India has long been the dominant source of demand for gold. It can consume a third of all world production most years. India produces little to no gold.   The Chinese also have an historic affinity for gold. It has only become legal to own gold in China during this current bull market, but the Chinese demand is exploding. In fact, in one quarter of 2009, it surpassed India in consumption and is not far behind on an annual basis. The United States is the third largest consumer, though lagging far behind the two leaders. Europe and the Middle East are other large buyers.

Whether purchased in bullion, coin, jewelry, or other form, gold is still mainly bought for gift giving for holidays or weddings, though investment buying is catching up fast. Buying season begins with Ramadan (currently observed in August) and the Indian Wedding Season lasting from September to December. In conjunction with the Wedding Season in India are the Hindu Diwali Festival and the Christmas Holiday season in the November to December time period. Also helping push demand is the end of the Indian harvest as the same time. Indians save in gold and silver, not bank accounts as in the West. Any excess profit from crops is used to purchase metal for savings.

The buying season culminates with the Chinese New Year celebrations in February, where gifts of gold are given for good luck in the new year. Indian Manufacturers typically restock in January and September: in January because of depleted supplies and in September in anticipation of demand. January and September are often the two best months for gold price appreciation.

From February to August the gold market is basically in the doldrums. However, there is a slight uptick in demand in the April/May timeframe. My theory is that this is springtime in the Northern Hemisphere when many engagements and weddings take place. It also corresponds to tax return season in the U.S. For whatever reason, the uptick is there but not anywhere near the Fall/Winter up-leg in demand and price. North America has its vacation season June through August, when many traders, investors, and others take time away from work. This is normally the bottom for both price and demand in the yearly cycle.

Historic Mining Stock Timing Factors

Gold stocks peaked in price long after the Dow/Gold ratio bottomed in both the 1930's and 1970's cycle.
The Dow/Gold ratio bottomed at 2 in 1932 while gold stocks peaked in 1936-38.
The Dow/Gold ratio bottomed at 1 in January of 1980 while most gold stocks peaked about a year later.
The Implications are that when the Dow/Gold ratio bottoms, move from physical metal to stocks. Two bulls for the price of one.

Gold Market Size

The gold market is small any way you define it. Precious metals are the smallest primary market when compared to the other primary investment options. The gargantuan Stock Market, Real Estate Market, Currency Market, and Treasury/Bond Market are each many multiples of the gold, silver, or other mineral markets. In fact, the entire Precious Metals Complex has a smaller market cap than single U.S. companies. According to Casey Research, the entire gold industry capitalization is smaller than that of Wal-Mart, Microsoft, or Exxon individually. They also point out that the Pharmaceutical Industry, the Commercial Banking Industry, and the Oil & Gas Industry are each six to ten times the size of the Gold Industry.

Not only that, but within the precious metals industry, the 'paper' market, according to John Hathaway, is some 35 to 100 times larger than the physical market. That is, for every one dollar of valuation of actual known physical bullion, there is 35 to 100 times the dollar value of gold stocks, ETFs, and other assorted gold derivatives.

He goes on to inform us that only 3% to 9% of investors have some precious metal exposure in one form or another.

He finishes by telling us that the market cap of all above ground gold equals about 1.4% of global financial assets.

The World Gold Council (2009) reports that gold stocks make up just .58% of total invested assets worldwide.

Egon von Greyerz points out that privately held physical investment in gold is only .7% of total world financial assets of $130 trillion.

According to Davos Sherman Okst, 0.8% of all global financial assets are invested in gold, gold shares, and ETFs.

James Turk, founder of GoldMoney, tells us that about 1-2% of invested money is in gold today.

Not to be overshadowed, Jeffrey Christian of the CPM Consultancy informs us that, in 2008, gold was only .6% of world wealth.

Yes, the gold and larger precious metals markets are very small, but do oscillate over time. They are currently as a historic low by most any measurement. This tells me that we are due for a swing back to at least the mean, if not an overvaluation of the sector at some point. It may take years to get there or it could happen overnight. No one knows. What we do know is that most markets do change direction eventually and return to the mean, if not overshoot. Patience is required.

Gold Supply, Demand, and Inventory

Supply

The U.S. Geological Survey - a division of the Department of the Interior - recently announced that there are now fewer than 50,000 tons of proven gold reserves left in the ground worldwide. Half of these reserves are thought to be in the nation of South Africa. About 7% are thought to be in China, the world's number one producer today. This compares to the 160,000 tons of already mined above-ground gold. This is another way of saying that more than three-fourths of known gold reserves have already been recovered from the earth. At current mining rates, that means the world will run out of mineable gold within 20 years. Of course, there will be more discoveries made in the next twenty years, adding to reserves. Also, that's at today's price. Uneconomic ore bodies become economic to produce with a rising price. But the fact of the matter is that the easily recovered gold and silver has mostly been mined and brought to the surface.

South Africa, the world's former and long-time top producer of gold, is experiencing some of the steepest production declines of any country. Production in that country has plunged nearly 95% from its peak to its lowest level in 86 years.

Adding to the supply crunch, big miners are simply not finding world-class deposits. Why? Simply because all of the elephant-sized gold deposits have already been found. The world has been trodden over and explored for thousands of years and the easy to mine, large lodes have been discovered and exploited.

In general, gold supply has been flat or falling during this ten year bull market while demand has been increasing. The inventory of World Central Banks was also decreasing until 2009. This is because they have been a huge source of supply to the market for many years, making up the deficit in the supply/demand balance. They have now become net buyers of gold in aggregate though some are still selling. It is thought that the world's Central Banks have sold perhaps half of all of their gold holdings in the last 30 years. They dare not sell the rest.

Production from mines has been in the neighborhood of 2400 tonnes per year over the last decade. Demand has averaged 4000 tonnes over that same period. The difference has been made up by Central Bank dishoarding (selling). That cannot continue forever and has indeed stopped. The implication is for a higher gold price in the future.

The situation for silver is much the same. The United States once possessed the largest silver hoard on the planet, measured in billions of ounces. Today it has none. Only India, China, and Russia hold silver in any quantity and they are thought to be not selling any longer. Furthermore, their stock of silver is severely limited. There are some 650 million ounces of silver mined each year on the planet and some 900 million consumed. The implication is for higher silver prices going forward.

Silver has been in a structural demand/supply deficit for over 60 years. The supply has come from existing above ground stock which is nearly exhausted.

Since demand for silver and gold has been increasing, one would assume that supply would increase to meet that demand. That has not been the case. The price of gold has risen five fold in this cycle, yet supply is flat to falling.

Why has the gold supply been waning throughout a decade long bull market?

One factor is the lag effect. It takes years for people to realize that the bull is here to stay. Because of the preceding two decades long bear market, miners simply were either unwilling or unable to throw resources at increasing production.

Many mines shut down during the gold bear market and have not been brought back on line for any number of reasons, one reason being a lack of maintenance during the shutdown time.

There has been a dearth of exploration for all those years which means no new discovery, and thus no new production. There has only been one 'world class' gold discovery in this bull market.

Another factor is that miners had to 'high-grade' ore to stay alive. They mined their best ore during times of low prices just to stay in business. Now that the price has risen, they have only lower grade ore left and can't produce more gold even when running the mine flat out.

Even when there has been a discovery of sufficient size to warrant the construction of a mine, it still takes from 7 to 10 years to build the mine from scratch. Some take even longer.

Then there are more restrictive laws and an emboldened environmental movement that simply did not exist to the extent they do today. These, along with always present geopolitical concerns, can preclude many would-be mines from ever processing their first ton of ore.

Finally, there is evermore discussion of, and evidence for, Peak Gold. Peak Gold, like its cousin, Peak Oil, is the concept that we've produced all of the easy resources and only the more difficult is left. That is not to say that we are running out of gold or oil, only that we have reached the maximum possible output. There will always be some amount of gold, oil, or any other commodity to produce, but there can only be one peak of production and then it's all lower production from that point forward. South Africa was the leading producer of gold for many decades but peaked in production decades ago. While there are many millions of ounces in the ground left to produce, all evidence point so South Africa never again producing more than it did for its peak year of production. "There is a strong case to be made that we are already at 'peak gold'. It is increasingly difficult to find ore."
Aaron Regent, President of Barrick Mines (The world's largest gold producer)
"Ore grades have fallen from around 12 grams per tonne in 1950 to nearer 3 grams in the U.S., Canada, and Australia."
Ambrose Evans-Pritchard, The London Telegraph 11-11-09

Demand
Virtually all gold demand is monetary demand. It is hoarded, hid, and saved. Gold is stored. Silver is stored and consumed.
Gold, being a monetary commodity, has counter-intuitive supply-demand functions. Unlike other commodities, when the price rises, oddly, demand rises as well. Investors become price chasers.
Silver is used for jewelry, industry, photography, and investment. Its demand rises in good economic times when the first three uses are in ascendancy. Its investment demand tends to rise in other than good economic times. In other words, its demand tends to be steady in most economic conditions. Because of its monetary value and close link to gold, silver demand also rises as its price rises.
India exerts the greatest demand for silver and gold, followed by China, and then the United States.
According to a recent report from the World Gold Council, China's gold jewelry and investment demand could double in the next decade to $29 billion. In 2009 China, at least for one quarter, overtook India to become the largest gold consuming nation on the planet. They are currently vying for the title of top gold consumer.
The U.S. consumes nearly all of its domestically produced silver in minting Silver Eagle coins. In fact, it's on pace to produce more Silver Eagles than domestic supply will allow.

"Sales of silver coins and medals jumped 63 per cent to a record 2,019 tonnes in 2008 while demand for gold coins and bars reached 837 tonnes, up 93.3 per cent on 2007." (GFMS, Silver Survey 2009)
"Demand for silver has continued to rise in 2009 with the US Mint seeing a near-70 per cent increase in coin sales in the first quarter compared with the same period last year." (GFMS, Silver Survey 2009)
Demand has continued to increase since their survey.

According to Goldfields Mineral Service (GFMS), a gold industry consultancy, for 2009:

- Mine production was up by +6%   (139 tonnes)
- Scrap gold supply was up by +27%   (305 tonnes)
- Jewelry demand was down by -23%   (491 tonnes)
- 139 + 305 + 491 = 935 tonnes
- Investment demand went up by +105% (to 1820t from 885t = 935t)

And according to the World Gold Council, from statistics it released in August 2010 regarding Second Quarter 2010 (year over year) demand for gold:
- Total overall demand is up 36%
- Investment demand is up 118%
- Supply is up 6%

Investment demand for the metals is now surging. It is the wildcard in the precious metals arena. If it goes viral, then the price goes parabolic.

Inventory
According to the World Gold Council (2009), World stocks of gold are broken down like this:
- Jewelry 51% (85,100t)
- Official Sector (Central Banks) 18% (29,700t)
- Investment (Individual) 16% (27,100t)
- Industry 12% (19,600)
- Unaccounted for 2%

There's really not that much out there. Most estimates put the number at some 160,000 tonnes of gold ever mined in all of history. It's said that all of the gold ever mined (above ground gold) could just about fit into two Olympic sized swimming pools. That may seem like a lot but read this.

According to Jeff Clark over at Casey Research:

- There are some 4.8 billion ounces (CPM Group) of above ground gold in the world and 6.783 billion people (U.S. census). Thus, .7oz each.
- This includes all jewelry, electronics, dental, religious artifacts, etc. which is 2.1B of the total.
- Private stocks = 1.1B ounces.
- Official Reserves (CB) = 1B ounces.
- Industrial use = .53B ounces.
- That leaves mine production and scrap to buy.
- CPM forecasts 122M ounces of gold will be mined in 2009.
- 0.018 ounce for each person on earth.
- Coin production will be only 5M ounces this year worldwide.
- Therefore, there is only 0.0007 ounce for each human to purchase per year.

Ted Butler is uber bullish on silver and sees it this way:
In 1959 there was
- ¾ oz. of gold per person
- 3 oz. of silver per person

In 2009 there was
- ¾ oz. of gold per person
- .15 oz. of silver per person

Not much when you look at it like that.

Only about 10-20% of all gold is held by world governments. Of this, the U.S. share is about one fourth. The U.S. has sold off some two-thirds of the gold it held at the close of World War Two.

Globally, Central Banks have about 10% of their reserves in gold. For Western Central Banks the figure is about 38%. The U.S., Italy, Germany, and France each have about two-thirds of their reserves in gold. China, Russia, & India have 2-5% of their reserves in gold. The amount of gold being accumulated by emerging economies has been steadily increasing.

The rest is in the hands of the people. Individuals own more gold than governments and are accumulating at a record pace.

What are the implications of these supply and demand dynamics?

Quite simply bullish in the long term.

The Dow:Gold Ratio

The Dow/Gold Ratio is the measure of how many ounces of gold it would take to purchase one 'share' of the Dow. With $1000 gold and the Dow at 10,000 the ratio would be 10:1 or just 10. We simply divide the Dow by the price of gold. The ratio was near 1 in 1980 (both the Dow and gold near 1000) and in the mid forties in 2000 (Dow 11,700 and gold $255). Its average value is somewhere around 10. It was generally rising in the 1980s and 1990s and has been falling most of this century. Over the last century, this ratio has tended to be on the upswing during times of economic expansion and on the downside during uncertain economic times, reached successive higher highs and successive lower lows on each cycle. It would not be surprising to see the next low below 1. Should the ratio again see parity, no one knows at what number the two would meet or cross. It could be at 5000. It could be at 20,000. It could be at any number. But when it does, we'll likely be nearing the end of the current gold bull.

Gold in Other Currencies

We know that gold is up some 400% (5x) since its low of 2001 and that the dollar is down some 30% on the Foreign Exchange Market (Forex) since then. But what of gold in other currencies? Has it done as well? The answer is yes. Gold has done about as well in all other major world currencies. The gold bull market is a worldwide phenomenon. The U.S. dollar, the Canadian Dollar, the Euro, and the British Pound have each declined some 70 to 80% against gold these last ten years. The CanDo and the Euro have done somewhat better than the U.S. and British currencies.

In fact, a study conducted by James Turk of the Free Money Gold Report found that gold appreciated the fastest in U.S. dollars (17.1% annually) from 2001-2009 as compared against 8 other major world currencies. This is another way of saying that the U.S. is winning the currency depreciation war. The next worst currency was the Indian Rupee with a depreciation against gold of some 17% annually on average over those years. Furthermore, the U.S. Dollar was the only currency in the study that fell against gold every year. All others had at least one year of outperforming gold during the study period. The currencies that held their value the best were the Australian Dollar and the Swiss Franc. Each only lost between 11 and 12% against gold during those years.

The story is much the same for silver. Again, the United States currency, the Federal Reserve 'Dollar' lost some 17.6% per year, on average, against silver.

I have an interesting chart that plots the value of gold in all world currencies combined as one line. It is overlain on another graph of the gold price in U.S. dollars. The chart begins around the turn of the century and ends in late 2009. The two lines on the chart cross a number of times but there is one interesting aspect that pops out at you when you look at it. The two lines start and end at almost exactly the same places. This tells me that gold is acting as a truly international currency and that is exactly what gold is; the one and only truly international medium of exchange. Gold is performing exactly as expected.

How High Could the Price of Gold Go?

Not 'How High *Will* Gold Go?' Nobody knows for sure. Anyone who says they know is a fool, has inside (illegal) information, or has a hidden agenda.

Or as Richard Russell writes: "How high will gold go? Wrong question, how low will fiat currencies go?".

The answer is not knowable as the future is uncertain. However, we can make inferences and educated guesses by looking at the past and surveying the present. After all, history tends to rhyme and there is nothing new under the sun.

Before we get to the question posed in the title, there are a couple truths the seeker needs to understand.

First, Gold is money. It has been throughout recorded history. It's desired. It's hoarded. It's flaunted. It's locked away for safe keeping. All know it has value intuitively and few part with theirs easily.

Some of the richest, most powerful, and well connected people on earth are Central Bankers. What do they keep in their vaults? Gold (and a few some silver). Why? Because they know the value of gold and that it is money. They don't keep rocks, or pigs, or wheat, or plutonium, or oil, or paper certificates in there, do they? Though each of these has its own value and utility, none is the best form of money. Gold is.

Second, Fiat Currencies (all of them) are the anti-gold. Gold is the anti-dollar, and the anti-Euro, and the Anti-Yuan, etc. It is in direct competition with currency. It's truly the canary in the coal mine. Only this canary gets larger and stronger as the currencies debase (read: inflate and die). Holding gold is a hedge against a falling dollar via inflation of the money supply.

Thus, the dollar and gold are highly negatively correlated. When the dollar moves down, gold is   normally up and vice versa. The dollar has been in a down trending market since the turn of the century. With dollars being created far in excess of expanding productivity and population, this trend seems likely to continue as each dollar created in excess degrades each existing dollar.

In a true gold or bi-metallic standard, each unit of currency would be backed and convertible directly by and to a unit of metal. Mike Rozeff calls this the 'Zero Discount Value (ZDV)' of gold and defines it as 'the total number of currency notes issued divided by the total number of ounces of gold held as an asset against that note issue.' That's not what we have today. One also needs to be able to convert those notes to specie upon demand.

So, if one accepts the above, that the money supply should be backed by a tangible asset, and that the best fit in this role is and has been gold, then one can more readily discern and accept the numbers below. All of the following prognostications have been published in 2009. Some are a forecast of where the analyst thinks gold will top at the conclusion of this bull market and some are only theoretical constructs. Even so, all are good for rumination.

Our first stop is at $875, which was the January 1980 all-time intra-day high ($850 close), which ended the great 1970's bull market. That number's no longer a candidate as it's in the rear view mirror.

Our next candidate is the government's CPI Inflation Adjusted number needed to equal the 1980 high. That number is currently in the $2300 range plus or minus change. In effect, we'd need a doubling of today's price to get there. But it's a moving target. To approach that number will take some time. By the time we get there, that number will likely have increased.

Moving on up, we have Andrew Mickey suggesting $3132 as a possible fair value gold in 2009. He figures that the median house price in 1980 was $47,184 and took 55oz. ounces of the yellow metal to buy. In 2009 the median house price was $173,000 nationally and took 146oz. to purchase at the average 2009 price of gold. If housing stayed constant, the price of gold would have to rise almost 3 fold from where it is today in order to buy the house for 55 ounces as in 1980. 1980 being the year the last bull market topped out. Using the same logic against automobiles instead of houses, he finds that the median car price in 1980 was some $4,800 (5.6oz.) and in 2009 was $19,145 (16.2oz.), giving us a target price for gold of $3413.

Arriving at $5246 as we climb the price ladder, this number comes to us by way of Jeff Clark at Casey Research. His number is calculated by dividing World Central Bank Reserves of $4.8 trillion by World Central Bank Gold Reserves of 929.6 million ounces.

The National Inflation Association suggests a possible price of $5400 if gold and the DOW met at the median of their current values (at that time). DOW 9800 and gold 1000. Add and divide by 2.

Thorsten Polleit figures that it will take $6000 gold to back the U.S. M0 (m zero) money supply with gold. M0 is the narrowest definition of the nation's money supply and consists of banknotes and coins in circulation. It is only a small percentage of the total money supply.

Dylan Grice of Societe Generale opines gold should hit $6300 if one takes the Federal Reserve Monetary Base of $1.7 trillion and divides it by the supposed U.S. gold reserves of 263M ounces.

If we get the same percentage rise in gold as we did in the 1970's bull market, the price would have to reach $6375. From a low of $35 to the $875 high is a 25 fold increase. Using $255 as the low and multiplying by 25 attains this number.

According to John Williams at Shadowstats, The price of gold would need to get to $7500 to reach its inflation adjusted high using the methodology for calculating inflation that was used during the 1970s.

Mike Rozeff uses the same methodology as Dylan Grice to arrive at $7725 but he uses a figure of $2.02 trillion for the monetary base.

James Turk has been writing for years that he sees an ultimate price of $8000 sometime between the years of 2013 and 2015. Wow. A price forecast and a timeframe!

Alf Field Believes gold won't enter a bear market until it trades for $10,000 per ounce.

Jim Sinclair is on record predicting a price twice as lofty at $20,000 per ounce. Since Jim is on record as predicting the previous golden bull would reach $900 years before the actual $875 high, one may want to pay close attention to his current forecast. It's also said that Mr. Sinclair's firm was the seller at the last top. He's certainly one of the top, if not the top gold analyst. Here's the quote from his website on how he arrived at this number.

"I recently completed the same mathematics that helped me so much in 1980 to determine the price that would be required to balance the international balance sheet of the U.S. Balancing the international balance sheet is gold's mission in times of crisis. I recently did the math again and was sadly shocked to see what the price of gold would have to be to balance the international balance sheet of the USA today. *That price for gold is more than twice Alf's projected maximum gold price.*" [italics mine]

http://jsmineset.com/2009/04/16/alf-fields-predictions-on-gold/

Jason Hommel over at Silverstockreport posted an interesting article concluding that it would take $28,500 per ounce of gold if we had to pay for oil with gold. Here are his calculations.

"I ran the numbers earlier this year, in March.

http://silverstockreport.com/2009/oil-not-money.html

At $40/barrel, the world spends $1.2 trillion, or $1,200 billion, on oil per year.

Oil is now $71/barrel. So $1.2 x 71/40 = $2.3 trillion spent on oil per year now.

Gold is now $1055/oz., which, at 80 million oz., is $85 billion on gold per year.

Thus, if all the world's new annual oil production was sold for all the world's new annual gold production, gold prices would have to rise by a factor of 2,300/85 which equals 27 times, or 27 x $1055 which implies a gold price of $28,500 per oz."

Getting back to Thorsten Polleit, he figures a gold price of $31,000 is needed to back M2 with gold. M2 is basically M0 plus Checking Accounts and Term Deposits. It's a broader measure of the money supply than either M0 or M1.

Jeff Clark again, over at Casey Research, sees a price of $31,822 to back all U.S. Foreign Debt with U.S. gold. $9.13 trillion divided by 286 million ounces (U.S. Official Gold Reserves).

More provocative, he surmises a gold price of $192,401 per ounce is needed to back all U.S. Liabilities (GAO number) by U.S. gold.

Adrian Douglas, proprietor of marketforceanalysis.com and advisor to the Gold Anti-Trust Action Committee (GATA) recently penned a piece posted at GATA's website titled 'Proof of Gold Price Suppression' (07/20/2010). He's looking for a gold price north of $50,000 once the fractional reserve gold market collapses.

He calculated the real dollar value of gold using two separate methods and finds similar prices. His premise is that President Nixon's executive order of August, 15, 1971 only temporarily (for 39 years so far) suspended dollar convertibility into gold and that the U.S. Treasury gold still backs the dollar even so. These are his main points.

Calculation #1:

- The supply of physical gold added by mine output is roughly 2200 tons per year.
- The LBMA reports net daily trading of 20 million ounces by member bullion banks.
- London is estimated to trade 90% of global volume so the total market is ~ 22.2 million ounces per day.
- Real physical gold supply (mine + scrap + dishoarding) is estimated to = 4000 tons per year.
- The ratio of total gold traded to physical gold traded is 180,555t/4000t = 45.
- For every 45 ounces of 'gold' traded, only one is real.
- The trading of gold is backed by only 2.2% real physical metal.
- If there is only one real ounce backing every 44 paper ounces, then the real price of that one ounce is: $1200 x 45 = $54,000. (He's using $1200 as the current market price of gold)

Calculation #2:

- The number of all issued dollars (M3) is 13.789 trillion.
- The POG at $1200 tells us that the treasury should have 11.5 billion ounces of gold to back the dollars but admits to only 261.5 million ounces.
- 11.5B / .2615B = ~44
- There should be 44 times more gold to back our dollars than there is. OR
- The POG should be 13.789T/261.5B=$52,831 OR
- The dollar is 44 times overvalued!

His Conclusions:

- The gold price is suppressed via fractional reserve bullion banking.
- The markets are selling 45 ounces of gold for every real ounce.
- The gold market is backed by 2.3% real gold.
- The fractional reserve suppression keeps the current POG at $1200.

- The USD purchasing power is 45x overvalued.
- Price suppression can be ended by taking possession of real physical gold.

"In testimony to the Commodities Futures Trading Commission (CFTC) in Washington, D.C. on March 25, 2010, Jeff Christian of the CPM Group, a consultancy, confirmed the suspicions of many that the London Bullion Metals Association (LBMA) was running a 100:1 fractional reserve gold ponzi scheme. This means that the exchange has on hand one ounce of physical gold bullion for every 100 ounces in contracts. There is only 1% of the gold available to fulfill all of the outstanding contracts. As the LBMA is the largest gold trading house on the planet, this is not insignificant news. What happens when 2% of those contracts stand for their gold and want it delivered to them? The exchange doesn't have it and will have to source it from elsewhere. Imagine what happens when word gets out about this and everyone wants their gold! I've simply multiplied the approximate price of bullion on 3/25/2010 ($1100) times 100 to get a price $110,000 per ounce. Yes it's overly simplistic buy nobody knows what the price will be when this scheme is widely publicized and understood. The price could even go higher."

Finally, perhaps the most obvious number is Infinity, as the dollar value goes to zero.

And what of silver?
I believe silver may outperform gold dramatically before the bull has run its course. Silver rose more than 38 fold in the 70's bull market; from a fixed price of $1.29 to $50 ($52.50 CBOT). Silver bottomed just above $4 in 2001. 38 x 4 = $152.
Interestingly, the Silver/Gold ratio bottomed at ~ 16:1 in 1980. In other words, you could exchange one ounce of gold for 16 ounces of silver near the end of that bull market. Today, the ratio is about four times higher (~64:1). Should gold get to $6375 and the ratio return to 16:1 at the top, silver will reach almost $400 an ounce. That's a 100 fold increase from its pre-bull low.
There's just one problem though. Nobody gives, nor can reasonably give, an accurate time forecast. In the next section, I'll attempt an educated guess as to what to look for as these numbers come to fruition, and discuss some signs of an approaching top.

As an appendix to this section I've included a link to price predictions of well known gold analysts as published by Lorimer Wilson in his July 2010 article 'These 72 analysts believe gold will go parabolic to between $2500 and $15,000!'. It's posted at many sites. Here is one link: www.gold-eagle.com/editorials_08/wilsonl071910.html. While I can't vouch for the accuracy of his data, the list does read as a who's-who of gold market personalities and it's helpful in that it shows the bullishness of the industry as a whole. I've only included the first 5 predictions to whet your appetite and to not infringe on Mr. Wilson's copyright. Enjoy.

Higher than $10,000

1. Mike Maloney: $15,000;
http://goldbasics.blogspot.com/2009/09/gold-should-reach-15000-oz-mike-maloney.html
http://goldsilver.com/news/newsID/8538/tPath/2/

2. Howard Katz: $14,000;
http://www.24hgold.com/english/contributor.aspx?contributor=Howard+S.+Katz&article=2241359014G10020&redirect=False

3. Silver-Coin-Investor.com: $7,000-$14,000;
http://www.silver-coin-investor.com/gold-and-silver.html

4. Jim Rickards: $4,000 – $11,000;
http://www.cnbc.com/id/34038650/Gold_s_Money_Value_is_4_000_to_11_000_Market_Strategist

5. Roland Watson: $10,800 (in our lifetime);
http://www.gold-eagle.com/editorials_05watson081605.html

Near Term Predictions
As a secondary appendix, I've included in this section near term (mostly 2010) predictions for the price of gold from some well known pundits. Although these forecasts will be old news by the time this book is published, I thought it would be helpful to look back to see who had the most accurate forecast. Most were made at the start of 2010 with gold around $1100.

- $1300 - $1500 at least – Nick Barisheff, BMG, Inc. (2010)

- $1350 – Goldman Sachs – Within 12 Months (2010)
- $1450 at least - Jennifer Barry (2010)
- $1500 – Merrill Lynch – Could top within next year (2010)
- $1500 – Jeffrey Nichols, Managing Director of American Precious Metals Advisors – Sometime during the year (2010)
- $1500 – Societe General - By Mid-Year 2010
- $1764+ - Jim Sinclair - On or before 1/14/2011
- $2000 – Rob McEwen, Chairman of USGold, former CEO of Goldcorp - By the End of 2010
- $2000 – James Turk of Goldmoney.com – Will reach sometime during 2010
- $2100+ - Citibank – Interim top (2010)

Signs of a Top for the Precious Metals Bull Market

Ok. I know. I may be a teeny bit early in thinking about a top right now being that we recently crossed the not-insignificant four digit barrier. But I think that we need to be constantly vigilant and thinking about what the circumstances of the top will look like when it arrives if we hope to recognize it when it inevitably does arrive. Though some are still questioning if we're in a bull market in the precious stuff, others are thinking maybe $1000 is the top, while still others are calling the gold market a bubble. I certainly do not. Let me be clear, I believe we're only about half to two-thirds through this bull time-wise, and only just off the bottom price-wise. Yes, I'm a gold bull.

Eleven signs that the gold market may be topping.
1.

All markets tend to fluctuate from bull to bear (or bubble to bust if you prefer) and back again over varying periods of time and for various reasons. Certain market sectors may be in alignment (stocks and bonds 1982-2000) at any given point in time or may be traveling in opposite directions in a big picture/long term view spanning years or even decades. Those sectors traveling together are said to be positively correlated while those in opposition are said to be negatively correlated. The dollar (as values on the foreign currency market against a basket of 6 major currencies) and gold are highly negatively correlated. When the dollar moves down, gold is normally up and vice versa. The dollar has been in a down trending market since the turn of the century. With dollars being created far in excess of expanding productive capacity and population, this trend seems likely to continue as each dollar created in excess degrades each existing dollar.
Clue #1: We aren't likely to see a gold top until the dollar stops its fall. With the U.S. Government's massive financing needs, bond sales (i.e. dollar printing) aren't likely to abate any time soon. Watch the dollar and the number of new ones created.

2.
The last bull market in gold and silver lasted from 1971 until 1980. The subsequent bear market in gold lasted about 2 decades, until the present bull began. The precious metals tend to run in sync with the general commodity cycles. Commodity cycles tend to last 15-20 years and sometimes up to 30 years.
Clue #2: We're about 10 years into the upswing with perhaps five or more to go. Furthermore, the nature of bull markets is that there occurs a 'blow off' (parabolic) top at the completion of the bull move (Think Nasdaq circa 1999-2000). This means that the big gains come in the latter stages of the bull. We've seen minor blow-offs but the big one should be ahead of us.

3.
Another measure to be mindful of is the multi-fold price increase of gold during the last bull market. We likely need to meet or exceed the percentage gains of the 1970's gold and silver bull markets. The price of gold rose from $35/oz. at the beginning of the seventies to $875/oz. in January 1980. That's a 25 fold increase in price. The lowest low of the 1980's/1990's bear market was $255. Multiply that figure by 25 and see that this bull market may not be over until we reach or surpass $6375.
Clue #3: We haven't yet arrived at $6375. Though only time will tell, this writer is of the opinion that we'll surpass this figure this time.

4.

A fourth measure is the Dow/Gold Ratio. This is a measure of how many ounces of gold it would take to purchase one 'share' of the Dow. With $1000 gold and the Dow at 10,000, the ratio would be 10. We simply divide the Dow by the price of gold. The ratio was near 1 in 1980 and in the mid forties in 2000. Over the last century, this ratio has reached successive higher highs and successive lower lows. It would not be surprising to see the next low below 1. Should the ratio again see parity, no one knows at what number the two would meet or cross. It could be at 5000. It could be at 20,000.

Clue #4: When the Dow/Gold Ratio nears 1 we'll likely be nearing the end of the current gold bull.

5.

Ibbotson Associates produced a widely circulated study in 2005 concluding that gold is the only major asset class that is negatively correlated to all other major classes. i.e. Bonds, Equities, Real Estate. These markets won't all turn on a dime at the same time. There will be lead, lag, and overlap. They aren't all precisely negatively correlated with gold either. However, in broad, general, terms they tend to behave in opposition. Think of the gold price flat to down in the 1980s and 1990s when Bonds, Stocks, and Real Estate were up.

Clue #5: When other asset classes have bottomed and begin to turn up, gold should be topping and turning down. (Caveat: Unless we see hyperinflation; In which case everything will rise in dollar price but gold should outperform).

6.

I remember reading (John Hathaway, I think) that in 1934 and 1982, 20-25% of all assets were in precious metals related investments. I also seem to remember James Turk saying that in 1900 40% of assets were in PMs. The market cap of all above ground gold today equals something like 1.4% of global financial assets. Don't nail me on these exact numbers but you get the idea. Think about this. If the amount of above ground gold is only appreciating at 1-2% per anum, and everyone wants in in a short timeframe, we'd have to have a 20 fold increase in the price of gold to rise from 1-2% of assets to 20-40%.

Clue #6: When a lot higher percent of all assets are denominated in precious metals, start looking for the golden exit.

7.

Worldwide gold production peaked in 2003 and is off about 10% from that peak. Largely because of the dearth of investment in the 80s and 90s gold bear market, production is lagging today even though we've had a 300% (4x) rise in the price of gold. Not only were the miners not exploring much for those two decades, they were also high-grading their mines just to stay in business because of the low price. Today, lower grade ore is what's left and supply can't respond to price.

Clue #7: Look for a multi-year sustained rise in mining output before the market tops. Supply needs to beat demand.

8.

All bullish pundit target numbers are met and/or exceeded.

Clue #8: Nowhere close. See previous chapter for those targets.

9.

The world comes to its collective senses and returns to sane monetary policy and stops inflating all currencies.

Clue # 9: Um... never was, ain't never gonna happen. All currencies today are fiat (not backed 100% by any tangible asset) and government are printing Yuan, Euros, Yen, and Rubles like mad. As Mike Maloney correctly point out: "Every government in the world is pursuing the same policy of currency debasement—and as a result—there is more than 10 times the currency circulating world-wide than there was in the 1970's."

10.

The mainstream papers and airways have gold as the lead story almost daily.

Clue #10: Nope. Maybe stories bashing gold or telling you now is the time to sell. How many stories have you read in Newsweek or the New York Times singing gold praises?

11.

Everyone you meet is talking about the gold market – how much money they're making – their next big score. etc.

Clue #11: People are still going to cash4gold parties. I see more of these commercials than buy gold commercials. A local community where I live just had a 'gold party' fundraiser at the local county fairgrounds.

One of the classic sign of a market top in anything is wide public involvement which means that people can't stop talking about it. There's well known story about Joe Kennedy Senior I believe it was, who was a well known and very successful stock investor in the 1920's. He had his shoes shined one day and, unsolicited, the shoe shine boy starts talking to him about the great investments and money he was making in the stock market. Joe knew right then and there it was time to sell. He did so and was out of stocks before the great crash of 1929. A 2010 poll of over 21,000 members of the general public by *Commodities Online* revealed that some 93% of respondents were bearish on gold.

No, we're not close to a top yet. The only way we could be (and not know it) is if there occurs an exogenous (black swan) event currently unforeseen by the masses. What could one of these events be? How about the U.S. or another major power suddenly implementing a gold, bi-metallic, or some sort of quasi-gold standard? Let's say the U. S. government announces that effective immediately they will now purchase gold in unlimited quantity from any source at $10,000 per ounce? Think that'll zoom the market price right up there in a jiffy? The 'downside' as I see it is that the bull market would be over and we'd be at a fixed price again. But no worries because we were all smart enough to buy at the ridiculously low price of a mere $1000 an ounce before that announcement. Right?

Chapter 7
Silver 'n Gold

"At all times and in all circumstances gold and silver are money."
Trace Mayer

Silver's Attributes

Silver has three huge attributes or qualities that make it special, valuable, and unlike any other metal: its versatility, its inelasticity, and its duality.

Versatility
"Silver is not simply a much more versatile metal than gold, it is the most versatile of *all* metals. In recent years, there have been more new patents issued for products containing or using silver than with any other metal. Because of this amazing versatility, *most* of the so-called market "experts" (especially in North America) have branded silver an "industrial" metal." *Jeff Nielson (6/18/09)*
Silver is often the best metal to use in varying applications because it does the best job for the least cost. For example, silver is the second best reflector of light. The first is Rhodium but it currently commands $2000 for an ounce. Silver, at $20, is one one-hundreth as expensive. Would anyone want to pay 100 times more for a mirror than they do now?
Silver is also one of the best conductors of electricity. Super-conducting wires use voluminous amounts of silver.
Silver is a biocide. It kills germs. Before modern refrigeration, people would put a silver dollar in their milk jug to help preserve the milk. Today, silver fibers are woven into undergarments to reduce odor by killing the germs that produce it. Many medical utensils and devices such as catheters are made of silver or coated with it.
Silver is the only catalyst available for certain chemical processes.
Silver is one of the most, if not the most, versatile of the metals and modern society could not exist without it.

Inelasticity

In most of the countless 'industrial' applications of silver, it is used in only trace amounts too small to be economically recovered. It is often used in solder to make electrical connections, using only a very small drop of metal. Because it makes up only a very tiny fraction of the manufacturing cost of a good, a steep rise in price will not prompt the manufacturer to find an alternative. For example, let's say that a clothes dryer uses one tenth ounce of silver in the manufacturing process. At $20 silver, that's $2 of the cost of the, say, $1000 dryer. Should the price of silver rise tenfold to $200 per ounce, the silver used in the dryer would be $20. While an $18 rise, it's still only less than 2% of the cost of the dryer. What would the manufacturer substitute for silver? The next most conductive element: gold? Not likely. So demand is said to be inelastic to price. Demand will remain relatively constant no matter the cost (unless, of course, silver were to rise to a price greater than gold).

Silver is also inelastic on the supply side. Because roughly two-thirds of silver is produced from other than primary silver mines, the silver supply does not rise or fall much with price. A certain amount of silver is always going to be produced as a by-product of non-silver mines no matter the price of silver. In other words, silver production cannot be easily increased in a shortage situation. Its production is inelastic.

Duality

Silver has the potential to do well in both an up and a down economy. "Silver is a unique metal that wins whether the economy is going well or is in bad shape. In the latter, the investor buys it as a hedge against the downturn in the economy and the markets. And if the economy improves, then the industrial demand increases." Chintan Parikh, CPM Group commodity analyst

There is always demand from one source or another. There is either industrial demand or monetary demand present. No other metal has quite this duality. Almost all of gold's demand is for monetary purposes and only a small fraction is for industrial uses (jewelry, tooth fillings, electronics). Copper's demand is almost entirely industrial.

These three characteristics make silver unique among the metals and thus valuable in that uniqueness.

Is Silver Money?

•   "To 250 million persons in 51 countries the word for money is the same as the word for silver and silver literally means money." *Silver Profits in the 80's*, by Jerome F. Smith and Barbara Kelly Smith, copyright © 1982, ERC Publishing Company, page 43.

•   "The major monetary metal in history is silver, not gold." Noble Laureate Milton Friedman in an interview with James U. Blanchard III for the 20th Anniversary New Orleans Investment Conference, November 7, 1993.

•   "Gold is the money of kings; silver is the money of gentlemen; barter is the money of peasants; but debt is the money of slaves." *Money and Wealth in the New Millennium*, by Norm Franz, copyright © 2001, Whitestonepress, page 154.

•   "American Eagle Silver Bullion Coins are affordable investments, beautiful collectibles, thoughtful gifts and memorable incentives or rewards. Above all, as legal tender, they're the only silver bullion coins whose weight and purity are guaranteed by the United States Government. They're also the only silver coins allowed in an IRA." U.S. Mint Website

•   The ISO (International Organization for Standardization) has set the standards for international currencies. Silver and gold are listed by the ISO as currencies.

•   Section 9 of The Coinage Act of 1792 defines a dollar as 371.25 grains of pure silver.

It has been used as money throughout recorded history so I'd say, yes, it is money if people use it as money.

Gold versus Silver Performance in a Bull Market

Silver has a tendency to underperform gold as a rally in the metals gets going. However, it tends to greatly outperform gold near the market tops. During the first two years of this bull market, silver did indeed lag gold. It then cought up to gold and tracked it the next couple of years, and then outperformed gold until early 2008 when the markets crashed. At its peak, gold was up nearly 250% in early 2008 but silver was up well over 300% at the same time from the beginning of 2002. As the metals both declined throughout the remainder of 2008, silver fell farther than gold from peak to trough. Silver fell nearly 60% while gold fell about half as much or 30%. Now on the way back up silver is again leading.

Here's a simplistic chart showing silver's leverage to gold. Notice that Precious Metal Related stocks tend to greatly outperform on the way up but terribly underperform on the way down. On the way up, many stocks leveraged the metals 3, or 4, or 5:1. But on the way down some pm stocks lost 90% or more of their pre-crash market value.

One other conclusion to be made is that when the economy is good, silver will tend to outperform.

When the economy is bad, gold will tend to outperform. This is because silver is also an industrial metal besides being a monetary metal. It is in great demand when the economy is rolling along but less in demand when the economy is in recession. Conversely, gold tends to be forgotten when times are good and remembered when times are bad. Even though it did fall substantially during the financial meltdown of 2008, it fell less than did the stock indexes, silver, or oil.

The Silver:Gold Ratios

There are a number of different ratios to talk about when comparing the two metals. Each can provide us with information regarding which metal is the better performer at any given point in time. The four being presented here are the production, inventory, price, and stock-to-flow ratios.

The Silver:Gold Production Ratio
Silver was originally 17.5 times more plentiful in the Earth's crust than gold. That's how Mother Nature desired it to be. The historic ratio of the two metals taken out of the ground was very close to this ratio until relatively recently. Today, the production ratio is less than half of what it had been for many centuries.

Silver is generally found closer to the surface than gold because of epithermal deposition. Some gold mines in South Africa are close to three miles deep; the deepest in the world.

The worldwide production ratio from 1493 to 1931 averaged about 13 ounces of silver mined for every ounce of gold. Presumably, this is due to the relative depth of each, and thus, ease of extraction, of the metals. The average from 1900 to 2003 was 7.64:1. Today it is just about 8:1. As you can surmise, there has been either relatively less silver or relatively more gold taken from the Earth this last century as compared to those previous.

In-ground geologic reserves are thought to be 7:1. That is, there is estimated to be seven mineable ounces of silver remaining in the Earth's crust for every mineable ounce of gold.

The Silver:Gold Inventory Ratio

In 1940 the Inventory Ratio was 10:1 and today it is 1:5. There were 10 billion ounces of known, above-ground, silver bullion in the world in 1940, of which half of that was in the United States. And at that time there was 1 billion ounces of gold in the world. Close to three-quarters of that total was located in the United States. These 1940 numbers roughly parallel the production numbers at that time.

Today there are estimated to be 5 billion ounces of gold in the world; a five-fold increase in only 70 years. Of that, the U.S. possesses about a fourth of the total officially. There are now thought to be as many as 1 billion ounces of silver bullion available in the world. This is on the high side of reliable estimates. Of this total, the U.S. officially possesses none. The U.S. sold off the last of its silver stocks by 2003.

So what we have is an industry that is still producing about 8 times the silver by weight as gold but the silver:gold inventory ratio continues to fall. Inventory ratios have changed drastically over the years; much more so than production ratios. Gold is hoarded. Silver is depleted. Almost every ounce of gold ever taken from the ground is still available in some form and at some price. Silver is consumed in industry and discarded due to its relative low price and the small amounts used in manufacturing. It's not economical to recover or recycle in the vast majority of instances; the one exception being photographic film. This bodes well for the price of silver in the future.

Historic Official Silver:Gold Price Ratio

I say 'official' because for much of history governments have fixed this bi-metallic ratio. The correct ratio is always the Black Market ratio. The price ratio is the number of ounces of silver it takes at its current price to purchase one ounce of gold at its current price. The ratio is near 64:1 as of mid-2010. It has fluctuated in a broad band from 20:1 to 100:1 over much of the last century. The modern low was reached near the peak of the last precious metals bull market. Silver is now undervalued as compared to the historic record as presented below.

90:1	USA	1991
51:1	USA	2007
17:1	USA	1980
15.68:1	USA	1800
15.5:1	France	1803
14.29:1	England	1806
12.5:1	Greece	323 BC
12:1	Ancient Rome	

Historic Fluctuations between 10:1 and 100:1 have been seen. The average has been 32:1 over last 200 years, but only 54:1 since 1970. The average ratio was 16:1 in the 1970's.

The price ratio can also be called the perception ratio because it's the market perception of what the metals are worth relative to one another. Even though inventory or production ratios may remain static, the price ratio will fluctuate greatly based on market perception of abundance or scarcity between the two. For example, the Price Ratio was 10:1 in Ancient Times, 15:1 during the Middle Ages, and 30:1 100 years ago. The Production Ratio remained fairly consistent during these times so there must have been other factors influencing the Price Ratio.

Many investors will play this ratio to their advantage over time, trading silver for gold at the lows and gold for silver at the highs. It is a viable long-term strategy if your goal is to increase the number of ounces of metal that you own. That should be your goal.

The Silver:Gold Price Ratio in Precious Metal Bull Markets

When the Price Ratio falls, both metals tend to do well.

Silver tends to underperform gold during the initial phase of a rally, and vastly outperform it during the late stage.

History shows silver outperforming gold as the precious metals market nears a peak. In other words, before gold has hit its high, the silver:gold price ratio will swing dramatically in favor of silver (fall). This is what happened in the late 1970s.

Watch for this to occur again as we near a peak in gold.

Stock to Flow Ratio
The Stock-to-Flow Ratio is the ratio of the amount of available inventory to the amount of annual consumption.
There have been some 160,000 tonnes of gold mined in history (by most estimates) versus, say, 2400 tonnes produced annually. Gold's Stock-to-Flow Ratio would be 66.67:1 using these numbers. There is one ounce of gold produced for every 66.67 ounces already above ground and hoarded.
Gold has the highest stock to flow ratio of any commodity which makes it ideal for use as money. Gold is accumulated. Other commodities are consumed.
Most commodities have Stock-to-Flow Ratios measured in days, weeks, or months (oil, corn). Silver's ratio is ~1.5:1. There are some one billion ounces in world inventory and some 667 million ounces mined annually, all of which is consumed (and then some).
Gold's Ratio is rising. Silver's is falling. Every year there is more gold added to world stockpiles. Every year the world uses more silver than is mined. The excess must come from inventory. Silver inventory had been declining for decades. The situation in gold can continue forever. The situation in silver cannot.

Metals Comparison: Gold versus Silver: Which is Better to Own?

Gold is known as the ultimate form of money; the king of money. Silver is generally thought of as gold's little brother or 'Poor Man's Gold'. It is said that:
Gold is the money of Monarchs,
Silver is the money of Gentlemen,
Barter is the money of Peasants, and
Debt is the money of Slaves.

Both have been used as money since forever. Historically, the price of gold has almost always been greater than that of silver. This is because silver is somewhere around ten to twenty times more plentiful in nature. Does this mean that we should only hold gold? I say no for a variety of reasons. One being that you get more (metal) for your money holding silver. Two being that the price of silver has more room to appreciate, both because of its relative low price and because of the current relatively high silver:gold price ratio. Does this mean we should only hold silver? I say no again. Gold is highly recognizable, highly desired, and coveted in all societies. Most World Governments and Central Banks hold gold but virtually no silver, save a few notable exceptions (Russia, China, and India). They know that gold is the ultimate money. Just as you would diversify your portfolio among asset classes and large/small cap stocks, etc., so too should you diversity between the metals. No one knows which will appreciate faster or further and be the superior investment going forward. I hold both. I'm simply going to throw some facts out for you to consider without passing judgment on what they mean as far as holding one metal or the other. In no particular order…

Gold is hoarded. Silver is consumed.

There is greater than 300 times the dollar value of gold in above ground form as there is silver.

According to the U.S. Geological Survey, there are fewer years of production of silver left in the ground than any other metal or mineral, including gold.

Silver is used in more applications than any other commodity (aside from petroleum).

Silver is rarer the deeper one goes in the earth's crust. Gold is more homogenous throughout the Earth's crust.

Much of the world's gold and silver comes as a byproduct of copper mining. Much more of the world's silver is a byproduct of mining lead and zinc.

About 30% of silver comes from primary silver mines. Approximately 70% is byproduct of other primary mines. Most gold is produced from primary gold mines.

There is less gold mined than silver, but there is more gold than silver bullion.

The Silver:Gold Price Ratio favors silver appreciation to return to historic norms.

Both have been selling near or even below the cost of production for the last 15 years.

Both are up about five fold since the beginning of this current bull market.

Silver is used in industry and for investment. Gold is used almost entirely for investment.

Both tend to rise and fall in price together. Their price movements are highly correlated.

Silver is more expensive or difficult to store (or hide) than gold because you get more for your money.

It would be easier for silver to rise higher on a percentage basis than gold due to the 'law of large numbers'.

In bull markets, silver always outperforms gold before it's over.

Only about 2% of the 160,000 tonnes of gold unearthed over the last 5,000 years has been lost and is unrecoverable according to Goldfields Mineral Service (GFMS) and the World Gold Council (WGC).

Most of the silver ever mined is gone for good.

Silver supply and demand are both 'inelastic'. This means that supply cannot be ramped up quickly when price rises.

The National Inflation Association (NIA) picked silver as its investment of the decade in December 2009.

Here are some fast facts.

There are 80 million ounces of gold mined annually and 650 million of silver.

5 billion ounces of gold have been mined throughout history and 44 billion ounces of silver.

15,000 - 30,000 tons (of 160,000) of gold are in Central Bank Storage cumulatively worldwide, depending on whose figures are used. There is very little silver in CB storage; probably counted in the tens of millions of ounces in totality. No one knows with any precision.

2 billion ounces of gold are in above-ground bullion form (i.e. the rest is in jewelry, artwork, etc.). 300 Million ounces of silver are in above ground bullion form.

2 billion ounces of gold in above-ground bullion forms @ $1250 an ounce = $2.5 trillion.

5 billion ounces of gold in all forms @ $1250 an ounce = $6.25 trillion.

300 million ounces of silver in above-ground bullion forms @ $20 an ounce = $6 billion.

1 billion ounces of silver in all forms @ $20 an ounce = $20 billion.

I'll finish by leaving you with these valuation numbers to compare.

In 1900 there were 1 billion ounces of gold at $20.00 = $20 billion.
In 1900 there were 12 billion ounces of silver at 65 cents = $7.8 billion.

The Price Ratio was $20.00 divided by 65 cents = 30 ounces of silver to 1 ounce of gold.
The Price Ratio in market cap was 20 billion divided by 7.8 billion = 2.5:1
The total amount of gold was worth 2.5 times more than silver in 1900.

In 2010 there are 5 billion ounces of gold and at $1250 per ounce = $6.25 trillion.
In 2010 there are 1 billion ounces of silver and at $20 = $20 billion.
The Price Ratio today is $1250 divided by $20 = 62.5 ounces of silver to 1 ounce of gold.
The Price Ratio in market cap is 6.25 trillion divided by 20 billion = 312.5:1
The total amount of gold today is worth 312.5 times more than silver.

Which is better to own? I own some of both.

Chapter 8
Precious Metal Ownership

"When you own physical gold or silver, you own a tangible asset.
Financial assets have counterparty risk, but tangible assets do not."
James Turk

Types of Metal Ownership

There are many ways to own precious metals. There are probably
more than you think. This section will have a cursory look at each of the
broad categories of possible metal ownership. Later sections will delve
into the nitty-gritty of each.

The first and probably the most recognizable form of metal are coins.
They come in all shapes and sizes and can often be bought below
market price. One advantage of coins is that they are highly
recognizable and relatively difficult to counterfeit – especially the older,
worn ones. It's also not very profitable to fake a small coin, just as it is
more advantageous to counterfeit a larger denomination bill ($20) than
a smaller one ($1).

The next type of metal is bullion. Bullion can refer to metal in pure or
nearly-pure form of any size, shape, or variety. Some coins that are
near-pure are known as bullion coins, as are 'rounds' manufactured by
companies. Bars are probably the most common form of bullion as they
are the type that is exchanged in the bullion markets. Bullion is
normally the cheapest form of metal one can purchase. This is due to
its large, uniform size and because it is what is traded on the
commodities exchanges.

In general, the smaller the amount of metal bought, the larger the
premium paid over the spot price (this is the price set on the
commodities exchanges) and the larger the amount of metal, the
smaller the premium. Quantity matter. Mining Companies sell metal 'in
the ground' at a discount to spot. Sometimes this discount is very great
due to the fact that it is still in the ground and may never see daylight.
Keep in mind that any form will have some premium, tax, brokerage fee,
shipping fee, storage fee, etc. attached to it. It's unavoidable.

Conversely to bullion, jewelry is the most expensive form of metal to own due to its high fabrication cost and because it is normally much less than 100% pure. It is not wise to invest in jewelry if you are investing in the precious metals.

So-called E-gold accounts hold real metal for you at a specified location. I call them hybrid ownership accounts because they are a hybrid of real metal and what I call paper metal. You own the metal but don't hold it. You have a paper title to some metal but it is not in your possession. Therefore it is both a metal and a paper holding. More on these hybrids in the next section.

Another way to own metal is via ownership of mining stock, metal mutual funds, or exchange traded funds (ETFs). Be aware that with each of these assets you may or may not have title to real metal and may or may not be able to have it delivered to you. Just because you own a portion of the un-mined metal of a company, does not mean you will ever see the metal yourself. You only own a piece of paper showing your stake in that entity.

Other forms of paper metal are warrants, which give you the option but not the obligation to purchase an equity or asset at a given price, and futures and options contracts, which may involve large scale delivery of the underlying commodity. As these forms of metal holdings are for highly skilled professional traders only, they will not be covered any further in this book.

Paper Metal versus Physical Metal

This section could be subtitled: Why is Holding Physical Gold better than holding Paper Gold? If we were looking at a Precious Metals Ownership Pyramid, the physical metal that you own and store for yourself would be the base. On top of that would be e-gold and carefully selected ETF shares. On top of that would be diversified metals mutual funds and large producing miners. Only at the very top would be the most speculative of holdings. Those would include futures, options, and smaller non-producing explorers (miners). It is always going to be safer to hold physical metal than paper metal. The reason to hold paper metal is for the leverage to a rise in the price of the underlying metal.

"…bullion is the only financial asset class you can own that is not simultaneously someone else's liability. When you own an ounce of gold, you own an ounce of gold. It's not just a piece of paper that conveys a right to it from parties that may or may not even exist if and when you want to turn their liability into an actual, unencumbered asset in your pocket." Doug Casey, Casey Research

Beware: Paper gold and physical gold are two different animals. Paper is a promise to pay – not the real thing. This includes stored bullion not in your possession. A receipt is not the same as the actual metal. Shares of equities can go to zero – bullion cannot. Bullion not in your possession can be confiscated much more easily than your hidden metal. Physical bullion is highly recognizable and desirable. People know what it is in any form and it can be exchanged in all countries at all times. You can always get at it when you have it in hand. There are no third parties involved. You will not get at your metal if there are bank runs or the entity holding your metal becomes insolvent. Also, sales are normally not reported when you sell your metal but normally are when another entity sells for you.

Here's a table of the main differences between physical and paper holdings.

Physical:	Paper:
Negatively correlated to financial assets	May be correlated to financial assets
Lower risk	Higher risk
No leverage	High leverage
No/low third party risk	Third party risk
Less subject to rule or law changes	Subject to rule or law changes
Taxes when sold	Taxes when sold
Can hold some forms in IRA	Can hold some forms in IRA
Easy Access	More Convenience
Possible Confiscation	Possible confiscation
Highly Recognizable	Fools Gold? Do you really know what you own?
Good anywhere	Must sell to profit
Highly Liquid	Not always liquid
Can never decline to zero value	Can decline to zero

"There are approximately 140 ounces of paper gold for every one ounce of physical gold." Trace Mayer 6/15/2009

In 2007, the last reported year, the LBMA, or the London gold market, exchanged over $20 Trillion in gold. Mining of new gold is only a small fraction of what is traded annually.

There are more paper claims on physical gold than there is physical gold. Physical Gold is likely leveraged 100:1 or more. This means that there is not enough gold to be delivered to everyone who has been promised paper gold. There may be 100 claims on each ounce of gold in existence. This leverage was confirmed by Jefferey Christian of the CPM Group at a Commodities Futures Trade Commission (CFTC) Hearing on March 26, 2010.

This is known as Fractional Reserve Gold. There is only a fraction of gold available for delivery. This is also how banks operate. All depositors' money is not kept on hand. Only a fraction is because, unless there is a bank run, not all depositors demand their money at the same time. Only a fraction do.

How do the players get away with this fractional gold scheme? Via unallocated accounts, ETF such as SLV and GLD that are not audited, and Commodity (Comex) contracts that are settled in cash and never delivered upon.

At 100:1 leverage, the system breaks down when more than 1% of claimants demand their gold. This happens when more than 1% of the holders of paper metal figure out the game and take personal delivery of their paper gold and turn it into real gold.

There is not enough gold in the world to provide the gold to those who think they own gold. We will see a modern day gold rush or run on gold at some point. Nobody knows when but it is coming sure as can be. Paper or metal?

Where can I Purchase Coins?

Virtually anywhere. Here's a few.
- Coin Shops
- Coin Shows
- Ebay
- Online Retailers
- Mints
- Refineries
- Bullion Banks
- Miners
- Pawn Shops
- Garage Sales

Personally, I prefer my local coins shop where I know the proprietor and have built a relationship of trust. In addition, because I'm such a frequent customer, he's been known to cut me a better deal on occasion. Also, I like the fact that there is a fixed location that I can visit. When buying online or at a coin show, it's not going to be as easy to track down the seller should you be dissatisfied with your purchase. However, you can just as easily get ripped off from anyone. Buyer beware.

Assuming you find honest coin dealer, as I'm assuming most are, he may give you 90-100% of the metal value on that day. Their offers vary widely based on their need or customer or refinery demand. Of course, the metal price is always changing too. There are many factors. They will normally buy at under the coin value and sell at a premium to someone else. This is their profit. And that's ok. They're businessmen and can't survive without a profit. That's the way it is everywhere. No one can give you 100% all the time. If they did, who would pay them more than 100% to give them a profit? Nobody. No one wants to pay more than something is worth.

A great source for locating a coin shop near you is at CoinInfo.com. www.coininfo.com/coin_dealers
There are hundreds of online retailers out there. Some are regional in scope but most are national or international. Some have been in business a very long time, while others have only opened for business during this bull market. Below I've compiled a list of some of the largest and most well known retailers. Some are refiners or mints, while most simply sell various product. They are selected but not necessarily recommended. Due your own due diligence.

- A-Mark Precious Metals   www.amark.com

- American Precious Metals Exchange   www.apmex.com

- Anglo Far East   anglofareast.com

- ASI   assetstrategies.com

- Blanchard Online   www.blanchardonline.com

- Border Gold   bordergold.com

- Brinks   www.brinks.com

- Bullion Direct   www.BullionDirect.com

- Bullionvault.com   www.bullionvault.com

- California Numismatic Investments   www.golddealer.com

- CMI Gold & Silver   www.cmi-gold-silver.com
- Coin Agent, The   thecoinagent.com
- E-gold   www.e-gold.com
- Fidelitrade   www.fidelitrade.com
- First Majestic   www.firstmajestic.com
- Gold Money   www.goldmoney.com
- Handy & Harman   www.handyharmancanada.com
- Investment Rarities   www.investmentrarities.com
- Johnson Matthey   www.matthey.com/about/preciousmetals.htm
- Kitco   www.kitco.com
- Liberty Dollar   www.libertydollar.org
- Miles Franklin   www.milesfranklin.com
- Monex Precious Metals   www.monex.com
- Northwest Territorial Mint   www.nwtmint.com
- Perth Mint   www.perthmint.com.au
- Rocklin Coin Shop   www.rocklincoinshop.com
- Royal Canadian Mint   www.mint.ca
- Royal Mint, The (UK)   www.royalmint.com
- SeekBullion   www.seekbullion.com
- Scotiabank   scotiabank.com
- The Silver Exchange
- Tulving   www.tulving.com
- United States Mint   www.usmint.gov
- USAGold   www.usagold.com
- Wexford Coin   www.wexfordcoin.com

How do I Know I'm Getting what I Paid for?

Or: How do I know I'm not getting ripped off. This is one of the most common questions that come up in my classes.

How to protect oneself: First, research what it is you want to buy. Knowledge is the key. You can never have enough information. Ask lots of questions. Purchase only recognizable coins or bars with recognized refiners' marks. Well known mint marks include A-Mark, Credit Suisse, Engelhard, Northwest Territorial Mint, PAMP, or Johnson-Matthey. Stay away from Numismatics (as defined in the Coin Categories section) unless you know what you're doing as they may be worth the effort to counterfeit and you'll likely be charged more than they are worth.

For large bars, buy only bars with a serial number, verified history, and weight. These are known in the industry as 'London Good Delivery Bars' because they have a known, traceable, verifiable history and therefore have minimal possibility of being tampered with.

Buy from a Reputable Dealer who's been in business for a long time. Make certain his business name hasn't changed multiple times over the years. If he's been in business a long time, chances are there's a good reason for that.

Make a small purchase and then try to sell the item back to the person you bought it from or to another dealer. If they are willing to give you your money back (or nearly so – dealers do have to make a profit on the spread) then chances are you have an authentic coin. Dealers have seen enough and can always tell the real deal from the fake.

Buy from Mints if you can. They are in business to sell metal, not to rip you off. They only sell and don't buy. They don't have to realize the spreads that a retailer does. And they have a fixed location and aren't going anywhere.

Buy Coins instead of bars. Coins usually aren't worth the time and effort to counterfeit. Coins are normally smaller than bars and have images on them. Bars are just large bricks of metal with numbers stamped on them. They lend themselves to trickery. If you do buy bars, buy small ones with well known marks.

There are a number of simple non-destructive tests that can be run against a piece of metal to help verify its authenticity. Not one is perfect, but used in combination, they should give the holder some level of comfort.

Weigh it. Gold and silver have specific weights.

Use Archimedes Principle which states that a known amount of water will be displaced by a known mass of material. If different, then it is not authentic.

Purchase a Fisch scale from www.fisch.co.za. It's a device that verifies a coin in 3 separate ways. They cost about $200.

Acid test kits are available for about $60. These are the same ones used in a jewelry store or pawn shop to verify the gold content of your jewelry.

Amazon.com has a fine selection of testers at
http://www.amazon.com/s?url=search-alias=aps&field-keywords=gold+tester&x=0&y=0

Gold is non-metallic. You don't want a magnet to stick to your bar or coin.

Though destructive, oftentimes a core is drilled through a bar to verify that it is indeed solid and one mass of like material.

Other more advanced tests include Electronic Resistivity test, Resonant Frequency test, Thermal Conductivity test, Flex test, and X-ray.
BullionAnalysis.com has recently come up with a new method of non-destructive testing that shows promise.

Have it professionally assayed. Leave it to the professionals. That's what they do. If they get it wrong you can always go back to them for restitution.

And finally, if the deal's too good to be true then it probably is. If someone is offering to sell you some precious metal at a price significantly below the spot price, walk away. There are no free lunches.

Coin Categories and Types

I've come up with 3 categories of coins for purposes of discussion. The 3 are: Face Value, Numismatic, and Junk.

Face Value coins are just that. The coin's value is what its denomination is. A one cent piece is worth one cent. A quarter is worth twenty five cents. There is no premium or discount to the value on its face. Obviously, the coins we use in daily transactions are these coins and I'll discuss them no further.

The second category is numismatic coins. I'm not interested in these either. These are the ones that sell for many times their face value because they are rare, or for some other reason, valuable. Some will use a definition of as little as 10 or 20% above face value to define a numismatic coin. They are not necessarily valuable because of their metal content. If they are made of a precious metal, that will increase their value, but most of the value of the coin is derived for reasons other than what they are made of. They may have no precious metal in them at all. Normally, there will be a big spread between the buy and sell price for the coin. You may want to get a coin book and look through your coins to pick out any of value you can. Yeoman's Blue and Red books are good for this purpose. However, I've never found any in my change or from those I've inherited. Most have been picked out of circulation long ago. But you never know. I'd stay away from numismatic coins unless you know what you're doing. Here's a pamphlet to send away for if you want to know more about buying numismatics.

The Professional Numismatists Guild booklet: "What You Should Know Before You Buy Rare Coins" Send $1 to them at 3950 Concordia Lane, Fallbrook, CA 92028.

The coins listed below have value because of their gold/silver content as opposed to today's zinc/tin coins. They are referred to as Junk (or Melt) coins in the industry. Again, I'm not talking about proof coins or rare medallions here. I'm talking about (mostly) old coins with silver or gold content. They derive most or all of their value from metal content and should have small premiums over spot price of 0-10%. Premiums, however, have become very volatile and have been over 25% for gold coins and as high as 100% for silver coins during the financial crisis of late 2008.

The Canadian mint recently produced a few gold coins that weighed a number of pounds each. One was recently sold at auction and only fetched the metal value of the coin (about $4 million I believe). There was zero premium paid due to its uniqueness. Even though it was newly minted and rare, I classify it as a 'junk' or 'melt' coin because that's where its value is derived, from its melted down value.

Common Gold and Silver Coins

Here are some common gold bullion coins. United States Eagles are the most popular. Listed next to the name of each coin is the country of production, the different weights produced, the karat, and the fineness of each. Fineness is a measure of purity. A coin that is .9167 fine is 91.67% gold and 8.33% other metal(s) (often silver or copper). The higher the fineness, the softer the coin. Other metals are added for hardness and durability. A one ounce Eagle and a one ounce Buffalo will both contain one ounce of gold. However, the Eagle will weigh more due to the addition of the other metal.

Eagles (US) 1oz 1/2oz 1/4oz 1/10oz (22k) (.9167 fine)

Buffalos (US) 1oz (24k) (.9999 fine)

Maples (Canada) 1oz 1/2oz 1/4oz 1/10oz 1/20oz (24k) (.999 fine)

Pandas (China) 1oz 1/2oz 1/4oz 1/10oz 1/20oz (24k) (.999 fine)

Krugerrands (S. Africa) 1oz 1/2oz 1/4oz 1/10oz (22k) (.9167 fine)

Sovereigns (UK) 1/4oz

Kangaroos (Australia) (.9999 fine)

Philharmonics (Austria) 1oz 1/4oz 1/10oz (.9999 fine)

In order to find what the eBay Gold Premiums are currently, go to this site.

24hgold.com/english/buy_sell_gold_coins.aspx?co_id=0

eBay is a good barometer. You should not be paying significantly more than the spread of the buyers and sellers on eBay.

Here are some common silver bullion coins. Again, United States Eagles are the most popular.

Eagles (US) 1oz (.999 fine)

Maples (Canada) 1oz (.9999 fine)

Pandas (China) 5oz 1oz 1/2oz (.999 fine)

Libertads (Mexico) 1oz (.999 fine)

Kookaburras (Australia) 1oz 2oz 10oz 1kilo (.999 fine)

Philharmonics (Austria) 1oz (.999 fine)

So-called 'Rounds' are also a popular way to invest in silver. They are produced by various private mints including the Perth Mint and The Northwest Territorial Mint, and are normally one ounce in weight.

In order to find what the eBay Silver Premiums are currently, go to this site.

24hgold.com/english/buy_sell_silver_coins.aspx?co_id=0

Old 'junk' U.S. silver coins are also a popular way to accumulate silver holdings. What's great about them is that their mint premium is long gone. They sell for strictly (the ones without numismatic value) the weight of silver each contains. And at times they've been known to sell for a discount to the spot price of silver. They are also highly recognizable and not worth the effort to counterfeit.

All U.S. dimes, quarters, and half dollars were made of 90% silver and 10% copper until (and including) 1964. After 1964, dimes and quarters contained no silver at all. Halves continued to be produced with 40% silver content until 1969. After that, they too contained no precious metal. One would think that these 40% halves would command about 40% or so of the price of the 90% but they don't. Because of added refining costs when melted, the 40% halves are less desirable and only command a price about half of what you would think, or only about 20-25% the price of the 90% coins. I prefer to deal in 90% coins only.

Many sites and shops sell $100 'face bags' of coins. A $100 bag would contain 1000 dimes, or 400 quarters, or 200 halves, or some combination that equals $100 of coin face value. Likewise, a $1000 bag would contain 10,000 dimes, or 4000 quarters, or 2000 halves.

The 90% silver coins contained just over .72 ounces of silver per $1 of face value when minted. Due to wear, the industry uses a standard of .715 ounces per $1 of face for all transactions.

So, if the price of silver is $20 per ounce on the commodities exchange and I pay a 5% premium, it would cost me $21 per ounce.

In a $100 face bag there are 71.5 ounces of silver. 21 x 71.5 = 1501.5. It would cost me approximately $1500 at $20/oz. silver to buy a $100 face bag. Plus tax if applicable.

More commonly, you're likely to be quoted a price per face. If a dealer is selling the same coins for $14.50 per face, we would divide 14.50 by .715 to get our cost of $20.28 per ounce of silver purchased.

Following are the content of silver per coin.

Dime = .0715 oz. per coin (Liberty dimes may have a slight premium over Roosevelt dimes)

~ 14 dimes make 1 ounce of silver

Quarter = .17875 oz. per coin

~ 5.5 quarters make 1 ounce of silver

Half = .3575 oz. per coin

~ 3 halves make 1 ounce of silver

From 1942-45 Nickels were made of 35% silver. No others.

Silver Dollars (Morgan/Peace) were also made of 90% silver but contain .77344 ounces of silver each. Many have premiums above the metal content.

A quick way of finding how much metal you have in your pile of coins is to visit the U.S. Silver Coin Calculator at

www.silvercoinstoday.com/silver-calculators/us-silver-coin-calculator

where you can enter the quantity of dimes, quarters, and halves you have, and the current spot price of silver, and get the dollar value of the coins. The calculator also lets you set various bid/ask price spread scenarios. It's a great way of finding a ballpark figure for your coins before you sell.

An equally helpful calculator is the Silver and Gold Payment Calculator at

It automatically enters the current metal spot value and calculates how much 'face value' in coins you need to sell to raise a certain amount of cash. In other words, in order to net $100 in cash, how much in 'face value' coins do I have to sell?

Premiums: Is it Possible to Buy At or Below Spot Price?

Yes and No. As will much in life, it all depends. As I've mentioned before, I've been able to occasionally buy below spot from a dealer. What likely happens is that the dealer bought at a lower price and the price of the metal has risen. He can now afford to sell below spot but still make a nice profit. It may be more advantageous for him to sell to you and move his inventory than to wait, ship to a refiner, pay shipping and insurance costs, receive a smaller premium, and wait again to get paid. He'd rather have the money up front from you hassle free.

Be aware that in normal times the premiums are usually around 5% but vary over time, between dealers, and depending on what you buy. It's been my experience that dealers will sell to you above spot and buy from you below spot, thus making a profit both ways.

Quantity and size matter. You're more likely to get a better price the more you buy and sell. Likewise, larger coins are going to have a smaller premium because they're worth more and the fractional coins (1/10 ounce Gold Eagle) are going to have a greater premium.

Buy what's out of favor at the moment. The market is always changing. Krugerrands were the hot coin back in the late 70's and early 80's. They're out of favor today. Eagles and Maples are much more in demand. Since you're buying metal you don't care. You just want the most metal for your money.

Buy dips. We've all seen market charts. They saw-tooth up and down no matter if a bull market or bear market. Buy when there is a price pullback from recent highs.

Shop around. Dealers sell what they buy from others. One dealer may have an abundance of what you're looking for or be more willing to move product for a smaller gain.

If you have a lot of excess money weighing you down, buy directly from the Commodities Exchanges in Chicago, New York, or London. This is where the price is set and you're always assured of getting the current price with no premium, though you will have to make delivery and storage arrangements ahead of time.

Finally, buy mining company stock. Typically, silver can be bought for $1 or less in the ground and gold for $50. Now that's a deal! Of course it's still in the ground and may never see the light of day but you are buying a claim on the metal for far less than the current price. So yes, it is possible to buy below the spot price of the metal.

Bullion and Commodities Exchanges

Bullion is normally the cheapest form of metal you can buy. This is because it is large in size and does not command a premium due to being imprinted or minted like a coin. It's just a lump of metal. Bullion Bars usually come in 1, 10, 100, 400, and 1000 ounce sizes as well as 1 kilo size. A bar should have both a weight and a serial number associated with it. Many will come with an assay certificate of authenticity. These are known as London Good Delivery' bars because they are the only bars accepted as settlement at the bullion markets. Bars come from various mints including Johnson-Matthey, Engelhard, and Handy&Harmon among others.

The major world commodities exchanges are the New York Commodities Exchange (Comex), the Chicago Board of Trade (CBOT), the London Metal Exchange (LME), the Tokyo Commodities Exchange (TOCOM), and the Shanghai Futures Exchange (SHFE).

The London Bullion Market is where members of the London Bullion Market Association (LBMA) trade billions of dollars worth of gold daily. It differs from the LME in that it trades physical gold whereas the LME is strictly for trading futures and options on gold.

The LBMA delivers more metal than all other exchanges. It clears more gold in a week than annual world mine production. It trades some $7.5 trillion of gold annually, making it the largest commodities trading market in the world. LME/LBMA stockpiles account for about 75% of the above-ground measurable supply of aggregate exchange gold when the stockpiles of the other major metal exchanges (SHFE and COMEX) are factored in.

Beginning in December of 2009, it has been widely published that they have been offering a 25% premium on contracts for cash settlement of those contracts. In October of that year, the Bank of England rescued the exchange by delivering 'less than London Good Delivery bars' against contracts standing for delivery to avert an exchange default. This tells me two things. One, there is nowhere near enough metal in the exchange vaults to deliver the promised metals, and two, England has so very little gold left if they are providing inferior gold bars. The exchange is also reported to be settling contracts with shares of the GLD ETF. This fund is thought to not hold the total amount of gold it is purported to. So, in actuality, there has been no settlement of these recent contracts. Read more about GLD and other Exchange Traded Funds in that chapter of this book.

The New York Commodities Exchange (Comex) holds about 2.5 million ounces of gold for delivery against contracts. Regular contracts for gold are 100 ounces each and have a delivery option. Comex Mini Contracts for gold are 33 ounces and can only be settled in cash. Silver contracts are 5000 ounces each.

Traditionally, less than 1% of contracts are delivered. The rest are rolled over to the next delivery month. Many more than 1% have been taking delivery since December 2008. This is a problem because it is thought that there is only a fraction of the metal available to settle a significant number of contracts.

A Buy\Sell Scenario

What follows is a realistic buy\sell scenario. You'll likely never realize the full gain of your metal purchase due to premiums, dealer profit, and taxes. Let's run through an example.

For our example, we'll assume the 'spot' (price on the commodity exchange) gold is $1000/oz when you buy. We'll further assume that spot goes to $2000/oz over some period of time and you want to sell at that time. What's your profit? It's not likely $1000. Here's why.

Assume a 7% state sales tax is applied to your purchase, the dealer markup is 10% on the buy and 10% markdown on the sale, and a 28% federal capital gains tax on any profit.

The numbers above may be a bit high but I'm trying to provide a worst-case scenario. In reality, many states do not tax coin purchases. It may be worth a trip to a neighboring state, or to buy them while on vacation, instead of from within your state if they do tax. Also, premiums may be as low as zero depending on the market at any particular time (or over 10%). However, gains on precious metals are taxed at 28% and not the 15% rate for equities.

So the buy price on our purchase of one ounce of gold when the spot price is at $1000 would be $1170. $1000 for the gold. $100 for dealer profit. $70 in state sales tax.

When we go to sell, we would net $1800. The sell price of $2000 minus the dealer 10% cut of $200.

Capital Gains would be applied to our $630 profit. ($1800-$1170=$630) The tax would be (630)(.28)= $176.40.

Your profit on a 100% rise in the spot price of gold is $453.60 ($630-$176.40) or a 45.36% return.

How to increase your return? Buy from an individual, not a retailer. Buy in a state with no sales tax on precious metals. Shop around at different coins shops. Time your buys and sells according to changing premiums (i.e. buy when premiums are low and sell when they're high). Don't report the sale on your taxes (Not advocated).

Where Do You Store Your Precious Metals?

There is no one-size-fits-all safest place. The easy answer is to not keep all of your metals in one place. Just as you would diversify your portfolio and diversify the types of metals that you own, you should vary your storage. There is always the chance that they could be stolen, confiscated, or lost due to third-party risk.

Broadly speaking, there are two basic storage possibilities. Either you store (hide) them yourself, or you pay someone else to store them. When you store them yourself, only you know where they are. There is no record or paper trail for someone to find them. But be aware that this advantage could be a disadvantage as well. If you are keeping them for your heirs, they need to know where they are or they'll never benefit from them. You will die one day. It would be awful should your life's accumulated savings be lost to your loved ones should you die unexpectedly. Because of this, I'd advise telling one, and only one, other person where they are. But do not write down where they are.

I would also break down storing your metal yourself into two sub-categories: storing them in/at your home and storing them elsewhere. Then I'd further subdivide into hiding or vaulting. If hiding, you'll want to hide them well. (duh) Do not hide in obvious places like the cookie jar or under your mattress or the top drawer of your desk. Be more creative. This is your hard earned wealth you're protecting.   One common way to hide them is to bury them in your yard. Perhaps this is obvious, but it should be property you own. If you so choose, be aware that metal detectors can locate metal up to four feet underground. Also, putting a nice big rock over them – one that needs a mechanical device to move - would be a good idea, as would pouring a thick slab of concrete over your buried treasure. These methods will greatly discourage not only a would-be thief, but will also discourage you from selling them before you really need them. They are your insurance and not to be given up easily.

If you choose option two, to vault them in your home, make certain that the safe you choose is too heavy for two or three men to move by themselves. Put it in the basement and bolt or cement it to the floor. A thief wants to take what you have and leave as soon as possible. He does not want to linger and spend excessive time trying to detach or remove your safe. No strategy is 100% sure to keep your metals safe, but you definitely want to stack the odds in your favor. One disadvantage to a large safe is that it must be delivered. Those delivery persons will know you have a large safe and where it is. (Gee, wonder what he'll put in it?) If at all possible, rent equipment and do the work yourself.

Some will advise not to store any valuables at home and I cannot argue with that. A safe or excellent hiding place is no match for a burglar surprising you in the middle of the night with a gun in your face. You will turn over your valuables in that situation.

The other option I mentioned was to store your metals elsewhere, other than your home. This may be on property that you own away from your home, it may be on remote public land (not recommended), it may be at your place of business (also not recommended), a boat that you own, a vacation cottage, or a storage facility. The list is endless.

When you have a company hold your metals for you, there are also a number of risks. Obviously someone(s) at the facility you are using knows who you are and what you have. There is a paper trail by necessity. This means that government and law enforcement may also know what you have.

Let's look at one of the most common forms of storage people use: Safe Deposit Boxes. Your valuables are largely safe from common criminals but there drawbacks. A safe deposit box restricts your access. You can only get to your assets during regular banking hours. This may not be convenient in an emergency. The reason you hold bullion is for emergencies. You may not have access when you want. Also, safe deposit boxes are not insured against robbery by the bank. You'll have to get your own insurance. And what if the bank closes for good when a 'bank holiday' is declared?

A safe deposit box compromises your privacy. It provides a generous clue for the government, in case it ever decides to repeat FDR's 1933 confiscation of gold. Putting aside confiscation, there are other reasons your valuables may not be safe within a safe deposit box. In 2008 in the United Kingdom, thousands of safe deposit boxes were forcibly broken into by law enforcement and the items inside confiscated. The stated reason was anti-terrorism (money laundering). In any event, the individual renters of the boxes were forced to prove ownership. If you must use a bank safe deposit box, put a photo copied purchase receipt with your name, date of purchase, and quantity inside of the box. Keep the original elsewhere.

There have also been thousands of cases in the state of California where 'dead' boxes that hadn't been accessed in a number of years were opened and the contents confiscated and sold by the state. Check on your possessions often.

One last issue related to the proper selection of a safe deposit box. Select one at a local bank. You don't want to be far away from your possessions.

You may want to look into storing your metal at a larger depository. These may or may not be local to where you live. Advantages over a safe deposit box are that the larger repositories specialize in storing metal and have vastly superior security measures. In addition to security issues, you'll want answers to these questions: How safe is the location/country of the facility? You don't want to be robbed upon leaving the facility. Can you even visit your metal? Under what circumstances can your metal be delivered? Do they offer segregated and insured storage? How will they deal with dynamic political/economic changes?

Don't be afraid to ask. You can never ask too many questions. If they don't like it, or you don't like their answers, move on to another facility.

The Commodities Exchange (Comex) in New York offers customer storage in at least two different warehouses. The bullion bank HSBC also offers space but have been culling their smaller accounts. Another option would be the well-respected VIA MAT facility in Switzerland. Many others have been popping up as the bull market progresses. None of the above or below are recommended facilities. Do your own due diligence and find one that best fits your needs.

- DasSafe www.dassafe.com (Germany)
- First State www.fsdepository.com (Delaware)
- Global Gold globalgold.com (Switzerland)
- Gold Switzerland GoldSwitzerland.com (Switzerland)
- Idaho Armored vaults www.goldsilvervault.com (Idaho and U.S.)

Confiscation Issues and Lessons Learned

It happened in 1933 and also during the Revolutionary and Civil Wars. Gold was confiscated (stolen) from the people by the United States Government. It was illegal to own, with certain exceptions, from 1933 until 1975. The reason it was confiscated was because gold was in circulation as money, or the dollar was backed by gold, during this time. Since 1971, there has been nothing backing the dollar.

It is estimated that only about 10-20% of gold held by citizens was ever turned in. Gold Certificates were also confiscated and became irredeemable.

That's history. I'm interested in learning the lessons of that confiscation. Here's what I've learned.

Confiscation validates the value of gold. Why would they take it from you if it wasn't valuable? They didn't confiscate cattle or land or chocolate chip cookies. They wanted gold. Gold has universally recognized value.

There was an exemption in that you could still hold small amounts. It was $100 (~5 oz.) per person. Gold was officially valued at $20.67 at the time of Roosevelt's Executive Order.

Many forms were also exempted. Jewelry, artwork, industrial use, and numismatic gold (coins with a +15% premium) were not taken. Think wedding bands, chalices, gold leaf, and dental gold.

Silver was not included. It obviously wasn't seen as a form of money even though it is.

No record exists of anyone ever being prosecuted. Maybe that's why such a small percentage was turned it.

Also exempt were gold mines, gold mining stocks, gold nuggets/dust, gold art, and religious objects.

Also exempt was gold held by U.S. citizens outside of the country. But those with a 'paper trail' were harassed to turn it in.

The price of gold soared 70% in 1934 via revaluation immediately after confiscation. Gold was officially re-valued to $35 an ounce. The government gave people $20.67 for their gold and then revalued it higher once it possessed it. Not only was gold confiscated, but the dollars given in exchange were severely degraded by the revaluation. Can you spell R-I-P-O-F-F?

History doesn't repeat but it does rhyme. Learn the lessons of history. Learn the lesson of the paper trail well.

I wouldn't count on the government not prosecuting anyone. However, it would not be economical for them to find every gram of gold hidden in every floorboard or cookie jar. That's very much a case of diminishing returns. What's far more likely is that they confiscate large, know hoards, and make a few well-publicized examples (prosecutions) to scare the rest of us into compliance.

I also would not count on domestic gold mines not being nationalized. After all, they probably hold more gold than Fort Knox. Foreign mining stocks may fare no better as foreign governments will be taking their cues from whatever the U.S. does.

So, will it happen again? I'd have to say overtly, probably not. Never say never, but I believe that covertly it has already begun. The fact is that the vast majority of American do not own any gold. They're stuffed to the gills with stocks, bond, dollars, and real estate. Most don't know how to spell gold – yet. You can't take something that isn't there.

However, let's talk about the Cash4Gold craze. The gold that people do own is in the form of jewelry. Gold is gold. That jewelry is easily melted into ingots and coins. All that jewelry being turned in is sent to refiners who melt it and sell it. Who do they sell it to? Quite simply, rich people in the know and Central Banks. I think our gold is being quietly and surreptitiously confiscated this way.

Then there's the matter of gold and silver Exchange Traded Funds. Many of these funds, including the largest, are thought by many informed individuals, not to hold the metal they are purported to. At some point, if they don't have the metal, they will default on their obligations to shareholders. Those shareholders who thought they owned gold will not. Even if they eventually receive dollars, they do not own, and may not be able to buy gold at any price at that time. In effect, they will have been defrauded. They will have had their gold taken from them. Confiscated.

There has been an ongoing tight physical market for both gold and silver since 2008. At times, buyers have not been able to get product at all. Mints have had slowdowns. The U.S. mint has suspended both gold and silver eagle sales numerous times the last 2 years. There has been reported waits of months for delivery of exchange contracts. This all adds up to shortage. If there is nothing to buy, isn't that a form of keeping metal out of the public's hands? Confiscating it before it gets to its intended recipient? The same goes for high premiums. If premiums go from 5% to 50% over spot, that has a discouraging effect on the buyer.

The final implementation of confiscation will probably be in the form of confiscatory taxes. If taxes rise to 90% on any profit I must report, then it will be discouraging and not worth the effort to hold the metal. Maybe they'll give us a timeframe where we can sell our metal at a lower rate before the new higher rate takes effect. Wouldn't that be generous of them... Not.

Taxes

I am not a tax professional and don't provide tax advice. Contact your tax advisor for guidance regarding your situation. Only use this section as a guideline. Reality may have changed since this was written.

State & Local Taxes may apply on purchase. My state had none until 2005. Now it costs me almost 8% in combined state and local taxes when purchasing coins. My local coin store owner tells me that he sells much more when he goes out of state to coin shows in states that charge no tax and that his sales are way down since implementation of the tax. He says that some of his customers will drive to a neighboring state an hour away to buy just to save paying the tax.

The IRS' perspective regarding owning physical gold, or any type of ETF backed by physical gold, is that you own a *collectible* rather than an *investment*. There's a difference for tax purposes. Gains from both investments and collectibles are taxed at your ordinary income rate if held less than 12 months. Investment gains are taxed at 15% if held longer than 12 months, but collectibles are taxed at a minimum of 28% if held longer than 12 months.

Collectibles include all denominations of gold bullion and numismatic coins, gold bars, wafers, rounds, or commemorative coins. Also included are ETFs such as GLD and SLV that are not closed-end funds. Electronic gold such as GoldMoney or BullionVault, and gold certificates such as those from Everbank or Perth Mint, are considered collectibles for tax purposes. Include any pooled metal accounts in this category as well.

The above applies to silver, platinum, and palladium as well.

In general, precious metal mutual funds are treated like any other mutual fund.

It can get very complicated with certain equities. The ETFs that don't own the metal get investment tax treatment, whereas the "asset-backed" ETFs get collectible tax treatment.

Again, use the above for reference only. Consult a tax professional for clarity and advice specific to your circumstance.

Reportable Transactions

The same disclaimer from the Taxes section applies to this section. I am not a tax advisor and do not provide tax advice. Consult a professional. Nothing in this section should be construed as tax advice from me to you.

Until recently there was no known 'gold registry', nor IRS reporting requirements for physical metal, so long as not in a financial account. There is still no reporting required for safe deposit box storage, whether domestic or foreign.

Slipped into the recent (2010) Healthcare Bill was a provision for dealers reporting any transactions of $600 or greater. Unless amended or repealed, this provision is set to become law soon.

Until then, you can buy metals in any size and pay with a check. However, for cash transactions over $10,000 you should file IRS form 8300.

When you **sell** to a dealer, the dealer is required to report any gold bar sale of 32.15 ounces (1 kilo) or more. Maples, Krugerrands, and Mexican Gold Onzas are reportable by the dealer to the government if sold in quantities of 25 or more. The dealer reports this on IRS form 1099B.

Gold and Silver Eagles, Australian Kangaroos, and Austrian Philharmonics are not reportable in any quantity.

Silver 'scrap' coins if over $1,000 face value and 1000 ounces in silver bars are reportable. 40% silver content coins are exempt.

Any 'suspicious' activity can be reported.

Gold Jewelry sales are not reportable.

This information is outlined in the Industry Council for Tangible Assets December 2004 Newsletter. They can be reached at 1-800-225-7531. The above information may be out of date by the time you read this. In today's environment, I'd suspect these requirements to change.

Holding Precious Metals in Retirement Accounts and IRAs

Once again, consult your tax professional or accountant for advice pertaining to your situation. Information provided here is believed to be correct but is for reference only and may be incorrect at the time you read this.

The 1997 Taxpayer Relief Act allows the holding of precious metals in retirement accounts with some caveats. The information below applies to all IRA types: Traditional, Roth, SEP, SIMPLE.

Gold (.995+), Silver (.999+), Platinum (.9995+), and Palladium (.9995+) bars and coins are allowed.

U.S. Gold, Silver, and Platinum Eagles and Gold Buffalos are allowed. Proofs are not. Notice that Eagles are allowed even though they don't meet the minimum purity outlined in the previous sentence. All other coins besides Eagles must meet the purity (fineness) standards.

Collectibles or numismatics are not allowed, nor are South African Krugerrands.

Most importantly, you IRA Custodian must allow metal to be held. Many custodians to not allow metal to be held within an IRA.

Custodians that do allow metal include Goldstar Trust, Sterling Trust, and Entrust New Direction. These are put her for informational purposes only and are not necessarily recommended.

For all IRAs, you receive cash on disbursement, not the metal, and it is taxed as ordinary income.

The following is from an article titled "Risks of Silver in an IRA" (10/22/2009) and written by Jason Hommel. It provides some food for thought.

Risks of Silver in an IRA:

1. Custodian theft risk
2. Custodian bankruptcy risk
3. IRA rule change risk
4. Confiscation by government risk
5. Third party common theft risk
6. Lack of IRA benefits risk
7. ETF custodian risk
8. ETF sponsor risk
9. Confiscation by government risk

You may want to diversify and not have all your eggs in one basket. This is not investment or saving advice.

Jewelry Sales and Cash4Gold

"For the first time in nearly 30 years, there are more people selling gold jewelry as scrap than buying new items. The high price of gold combined with the economic downturn has encouraged people to raise extra cash by selling everything from family heirlooms to tooth fillings."
"Gold Sold for Scrap Outstrips New Purchases" The London Times (2009)

This is the first time this has happened since 1980. More gold is being sold than purchased. I suspect that people are running out of scrap jewelry to sell, although about half of all gold ever mined is now in the form of jewelry. So there is still a lot out there.

The question we need to answer is: are those gold buying companies such as Cash4Gold and Gold Buyers of America really legit or just scams?

As with so many things in life, it depends.

There has been a tremendous proliferation of the 'Sell your old gold jewelry and receive hundreds of dollars' commercials recently. People are holding gold parties like the old Tupperware parties – only this time they're selling, not buying something. What's going on? Why the sudden interest? Why are these companies so interested in your gold? Can they really give you a fair price?   There's certainly a new 'awareness' of the gold and silver markets out there, but not much analysis or expert advice.

Let's examine this phenomenon logically. Why would someone want to pay you for your gold? Logical answer: Because they will somehow profit from it. How so? In one of two ways. They will either pay you less than they can turn around and sell it for (i.e. not pay you what it's worth) or they are hoarding it for higher prices. I think a little of each is going on but certainly more of the former.

Is this legal? Yes. Is it ethical? Maybe. Yes it's ethical if an educated buyer and an educated seller agree on the terms of sale. No it's not if the buyer misleads the seller.

Just as the coin dealer has to make a reasonable profit by selling at a premium to you, so a gold buyer needs to make a profit. The question becomes: what is a reasonable profit? And the answer to that, like artwork, is very subjective. Is a 50% profit too much? How about 100%? Perhaps it's reasonable if the buyer is helping someone by buying what no other buyer will, or traveling a long distance to buy from someone who doesn't drive and can't get out. I'm not going to pass judgment. Suffice to say, buyer beware. Educate yourself and shop around just like you would for any other purchase or sale.

Most important, you'll want to understand karat. Karat is a measure of purity or fineness. Karat measures how much gold is contained in a given item. Here's a table.

Karat	Pure Gold Content
24	100%
22	91.7%
18	75%
14	58.3%
12	50%
10	41.7%

The buyer only cares about the gold content of your jewelry. He does not care one bit about how beautiful it is or how intricate the design. It's all getting melted in the end. Normally gold is combined with silver for hardness. Silver sells for about 65 times less than gold. The silver content is inconsequential in the transaction. The gold content probably accounts for 90+% of the value of the item.

Let's do a little exercise. Say gold is selling for $1000 an ounce. Gold is priced for pure (.999 fine or 24k) bars sold on the commodities exchanges. Let's say we have 2 gold chains. One is 24 karat and the other is 12 karat. Each weighs ¼ ounce. How much are they worth? The first one would be worth $250 and the second $125. How much would we get for them? A good rule of thumb is that you're lucky to get half of the value at your local pawn shop, jewelry store, or gold party. You might get about $175 for both. While gold is selling for $500 for a half ounce, you're actually getting about a third of that.

If you think it through, what they pay makes more sense. The buyer has to make his cut. Then it needs to be shipped (and insured) to a refiner. It takes a lot of effort and energy to melt and separate the gold from other metals and then form it into ingots. The smelter also gets its cut. Then the refined gold has to be shipped again to wherever it's going. With that in mind, it's not surprising that they pay so little relative to the prevailing price.

However, there are better ways and worse ways to sell your jewelry. As stated before, you should be able to get about half of the current gold price if selling to a jeweler or pawn shop. What you can get is going to vary widely, so shop around. Anywhere from 25-65% isn't surprising.

Well, what about the companies that advertise on TV to mail in your gold? A couple of years ago the television show Good Morning America did just that. They received 16% of the value of the weight of their gold. This is common. I continue to hear and read stories about people getting 15-30%. Besides that, once you ship off your valuables, how do you get them back if you don't like the price? It's not easy once they have your gold.

There may be a far better solution. Send your metal directly to a refiner. Yes, it's possible. Refiners will pay you 95+% of the value of your gold. This is where the gold partiers and pawn shops sell it anyhow. Cut out the middle man and ship direct. The main problem in doing so is that the refiners likely have a minimum amount of gold they will accept. You may need to pool your gold with friends. Also, there will probably be a refining or assay fee of about $30 per sale. And don't forget shipping and insurance costs. Most buyers will not accept gold plated items but will accept gold filled items. Still, this will probably be the most cost effective method for you to sell your gold.

Two companies that were accepting metal from the public at the time of this writing are listed below.

Dillon Gage Refinery 888-436-3489
www.dillongage.com/Metals/RefiningServices/tabid/31/Default.aspx

Pooled Accounts versus Allocated Accounts

An account that keeps track of your personal gold ownership but stores the actual bullion in a vault with other member's gold is known as a pooled account. Your gold is part of a centralized stash, along with that of any number of other customers. You have a claim on part of the metal but not on an individual bar or coin. Pooled accounts may be good for owners of sufficiently large quantities of metal such that delivery and private storage are impractical. Pooled accounts are cheaper than Allocated accounts.

As you may have guessed, with allocated accounts, you own a specific pile of metal in a specific location and your bars have specific serial numbers. Because of the added overhead, allocated accounts are more expensive than pooled accounts.

The advantage of allocated over pooled is that you have a claim on an asset. If the company goes bankrupt, you still get your metal. In a pooled account, you may be an unsecured creditor of the company since your name is not associated with any specific asset. Also, it's not unheard of for a company to lease metal from a pooled account to earn extra income. This is known as fractional reserve gold. They will only keep a fraction of the gold on hand that they think customers will want at a given time. There may be ten times (or more) the claims on the pooled gold than there is gold in the pool. Furthermore, this lending of gold acts in the same way as selling. Whenever something is sold, it has a depressive price on that item. Whenever bought, it has a supportive effect on the price. So, when you are buying into a pooled account, the company may be using your funds to actually depress the price of the commodity you are trying to profit from.

This is exactly what Morgan Stanley was doing with silver it was supposed to be storing for clients. It settled a lawsuit with those clients in 2007. Morgan ended up paying the clients million of dollars to settle. There are any number of differences in accounts, so once again, read the fine print, shop around, and compare. I just want you to be aware of them.

Companies that Store Metal on Your Behalf

While these aren't the only ones, they are six of the largest and well known. Do your own due diligence before investing.

- BullionVault   bullionvault.com
- EverBank   everbank.com
- GoldMoney   goldmoney.com
- Kitco   kitco.com
- Perth Mint Certificates   perthmint.com
- Gold Bullion International   bullioninternational.com
- Security Center   securitycenterneworleans.com

Bullionvault's London-based facility stores only allocated metal in bar form, in an offsite vault through Via Mat in Switzerland. Purchases may be made in any size with the minimum purchase being one gram. The company will deliver only 400 ounce bars and for a fee. The trading fee is typically 0.4% from spot, with a maximum commission of 0.8%, falling to 0.02% for dollar amounts above $30,000. There is a custody (storage) charge of 0.12% per annum.

Everbank's metals accounts are available in either holding accounts (allocated) or pooled accounts (unallocated). Gold is offered by the ounce, in bars or coins. The minimum deposit is $5,000 for a pooled account and $7,500 for a holding account. The trading fee is approximately .75 - 1% above the spot price of gold when you buy or sell. There are no management, insurance, or storage fees for pooled accounts. There is a 1.5% storage fee for holding accounts. You may only take delivery of metal from a holding account. A pooled account must first be converted to a holding account if you want the gold delivered and a fabrication fee is charged for the conversion. There is also a delivery fee. Accounts are FDIC insured.
In February of 2010 Everbank sent the following to holders along with a Personal Account Terms, Disclosures and Agreements Booklet. In the accompanying letter, this appears under "Non-FDIC Insured Metals Select Changes"
'Section 6.3.7. General Terms: We have added language clarifying our right to close your account. We may close your Metals Select Account at anytime upon reasonable notice to you. If we believe that it is necessary to close your account immediately in order to limit losses by you or us, we may close your account prior to providing notice to you. Notice from us to one of you is notice to all of you. If we close your account, we reserve the right to convert your Precious Metals to U.S. dollars and tender the balance to you by mail.'

I understand that Everbank quickly retracted this section. However, let it be a reminder that metal not held in your personal custody is always subject to third party risk.

GoldMoney accounts are backed by physical gold or silver bullion stored in London or Switzerland. The company is headquartered in Jersey, British Channel Islands. All metal is allocated in your name. There are no unallocated accounts. There is no dollar minimum but there is a one gram of gold minimum purchase. There are no storage fees. An account fee is fixed at 1/10 gram of gold per month no matter the size of your holdings. Proceeds are payable in US$, C$, Euro, or British Pound. Metals are independently audited twice a year. One can switch storage locations or swap gold for silver (or vice versa) online. You can take delivery of your metal for a fee and there is a 400 ounce bar minimum for delivery. GoldMoney can also be purchased through Kitco.com. See IRS form TD F 90-22.1 for reporting requirements if account exceeds $10,000.

Kitco does not store allocated metal, but will arrange with HSBC New York to store your allocated gold there, subject to HSBC's storage fees. Pooled (unallocated) accounts have no storage fees and no minimums. Pooled gold can be converted to metal for a premium, plus shipping and handling fees. The premium ranges from $17 to $112 per ounce depending on the kind of coin or bar.

Perth Mint Certificates are a government backed bullion storage program. The gold is vaulted and insured by the state of Western Australia. There is a US$10,000 minimum for an initial purchase. There is a one-time $50 certificate fee. There are no storage fees for unallocated metal and a 1.5% per annum fee for allocated. This program allows you to purchase specific coins or bars from ½ ounce up. The trading fee is about 1% on the buy, 0.5% on the sell.

Gold Bullion International is a lot like GoldMoney. Metal is stored in allocated accounts at your choice of London, New York, Zurich, or Salt Lake City. Owners can take delivery of their metals. The bullion is regularly audited on a quarterly basis. The minimum purchase is a 1 Kilo bar (~32 troy oz.).

Security Center is a private safe deposit box facility and not a bank. It is located in New Orleans in the former Federal Reserve Bank building. The company has been in business for over 30 years. It offers a 24 hour vault access and a double key locking system. There is an option for providing no customer identification if one so chooses. Security Center is not subject to bank or reporting regulations. Bullion shipments can be received via mail.

Should you simply want to vault your metal in a secure location, consider these additional options.
- **Global Gold**   globalgold.ch
- **GoldSwitzerland**   GoldSwitzerland.com
- **Idaho Armored vaults**   www.goldsilvervault.com
- **VIA MAT**   viamat.com

Chapter 9
Precious Metals Equities

"A mine is a hole in the ground with a liar standing beside it."
Mark Twain.

Mining Company Leverage

"A mine is a hole in the ground with a liar standing beside it."
Boy is that statement ever true. While there are very many reputable mining companies, the industry seems to attract a disproportionate number of con artists. In general, the larger the company, the less likely it is going to be a scam. It is said that only about one in one thousand exploration companies will eventually become a producing mine. It's extremely difficult to turn moose pasture into a gold mine. Not only that, but the industry as a whole seems to have more than its share of ups and downs. Furthermore, the associated stocks can often be extremely volatile, both on the upside and the downside. Be very, very careful when investing in the mining sector.
Heed the words of Nick Barisheff of Bullion Management Group and one of the wisest cookies out there.
"While mining stocks can provide attractive returns, they simply do not have the same risk-reward relationship or non-correlation to traditional financial assets as an investment in physical bullion. Physical bullion in allocated form is the lowest risk way to invest in precious metals. Unlike mining stocks, bullion is not subject to changes in production costs, management skills, availability of financing or exploration success. Allocated physical bullion provides the investor with unencumbered ownership because there is a huge difference between owning actual gold and owning a paper proxy such as an ETF or certificate."

In case you missed it, let me translate what he is saying. He said that bullion in your physical possession should form the foundation of your precious metals investment. Only when you have your bullion procured and safely stored should you look to mining equities. Any form of paper gold inherently has third-party risk associated with it. Furthermore, he is telling you that paper gold does not necessarily perform in the same way as bullion. You hold bullion because it is the anti-dollar and moves opposite of traditional sectors like market indices, real estate, bonds, and cash. Only physical bullion provides this function. Paper bullion tends to move with the stock markets, not against them. He is sending a warning you should not take lightly.

Then why invest in miners at all? One word: leverage. In aggregate, the mining sector provides returns of between 3:1 and 5:1 over gold. Should gold rise 10% over a given timeframe, the associated gold equities (mining stocks) will likely rise 30-50% over the same timeframe. This is how leverage works with the miners.

Let's say the gold price is at $1000 an ounce. We're interested in investing in the ACME mining company. It costs ACME $500 per ounce of gold to mine, refine, and ship ore from their mine, leaving a nice $500 profit per ounce at $1000 gold. Let's say the price of gold increases to $1100 an ounce. The bullion that we bought at $1000 has now increased $100 and given us a 10% profit. Very nice. Assuming production costs are static at ACME (a fair assumption), the company profit is now $600 per ounce. Profits have gone from $500 per ounce of gold produced to $600. That is a 20% increase in profit. The stock price should reflect that increase and also appreciate by 20%. This example would give us 2:1 leverage to the price of gold.

This is a very realistic example. Many miners produce gold for about $400-$800 an ounce today (2010).

Here's a quiz for you.

Which company would you rather own in a rising market? Silver miner A (SMA) or silver miner B (SMB)?

SMA has mining costs of $5 per ounce of silver taken from the ground. For SMB it costs $9.

Assume a correct and efficient market price per shares and all else being equal.

Let's say the price of silver (POS) doubles from $10/oz. to $20/oz.

For SMA:
@$10 POS   Profit = $5/oz.
@$20 POS   Profit = $15/oz.
Profits Tripled (3x).
Profits drive SMA stock price up 3 fold.

For SMB:
@$10 POS   Profit = $1/oz.
@$20 POS   Profit = $11oz.
Profits up 11 fold (11x).
Profits drive SMB stock price up 11 fold.

You actually want to own the high cost producer in a rising market. In a bull market, those with high production costs have the greatest leverage.
In a bear market, those with the lowest production costs fare the best because they can absorb the lower price. A high cost producer may end up producing at a cost that is above the current spot price and won't survive long.
But watch out! Leverage works both ways. During the financial meltdown of 2008, gold went from over $1000 an ounce to under $700, losing more than 30% of its dollar value. The gold stocks, as measured by the XAU index lost more than twice what gold lost. Not only that, some of the smaller gold stocks lost more than 90% of their market price and have not recovered 2 years later.
Let's look at the lessons learned and talk about timing.
When the price of gold is in a general upturn, the major producers (large gold companies) tend to rise first, then the mid-tier producers, then the juniors, and then the more speculative shares.
In a downtrend they all tend to go south at the same time. But the smaller companies will fall far harder than the Majors.
From a wider perspective, all miners tend to outperform gold during times of economic stability. Gold outperforms the miners during times of economic crisis. Gold becomes a haven in times of crisis just as bonds and cash have tended to do. This does not necessarily mean that gold will rise in times of crisis, as pointed out above, it may fall less than other investment classes, thus outperforming them. But it still outperforms equities. During these turbulent times, gold stocks tend to act like stocks and not gold. The baby gets thrown out with the bath water. Even 100% bullion funds like the Central Fund of Canada (CEF) suffer. Gold in your hand is gold in your hand and nothing else is.
Seasonally, according to Casey Research, gold stocks, as measured by the HUI stock index, have done best in May, November, January, August, and September. They've done worst in October and July. This is on average for the years 2001-2008. Not much of an actionable pattern there.

While gold is very inversely correlated to the dollar and all other major asset classes, it is only somewhat correlated to gold stocks. According to figures published at edegrootinsights.blogspot.com, the coefficient of correlation of gold to gold stocks during the current bull market has been only .68 (point six eight). This tells us that there is some relation between the two but only about two thirds of the time can the moves in one predict the moves in the other. So, about two thirds of the time gold stocks follow gold and about one third of the time they follow general equities or are doing their own thing. During the 1970's gold bull market the correlation was much stronger at .94 and during the 1930's the correlation factor was .82.

Inflation and Mining Equities
Precious metal equities outperform ahead of re-inflation (quantitative easing), while the rest of the commodity sector outperforms during the ensuing inflation. Gold tends to anticipate inflation. When inflation begins to take hold, the precious metals market has already anticipated it. Inflation raises the cost of everything. As the cost of steel, oil and labor rise, it hurts the profit margins of gold producers.
Gold stocks perform best when their margins are expanding. That can happen when the price of Gold stays flat and cost inputs (oil, steel, labor) fall. It can also happen when gold rises faster than rising cost inputs.
Hence, gold companies outperformed during the deflation and early re-inflation of the 1930s.
But there are, of course, many other variables weighing on precious metal equities and any single equity can buck the larger trend. Mining stocks can be adversely affected by many factors, both internal and external, besides the price of bullion. Variables include general economic conditions, stock market volatility, performance of company management, geopolitics, environmental issues, mine life and exploration success, production costs, and increases in labor and energy costs among many others.

Mining Company Risks

Remember, a mine is a wasting asset or a 'burning match'. It has a finite lifetime unless additional resources are found or otherwise obtained. Mines run the risk of running out of mineable ore. They must always stay one step ahead of production. Gold mines normally have about a 15 to 20 year known supply of available ore to mine. If less, the stock will likely suffer. Exploration and/or acquisition must be ongoing. This is known as property risk.

Another risk is financial risk. Does the company have enough cash on hand to remain profitable and pay its bills? Can it raise enough funds to continue with its exploration program? Does it have a line of credit it can draw upon or will it need to dilute its outstanding shares in order to raise cash?

Then there is management risk. Look at the track record of management. How much experience do they have? Have they done what they said they would do in the past? Were schedules met or did they slip? How many shares of the company do they own and are they buying more or selling more? Also, they need to possess both geologic and capital raising skills.

Often overlook is the potential for the company to be nothing but a scam. It happens quite often in the mining business. See the quote from Mark Twain at the beginning of this section. There is some truth in it. In the 1990's there was a company named Bre-X that turned out to be a huge scam. The company kept reporting spectacular drill result after spectacular drill result. The share price took off and increased many fold in a short period of time. It turned out that the company had been 'salting' their drill results with specs of gold to make them assay better. When the scam was finally exposed, the stock price crashed and millions were lost by investors.

There is also market and commodity risk. There was no change in the fundamentals of gold when the stock markets crashed in 2008. The good was sold along with the bad to raise cash. Gold got caught in the maelstrom. Mining companies do not set the price of the underlying commodity. They live and die by price fluctuations.

Hedging is the process of 'forward' selling a commodity to lock in today's price. If the price stays flat or falls, it's a good deal. But if the price of the commodity rises appreciably, it's a bad deal. There are still companies out there that sold the gold they are mining today for hundreds of dollars less an ounce than today's price. You'll want to make certain your stock is either un-hedged or lightly hedged.

One more hugely important potential risk is geo-political risk. Just as there are better and worse neighborhoods to live in, there are better and worse places to open a mine. Location, location, location. Obviously, once a mine is in place it cannot be moved. Miners must be very particular in their selection of country, province, or state.

A survey by McMahon and Vidler (2008) found Canada, Australia, and The United States to be the most mining friendly locations respectively. Eurasia, Latin America, Africa, and Oceania were seen as less friendly. The Fraser Institute (fraserinstitute.org), in its *Survey of Mining Companies: 2010 Mid-Year Update*, lists the top ten most mining friendly jurisdictions as Alberta, Finland, Quebec, Yukon, Saskatchewan, Chile, Newfoundland and Labrador, Botswana, Alaska, and Nevada. Their bottom ten are Ecuador, Mongolia, Kazakhstan, Bolivia, Venezuela, Zimbabwe, Russia, Colorado, Indonesia, and Tasmania.

The U.S. is currently looking at revising the still in-effect mining law of 1872. The revisions being talked about include a 10% tax on gross profits. Keep in mind this is gross not net and may wipe out numerous miners if implemented. Within the United States, about half the gold produced in the country comes from Nevada, and the state is very friendly to mining interests.

Australia recently passed a confiscatory mining tax of some 40%. It's yet to be seen how this will affect their mining industry.

In the early 1990s, after decades of not allowing foreigners to have a controlling interest in Mexican miners, the law was changed. Foreign companies have been inundating Mexico seeking to buy up long dormant properties. Mexico is now known for its respect for mining and its supportive mining law. It also has a long mining history and tradition dating back centuries, not to mention low costs.

The Canadian Province of Quebec is perhaps the most mining friendly jurisdiction on earth. The province reimburses companies for 50% of their exploration expenses. In effect it allows miners to cut their exploration budget in half or double the amount of exploration they perform.

What are some of the most un-friendly places to mine?

Mongolia recently instituted an excessive windfall profit tax. I understand that it is being revised but it still sounds bad.

Uzbekistan claimed that the largest U.S. gold miner, Newmont, owed the government taxes. Reportedly, the government stole cash and bullion, and when that wasn't enough to pay off the supposedly owed taxes, they expropriated (nationalized) the gold mine.

Uzbekistan also annulled Oxus Gold's previously issued license to develop the Khandiza polymetallic deposit.

In Venezuela, "The Venezuelan government plans to nationalize the Las Cristinas gold mine, which is estimated to have the largest gold deposits in the country and is currently conceded to the Canadian company Crystallex." That quote comes from the Minister of Basic Industries and Mining (MIBAM), Rodolfo Sanz.

The country of Fiji seized the Vatukoula mine belonging to Australia's DRDGold.

In Russia the environmental agency revoked two mining licenses owned by Peter Hambro, the London-listed gold producer.

Other countries on the 'bad boy' list include China, Ecuador, Bolivia, and Zimbabwe.

A leopard doesn't change his spots nor a zebra his stripes. If they did it once they can do it again. While many large miners hold claims in numerous locations, try to pick only those with primary interests in friendly countries.

Mine Development and Production

The development of a mine is a seven to ten year arduous process. In the beginning there is moose pasture. A lonely soul wanders along kicking rocks for clues as to what may lie below. If warranted, exploratory trenching or drilling will be done, and then additional, ongoing infill drilling as necessary to better define the deposit area. Exploration takes years before a mine begins production and continues for the life of the mine. Leases and rights of way must be secured. A feasibility study must be completed. It will cover all facets of building and running the mine and must satisfy owners, investors, and lenders that a mine would be possible and profitable with no major roadblocks. It's similar to a business plan for a startup company. Baseline and ongoing environmental studies need to satisfy government regulatory entities. Engineering and procurement activities, as well as construction of road and utilities, are ongoing activities at any mine site. Actual mine construction and/or improvements can require hundreds of millions or billions of dollars to finish. Startup production problems are not unexpected and continuous refinement is the norm. National 43-101 (Canadian) resource estimates need to be compiled at regular intervals to keep investors and lenders investing and lending.

Permitting is another years' long process that needs to be kept abreast of in conjunction with all other mining functions. There may be dozens or even hundreds of permits to obtain. Fund raising (financing) never ceases. If the money flow stops, work on or at the mine ceases. And finally, community relations must be forever kept up, as bad relations can indeed shut down a mine.

Not every mine that is started is completed. Not every mine that is completed goes into production. Not every mine in production stays in production until its resources are exhausted. There are seemingly infinite examples to choose from. Mining is a difficult, dirty, resource intensive, money intensive, complex, dangerous business. It is difficult to extract minable ore at a profit, yet mines are so vital and necessary to everything we own and our standard of living that they are absolutely indispensible.

Productive mines can stay producing for many decades or even centuries. But they are wasting assets. By that I mean, that unless reserves are somehow replaced, the more ore that is taken from the mine, the quicker the life of the mine diminishes. A mine with a 20 million ounce resource is going to last half as long if production is 2 million ounces a year instead of a million. Who wants to be holding the stock when the last ounce is produced? Once it stops production, the mine has no value other than salvage.

Now, how does a mine replace mined ounces? First, a rising gold (commodity) price can convert known resources into economical reserves. Mineable ore is rarely evenly distributed in any property. It may be twice as concentrated in one vein as compared to another close by. Ore that was unprofitable to mine at a lower price now becomes economical. Mine life can be extended years just by a rising price of the underlying commodity with no further exploration.

A second way to expand mineable ore is via discovery (drilling) at existing operations. Most mines cover only a very small part of a claim or land holding. Land nearby the mine is often like land the mine sits on and will have like metals.

A less likely way to find additional ore is through grassroots exploration projects. These would be projects that are exploring new, never before explored (or never explored with the latest mining techniques) areas. Keep in mind that these types of projects have very long lead times and are very uncertain in nature.

Far more common are mergers and acquisitions. It is much easier, and often more profitable, for a large mining establishment to absorb a smaller one. This gives the large company known, verifiable, additional ounces to work with at a fraction of what it would have cost them to find those ounces themselves from scratch.

Gold 'in the ground' is valued at about $50 per ounce on average for a small miner. Silver 'in the ground' is valued at close to $1 per ounce. What a great value for a company that already has infrastructure in place close to the deposit. Even if they had to pay two or three times these amounts, the profits will be huge.

Let's say that a merger or acquisition is not possible for a mining interest. What are some ways that they can increase revenue to stay in business?

A rising price for the underlying commodity will increase profitability, all else being equal. A rise in production, either via processing more ore or by efficiency gains will help the bottom line. In good times (high prices) miners will take the lower grade ore and during bad times (lower prices) they will 'high grade'. This helps ensure a steady income and the longest possible mine life. Less appealing is selling more shares or taking on more debt which will also increase revenue, though not in desirable ways.

According to gold guru Jim Sinclair, it takes $500 to $600 to pull an ounce of gold from an underground mine, $300 to get a like ounce from an open cut mine, and only $22 to $75 to get one from a surface mine. Even though annual gold industry exploration budgets have risen more than 3 fold since the turn of the last century, the resources found in new discoveries are down some 80-90%. (Agorafinancil.com).

I think it's obvious why takeovers are so advantageous to larger miners.

Miners

For mining equities, in general, the bigger the better. By better I mean more conservative, more stable, less volatile, better management, and a 'going concern'. Large companies are well known, well researched, and rated by research firms. Each has had many years or decades to prove itself and prosper. The longer in business, likely the better the business model. There are normally fewer surprises with large miners than with small. The smaller entities are just about the opposite. They have short track records and are unproven. The market will discount their stock value because they are 'unknown' to the mainstream. Furthermore, large enterprises often have real assets to back their valuations, where smaller ones are only paper tigers with little more than hope keeping them afloat.

Another way of distinguishing between miners is whether they are 43-101 compliant. This is the Canadian Institute of Mining, Metallurgy, and Petroleum (CIM) classification system under National 43-101 regulations. It became effective February 1, 2001. This standard is a codified set of rules and guidelines for reporting and displaying information related to mineral properties. It applies to any company listed on a Canadian stock exchange. Since over half of the world's mining concerns trade there, it has become a de-facto worldwide benchmark. Many gold funds and retirement accounts cannot own miners that are not a certain market size or do-not have 43-101 resources.

The following are some best practices to follow when considering entering into the realm of mining equities. Always remember that mines are wasting assets. They deplete themselves. Don't stick with one forever. Situations can change quickly in the mining business. Buyouts and takeovers occur with regularity. Mines flood. The large uranium miner Cameco had its main mine flood a few years back and saw a precipitous decline in its share price because of it. Only allot a small portion of your funds to the most speculative miners. Remember, the downside could be 100%. I've seen this happen with numerous mining shares over the years. Pay close attention to the commodity market associated with your miner. There is often a one-to-one relationship with a share and its underlying commodity. Pay close attention to energy costs. Energy accounts for about 25% of a mines cost. Labor relations are another biggie to keep abreast of as well.

Silver and Gold Miners by the Numbers
There are about 5 times as many primary gold mining stocks as silver
mining stocks as listed on the US and Canadian exchanges. The silver
miners account for only some one seventh of global silver production.
Only about the same fraction of these silver miners actually produces
silver. The rest are of the junior/explorer variety. The value of all listed
gold miners is more than 20 times that of silver miners. There are
literally hundreds of companies that have market caps greater than all
the silver miners combined.

Classes of Miners

Producers
Producers are those miners that are currently retrieving ore for market.
They tend to be the larger companies but not always. They tend to
offer geographic diversity. Most have been around a long time. Keep
in mind that most mines produce many different metals.
We're interested in primary gold/silver mines. These mines can be
divided as follows.
Large: > 1 million ounces of annual gold production
(Produce half of all globally mined gold)
Mid-Tier: 200k – 1m ounces
(Produce about 10% of mined gold)
Small: < 200k ounces of production
The average producing mine has about 10 years of reserves.

Developers/Near Producers
One rung down is the Near Producers. They tend to have proven
resources and some infrastructure. They often have plans to begin
production in the near term (1 or 2 years). They usually, but not always
will have a Feasibility Study completed. Their share price will normally
rise when production does begin. They offer higher leverage than
Producers but more uncertainty. There was a high-flying Canadian
company by the name of Nova Gold that was a Near Producer in 2008
when their plans fell through. They had committed many millions to
their mine infrastructure and had their financing in place. Then they
decided conditions weren't right and put production on hold. Their
share price subsequently tumbled over 90% in short order. You can
never be certain of anything in mining.

Explorers/Juniors

While there is no definition of a junior, analysts know one when they see one. These tend to be the small, underfinanced and over hyped companies. Only a small fraction will ever see production. More likely they will go bankrupt. If lucky, they may get a good buyout offer from a Major. They are normally several years or more from production, if it ever happens. These ventures may or may not have proven resources and may only have title to land or nothing at all. Likely, they do not have any infrastructure. Their stock price is low for good reason and is probably a penny stock. What they do have is high leverage to a major discovery, should it occur, and they may get bought out at a nice premium.

Moose Pasture
See Mark Twain.

Mining Companies

I cannot overemphasize the following. These are selected but <u>Not Necessarily Recommended</u> precious metal related stocks and funds. Do Your Own Due Diligence! I do not share in your profits and am not responsible for your losses. Your money is yours and mine is mine. Do not invest in any company solely because you saw it listed in this book. These are the largest-cap primary gold miners widely available for trading at the world's major stock markets.

Agnico-Eagle Mines (NYSE:AEM) - Canada
AngloGold Ashanti (NYSE:AU) - South African
Barrick Gold (NYSE:ABX) - Canada
Buenaventura (NYSE:BVN) - Peru

Eldorado Gold (AMEX:EGO) - Canada
Freeport McMoRan Gold (NYSE:FCX) - US
Golden Star (AMEX:GSS) - US
Gold Fields (NYSE:GFI) - South Africa

GoldCorp (NYSE:GG) - Canada
Harmony Gold Mining (NYSE:HMY) - South Africa
IAM Gold (NYSE:IAG) - Canada
Kinross Gold (NYSE:KGC) - Canada

Lihir (Nasdaq:LIHR) – Papua New Guinea
Newcrest (Australian:NCM) - Australia
Newmont Mining (NYSE:NEM) - US

Northgate Minerals (AMEX:NXG) - Canada
Randgold Resources (Nasdaq:GOLD)
Yamana (NYSE:AUY) - Canada

As you can see, there are more located in Canada than anywhere else.
This does not mean that all or any of their actual mines are located
there. This is where the company is headquartered. In fact, it may have
no mining operations in the country at all. Most of these firms are
international and have many mining operations in many countries.
Within Canada, a disproportionate number of mining companies reside
in the Vancouver area.
According to Goldfields Mineral Service (GFMS), in September 2009
these were some of the market capitalizations of these companies per
ounce of gold held in the ground: Barrick $194; Goldcorp $507; Kinross
$302; Newmont $237; AngloGold Ashanti $92; Gold Fields $45; and
Ashanti $26.
The 10 Best Rated Precious Metals Stocks based on the number of
positive brokerage analyst ratings was compiled by cnanalyst.com in
July 2010. Here are their results. Corporations are listed in order with
the best stock pick first.

Barrick Gold Corporation (NYSE:ABX)
IAMGOLD Corporation (NYSE:IAG)
Yamana Gold Inc. (NYSE:AUY)
Goldcorp Inc. (NYSE:GG)
Silver Wheaton Corp. (NYSE:SLW)

Kinross Gold Corporation (NYSE:KGC)
Eldorado Gold Corporation (NYSE:EGO)
Newmont Mining Corporation (NYSE:NEM)
Agnico-Eagle Mines Limited (NYSE:AEM)
Aurizon Mines Ltd. (AMEX:AZK)

The largest-cap primary silver miners are:

Coeur D' Alene (NYSE:CDE) - US
Hecla (NYSE:HL) - US
Industrias Peñoles (IPOAF.PK) - Mexico

Pan American (Nasdaq:PAAS) - Canada
SilverCorp (AMEX:SVM) - Canada
Silver Standard (Nasdaq:SSRI) - Canada

Be warned that these are not necessarily the largest silver producers.
They are the largest miners that have silver as their primary output.
Between 2/3 and 3/4 of all silver comes from other-than-silver miners.
Most silver comes as by-product of lead/zinc mines, copper mines, or
gold mines, in that order.
Ten of the world's top 14 silver producers (over 10 million ounces per
year) are big base metal operations. The 14 are BHP Billiton, Peñoles,
KGHM Polska, Minera Volcan, Kazakhmys, Pan American Silver,
Goldcorp, Buenaventura, Polymetal, Southern Copper, Hochschild, Rio
Tinto, Teck Cominco, and Codelco.
The world's largest mining companies are:
BHP Billiton (NYSE:BHP) - It is the largest mining company in the
world. You get diversification in one stock. It is an Australian company.
Rio Tinto (NYSE:RTP) - It is also one of the largest mining companies
in the world and you also get diversification in one stock. It is UK
owned.
Teck Cominco (NYSE:TCK) - It is another very large mining company.
It has Canadian owners.

Junior Mining Companies

Junior mining companies (Juniors) can be thought of as 'feeder'
companies to the major miners. More often than not, if they don't go
bankrupt, they are bought by a Gold Major rather than begin mining
operations themselves. Today, Juniors perform about half of all mineral
exploration. The Majors have relied on them more and more for new
discoveries as time progresses. The term 'Juniors' is often used
interchangeably with 'Explorers', as that's what Juniors do. They
traditionally explored 'virgin' land for minerals but that is changing.
Today, most tend to explore is areas adjacent to or near current or
previously operating mines. As there are many thousands of current
and former mines about, the best place to look for gold is where it has
already been discovered. Why spend countless days and dollars
looking where no one thought to before when you have a much better
chance of finding what it is you are looking for right next to a known
deposit. Besides the obvious, there is likely to already be infrastructure
in place and a capable workforce nearby to exploit.

While there is no definition of what a junior miner is, gold junior miners can generally be thought of as those that have market caps less than a quarter million dollars. About half have market capitalizations of less than ten million dollars. Most are 'penny' stocks trading at less than one dollar per share. Many trade for a fraction of a penny per share. The ultimate fate of a Junior can be one of four.

They can go into production. This is rare for a Junior to attempt as the set of skills for drilling and exploration is quite different than the set of skills needed to construct and operate a mine. Most Juniors have no intention of ever becoming a mining company.

They can get bought by a Major. This is far more likely than production. Majors must continually replenish ore as it is mined either via their in-house drilling and discovery process or by buying ounces through acquisition.

Many small exploration companies simply flounder. Heed the words of Mark Twain: "A mine is a hole in the ground with a liar standing beside it." All too many of these companies end up in this category. They simply finance exploration operations through share dilution. Unless they can find enough mineable gold to construct a mine or sell out, they end up in this state of limbo for many years or decades, their stock price falling all the while. Normally it's an easy transition for floundering companies to transition into the fourth possible destination: bankruptcy.

More Juniors fall into this category than any other, perhaps all other. It is said that perhaps only one in one thousand junior exploration companies will make the transition to profitable miner. You would do well to heed the words of Mark Twain or Mickey Fulp. The following is from a missive by Mr. Fulp from September 10, 2008.

"Don't forget that most junior resource companies are simply "mining the stock market". Few have potentially viable Resources let alone economic Reserves. Most don't want to be miners. Of those that aspire to this difficult goal, perhaps 1 in 15 will ever develop a project with Mineral Reserves, and more than half of those will fail for one reason or another. Assuming those numbers are more or less correct, about 100 of the 1373 Venture Exchange exploration and mining juniors will define a Reserve and less than half of those, perhaps 30 or 40 at most, will develop a profitable mine for their shareholders or, more likely, the bigger company that takes them over will develop said mine."

Junior stocks selection criteria

There is no check-list of specific metrics to follow when selecting a Junior to invest in. It's as much art and experience as science due to the fact that each and every mining project is different. No two are alike and normal methods of valuation don't always apply. But there are things to look for to increase your odds of success.

Companies already producing ore or moving toward production in the next year or two are safer than those not producing.

Those with quality properties in politically stable areas are better.

Those with vital infrastructure on site or close by and good road access are better.

Those with proven and probable resources are better.

Management with a track record of success is better. In general, it's better to have a mediocre property with excellent management than the other way around.

Those with a healthy balance sheet, cash on hand, lines or credit, or the ability to easily raise funds are better.

Those that have a completed feasibility study are better.

The three most important factors in selecting any junior resource company are Share Structure, Management, and Projects. Try to have excellence in all three.

For pricing Juniors that are not yet producing, only buy them for up to ten percent of "in situ metal value" (on site or in the ground). If you have a million tonnes of ore in the ground worth one hundred dollars per tonne, you have a one hundred million dollar company for market valuation purposes.

The Majors have paid between twenty and thirty percent of in situ metal value in past buyouts.

According to James & Dashkov in *What's a Company's Gold Worth?*, published in January of 2010:

- A survey was conducted of 90 Mining Companies with mostly gold resources and listed on the Toronto Stock Exchange.
- They used 43-101-compliant gold resource estimates.
- The average worth of gold in the ground was:
- US$20 per ounce for Inferred
- US$30 per ounce for Measured & Indicated
- US$160 per ounce for Proven & Probable

These are averages and every mining project is different. They should be used as guidelines only for company valuation purposes.

Junior Seasonality

There is a definite seasonal pattern to exploration companies, but that doesn't necessarily equate to a price pattern. They all move on their own merits and the daily change in the price of gold tends to have only a marginal affect on them. Nonetheless, this is what the annual pattern looks like for most junior miners.

Drilling results move the Junior's share price one way or the other. Drilling takes place from Spring to Fall in both hemispheres. In the tropics, drilling may continue year round.

Cores normally take months to be assayed.

The drill results are normally released via Press Release during the ensuing Fall to Winter time period.

Resources are re-calculated by the company and released in the Winter to Spring period.

Wash. Rinse. Repeat. The cycle continues for another year.

The best period for speculation is just prior to the news of drill results and the second best is just prior to news of resource numbers based on the drill results.

Why *should* Precious Metal Junior Mining Companies appreciate, in aggregate, from here?

- Gold resources and grades in the world's largest mines are in a persistent state of decline. This has led to a flat-to-falling supply of gold for a decade now.
- Senior companies will need to buy more reserves and will need to buy the smaller companies reserves. These Major producers have continually cut back on exploration staff and projects for many years and can only replenish supply buy buying out other miners.
- There is an ongoing shortage of new gold projects and production from old. New mines are not being opened, and new reserves discovered, apace with what's being extracted from older mines.
- There have been few major discoveries in the past two decades.
- Most drilling is now done by smaller companies.
- Few investors have any position in gold or gold companies. The ones they do are in the Major companies which are, therefore, fully valued. As the bull market progresses, investors will increasingly look down the food chain to the medium, and then small cap miners.
- Most small cap miners are at historic low valuations.
- Because of their size and undervaluation, Juniors have great leverage and represent a perpetual option on the price of gold.

Be careful out there. The Juniors are notoriously volatile. They can double or more in short order or can fall to zero just as quickly. It's said that they are the most volatile of all stocks and I agree. Here's a look at what they can do for you. These were the best performing Juniors in the last gold bull market. Here's how they fared.

Stock Price in 1975:
- Bankeno $1.25
- Steep Rock   .93
- Mineral Resources   .60
- Wharf Resources   .40
- Azure Resources   .05
- Lion Mines   .07

Stock Price in 1980 and resulting increase:
- Bankeno $430   344x
- Steep Rock $440   473x
- Mineral Resources $415   691x
- Wharf Resources $560   1400x
- Azure Resources $109   2180x
- Lion Mines $380   5428x

That is, Bankeno increased by some 34,000% in five years. Would you have held the entire way?
It can work in reverse though. Here are a few from this current bull market and how they fared from high to low. Look them up and see.
- Sino Silver $3.00 down to $.03
- Abcourt Mines $1.11 down to $.06
- Gemini Exploration $.095 down to $.0004

And did I say to be careful out there?

Royalty Companies

Royalty companies are not miners and own no mining properties. They have somehow acquired the rights to royalties to other companies mining output. The contracts may be for a fixed amount of metal, be bounded by a certain time frame, or be in effect for the life of the mine. They tend to be long term in nature. All agreements are as different as the companies involved. Commonly employed are net smelter royalty agreements. This entitles the royalty company to a net percentage of what is actually refined at the smelter.

Royalty companies are seen as low risk because they normally get paid first. The only way they don't get paid is if the miner goes out of business or for some reason stops producing metal.

Royalty companies have low overhead because they produce nothing and have no infrastructure. This means they have no exposure to rising capital costs. But they do have full exposure to rising metal prices and are protected from falling prices.

Typically, these stocks trade at a premium due to their desirability and safety.

Here are some of the largest and best known.

Franco-Nevada (Toronto:FNV) - Gold in Nevada.
Gold Wheaton (Vancouver:GLW) - Gold and Platinum.
International Royalty Corp. (AMEX:ROY) - Base and Precious Metals (Nickel).
Royal Gold (Nasdaq:RGLD) - Gold; Well Diversified Properties.
Sandstorm Resources (Vancouver:SSL) - Gold Royalty.
Silver Wheaton (NYSE:SLW) - 100% Silver Leverage.

Exchange Traded Funds

"A security that tracks an index, a commodity, or a basket of assets like an index fund, but trades like a stock on an exchange." *Investopedia* Exchange Traded Funds (ETFs) aim to track or trade the underlying commodity. They are securities and may or may not have actual physical metal in storage backing them. They often trade both above and below their respective Net Asset Values (NAV).

An advantage of owning an ETF is that Funds and Institutions that cannot own commodities can own ETF shares. This exposes ETFs to potentially vast sums of money. A disadvantage is that they are taxed at a 28% collectible rate, not 15% capital gains rate no matter how long owned.

The issue, as I see it, is to make sure yours has the goods.
According to Jeff Nielson:
"Bullion-ETF's claim they can purchase gold and silver with *no premium*, and in *infinite amounts* - and then store these vast hoards of gold and silver at **zero cost**. How can this be possible?"
"With only a few, rare exceptions, **no "bullion-ETF's" hold <u>any</u> gold or silver**. Instead, all they hold are "paper promises" to deliver gold."
Make sure yours is audited regularly.
Authors John Rubino, Dave Morgan, and James Turk all urge caution. These are some of the largest and most well known precious metal Exchange Traded Funds. As always, these are selected but not necessarily recommended Funds. Do your own thorough research. The Stock Exchange the fund trades on and its trading symbol follow the equity name. The year in which it began trading follows that.
Central Fund of Canada (AMEX:CEF) (1961) Holds 100% Gold and Silver bullion. It's a closed-end fund that's made up of 59% gold and 34% silver. Audited twice yearly. Almost always trades at a premium to spot (market) price of metal (NAV). The premium to NAV has been as high as 30%.
Central Gold Trust (AMEX:GTU) (2006) Gold Bullion
Claymore Silver Bullion Trust (TORONTO:SVR.UN)
Elements MLCX Gold Index ETN (AMEX:GOE)
ETFS Silver Trust (NYSEArca: SIVR) (2009)
ETFS Physical Swiss Gold Shares (NYSEArca:SGOL) (2009)
E-TRACS UBS Bloomberg CMCI Gold ETN (NYSE:UBG) (2008)
E-TRACS UBS Bloomberg CMCI Silver ETN (NYSE:USV) (2008)
Global X Silver Mines ETF (NYSEArca:SIL) (2010)
Horizons BetaPro COMEX Gold ETF (TORONTO:HUG) (2009)
iSHARES COMEX Gold Trust (NYSE:IAU) (2005) Gold Bullion. Trades at a premium.
iShares Silver Trust (NYSE:SLV) (2006) Silver Bullion. No independent audits. Can lease its silver. Doesn't segregate or allocate silver.
Market Vectors Gold Miners ETF (NYSE:GDX) (2006)
PowerShares DB Gold (NYSE:DGL) (2007) Gold Bullion.
PowerShares DB Precious Metals (NYSE:DBP) (2007) Precious Metals. 80% Gold. 20% Silver.
PowerShares DB Silver (NYSE:DBS) (2007) Silver Bullion.
streetTRACKS SPDR Gold Shares (NYSE:GLD) (2004) Gold. No independent audits. Can lease its gold. Doesn't segregate or allocate gold. Tracks 1/10 ounce per share.

NAV

ETFs are structured to keep the share price very close to the net asset value (NAV). They buy or sell shares and metal to attempt to keep the NAV constant. They try to track the price of bullion.

Shares of closed-end funds can trade at a steep discount to NAV or at a premium depending on market sentiment. Those who buy at a discount and sell at a premium to NAV will get an added kicker on their investment.

Goto http://www.centralfund.com and click on "Net Asset Value" to find current NAV of the CEF fund.

GLD

According to James Turk:

Ever since the Greenlight Fund said they were swapping from paper gold to 'real' physical gold there's been a steady sell off in GLD holdings. According to TickerSpy, since Greenlight announced their change the following funds have sold out of GLD.

Augustine Asset Management - 1.9m

Churchill Management Group - 0.4m

CI Investments - 424.7m

Manley Asset Management - 1.1m

Pate Capital Partners - 4.54m

TD Securities - 2.0m

United Financial - 7.1m

GLD does not prove that the gold they purport to hold actually exists, nor do they verify its quality, by way of independent third party audits. The same gold in GLD may be owned by two people because of short selling.

Even if GLD were in reality backed by gold, there are too many parties between you and the gold to claim that you really own it. They employ sub-custodians to hold the fund's gold and those sub-custodians may employ sub-custodians of their own. So while you may have "access" to the gold price through GLD, you do not have access to any physical metal that it may be holding.

James Turk from his article "The Paper Game"

www.financialsense.com/editorials/turk/2007/0305.html

And from Jim Willie:

"The COMEX can legally use Street Tracks GLD shares from their Exchange Traded Fund to satisfy short futures contracts.

Evidence points to the GLD gold bullion inventory taken to satisfy the London demand for gold delivery.

GET OUT OF THE 'GLD' AND 'SLV' FUNDS, WHICH ARE IN ALL LIKELIHOOD DEEP FRAUDS THAT HOLD SHRINKING BULLION IN DEPOSITS. In time the GLD might be exposed as having little or no gold, and certainty inadequate amounts to back their fund for legitimacy."
This is taken from the writings of Jim Willie at
http://news.goldseek.com/GoldenJackass/1256173200.php

Buyer beware.

Precious Metal Funds

I must reiterate the following: These are selected but <u>Not Necessarily Recommended</u> precious metal related stocks and funds. Do Your Own Due Diligence! I do not share in your profits and am not responsible for your losses. Your money is yours and mine is mine. Do not invest in any company solely because you saw it listed in this book.

Double Your Pleasure
The following funds endeavor to double the move in the underlying commodity, either up or down.

Long (Bullish) Precious Metals Funds
- Horizons BetaPro COMEX Gold Bullion Bull Plus ETF (TORONTO:HBU)
- Horizons BetaPro COMEX Silver Bull Plus ETF (TORONTO:HZU)
- PowerShares DB Gold Double Long ETN (NYSE: DGP)
- ProFunds PM UltraSector (PMPIX) (2002) (1.5x)
- Proshares Ultra Gold ETF (NYSE:UGL)
- Proshares Ultra Silver ETF (NYSE:AGQ)

Short (Bearish) Precious Metals Funds
- DB Gold Short ETN (NYSE:DGZ)
- Horizons BetaPro COMEX Gold Bullion Bear Plus ETF (TORONTO:HBD)
- Horizons BetaPro COMEX Silver Bear Plus ETF (TORONTO:HZD)
- PowerShares DB Gold Double Short ETN (NYSE: DZZ)
- Proshares Ultrashort Gold ETF (NYSE:GLL)
- Proshares Ultrashort Silver ETF (NYSE:ZSL)

The following precious metals funds are some of the best known and widely traded. Each is different in some way from the next. Each will have different weightings of stocks to bullion. Some like foreign securities and some like domestic. Others only have a portion of their holdings in precious metals and will hold other natural resources as well. Just be aware that, should you be looking for 100% gold exposure, you may not get that with certain funds.

- American Century Global Gold (Nasdaq:BGEIX) (1988)
- BMO Jr. Gold Index (Toronto:ZJG)
- ETF Securities Silver Trust (Nyse:SIVR) (2009)
- ETF Securities Physical Swiss Gold Shares (Nyse:SGOL) (2009)
- iShares TSX Global Gold (Toronto:XGD) (2000)
- Fidelity Select Gold (FSAGX) (1987)
- Global X Silver Miners ETF (NYSE:SIL) (2010)
- Millenium Bullion Fund - for Canadian RRSP and RRIF Retirement Funds
- Paulson & Co. Gold Fund (2010)
- Rydex Precious Metals Fund (Nasdaq:RYMNX) (2005)
- Silver Bullion Trust (Toronto:SBT-U)
- Sprott Asset Physical Gold Trust (NYSE:PHYS) (Toronto:PHY) (2010) 100% Physical Gold Bullion   sprott.com
- Tocqueville Gold Fund (Nasdaq:TGLDX) (1999) tocquevillefunds.com
- U.S. Global Investors Gold and Precious Metals (Nasdaq:USERX) (2004) - Gold Stock Fund invests in producing companies only.
- U.S. Global Investors World Precious Minerals (Nasdaq:UNWPX) (1988) - 80% Producers - 20% Juniors   usfunds.com
- USAA Precious Metals and Minerals Fund (Nasdaq:USAGX) (1988)
- Van Eck Global Junior Gold Miner ETF (GDXJ) (2009) – 38 Juniors/Explorers   vaneck.com

This last group I would classify as 'non-traditional investments in gold' funds. They are a mish-mash of other options available to you.

- AIG World Gold Fund   A fund of gold funds.
- DSP Blackrock World Gold Fund A fund of gold funds.
- E-gold e-gold.com Like GoldMoney. Digital gold.
- First Majestic firstmajestic.com Silver Mining Company. Buy Direct from the mine.
- Liberty Dollar libertydollar.org Silver denominated coinage.
- Masters Fund   Seeks to maximize returns in gold, not in dollars.
- Phoenix Silver phoenixdollar.com Silver denominated coinage.
- SeekBullion seekbullion.com   Online Bullion Auction site.

Diversify, Diversify, Diversify

Just as you would diversify between classes of stocks and between asset classes themselves, so too should you diversify within the precious metals sector.
The four most common of the precious metals are gold, silver, platinum, and palladium. There are many nice coins and rounds made of platinum or palladium you may want to consider.
It's also not a bad idea to have different forms and sizes of metal. Think about owning coins, bars, rounds, or even jewelry of a single metal.
Actual gold nuggets make nice conversation pieces or gifts.
Consider diversifying the storage of your metals between home, a safe deposit box, and a depository. Don't put all your nuggets in one location.
Look into e-gold solutions such as BullionVault, GoldMoney, or the like.
Own a smorgasbord of Miners, Funds, and possibly certain reliable ETFs.
And don't forget to spread your wealth among Producers, Near-Producers, and a smattering of Juniors and Explorers.
Diversify, Diversify, diversify.

Portfolio Allocation per the Pros

"Investors can potentially improve the reward-to-risk ratio in conservative, moderate, and aggressive asset allocations by including precious metals with allocations of 7.1%, 12.5%, and 15.7%, respectively. These results suggest that including precious metals in an asset allocation may increase expected returns and _reduce portfolio risk_." _Ibbotson Associates_

Traditionally, many investment advisors have advised perhaps 5 to 10% of one's portfolio be allocated to precious metals. That's changing. There seem to be two camps. Those in the know about the bull market are advising more, sometimes much more than 10% be invested in gold at this time. Those still stuck in the stocks and bonds (and real estate) paradigm are not recommending any. If you averaged all advisor recommendations together, you'd probably come up with an average somewhere about the norm. However, as per the last chapter, more and more 'traditional' advisors are turning toward gold.

In 2009, an organization named Efficient Frontier undertook a study to find the optimal amount of Gold and Precious Minerals that one should hold to provide maximum return for minimal risk. The period of study was from 1971 to 2009. They found the optimal holding of gold in a portfolio during that time to be about 15%. One would have actually done the best with a 50% holding of metals during that period but with greater volatility.

In addition to the two advisories mentioned already, Wainwright Economics suggests anywhere from 18-47% be in precious metals during inflationary environments. Casey Research sees 33% as the way to go while the company's founder, Doug Casey, admits he's been 100% in gold for his personal account since 2008. And the Dean of them all, Richard Russell has let it be known that he's now 50% in gold in his personal portfolio.

One thing that advisors seem not to do is to differentiate between physical metal allocation and paper metal. Paper gold being anything other than fully paid for, allocated, insured, in your possession, physical metal. Paper gold includes mining company shares, unallocated gold accounts, futures contracts, and any other form of precious metal investment where you don't own actual physical bullion in your name (or better yet, in your hand). In the Paper Metal Versus Bullion Chapter, we'll get into the differences.

In short, I would want to diversify within this sector no matter what your percentage allocation to metals. You may want to diversify by holding a portion in gold, silver, platinum, and palladium. All are considered precious metals along with certain other rare earth's such as Osmium or Rhodium.

You may want to look at holding different forms of the metals such as coins, bars, rounds, or jewelry.

How about diversifying the storage of your loot between your home, a safe deposit box, and a depository?

How about a portion in an audited E-Gold account such as Bullionvault, Everbank, or GoldMoney.

Don't forget individual mining company stocks, precious metals funds, and exchange traded funds (ETFs) too. And within the mining companies there are producers, juniors, and explorers to consider.

Whatever you percentage strategy, there are still a couple of truisms no matter what you are investing in. Diversify, Dollar Cost Average, and Hold for the Long Term. As long as you have the trend correct, these are your three best amigos.

Precious Metal Market Indexes

Precious Metal resource companies are primarily traded on the dominant Canadian Exchanges in Toronto and Vancouver. To a lesser extent, they trade on the AMEX Exchange in the United States. Many will trade on a combination of exchanges or even all of the primary exchanges. However, they will have somewhat different symbols on each exchange.

To better evaluate the mining sector, a number of stock indexes have been constructed so as to more easily track the sector as a whole or in part. There are six indexes. The first three can be accessed in real time by entering the karat symbol (^) before the index name in the search box at finance.yahoo.com. (For example: ^HUI)

The **HUI** index is the primary mining index of unhedged gold and silver miners. It is also known as the AMEX Gold BUGS Index. The acronym BUGS comes from "Basket of Unhedged Gold Stocks". Presumably, this is also where the term 'Gold Bug' originated. Unhedged miners are mining companies that have not sold forward their gold. When a company hedges, it sells future production at today's price. In a falling market, this benefits the miner. In a rising market, the miner loses. Hedging has not been a good idea for at least the last 10 years for precious metal miners. All companies included in this index are supposed to be unhedged but this is not true. Barrick Gold has hedged its production for much, if not all, of the current bull market.

The HUI is a modified equal dollar weighted index of 15 gold mining companies. The 3 largest companies (Goldcorp, Barrick, and Newmont) make up over a third of the index by weight. The five largest comprise about half of the index while, the remaining companies make up the other half. The weightings do vary regularly. See: http://amex.com/othProd/prodInf/OpPiIndComp.jsp?Product_Symbol=HUI for current rankings.

This index provides the narrowest cross section of the six indexes and is heavily skewed to the biggest gold and silver companies. Approximately 99% of the index resources are in gold.

The **XAU** index is comprised predominately of the largest 'Blue Chip' gold and silver miners. Many of them are hedged but many have closed their hedges and are currently unhedged.

The XAU is also known as the Philadelphia Gold and Silver Sector Index. It contains 16 large and medium cap weighted companies engaged in the mining of gold, silver and copper. The same 3 large companies (Goldcorp, Barrick, and Newmont) that top the HUI make up about half of this index by weight. The largest 5 make up about two thirds. For company updates to the index see: www.nasdaqtrader.com/Dynamic/PublicIndex/XAU.txt.

Approximately 92% of the index resources are in gold and about 5% in silver.

The **GDM** index is also known as the AMEX Gold Miners Index and is a modified market capitalization weighted index of 31 silver and gold mining companies. This index represents the largest cross-section of precious metals mining companies throughout the world. For current index updates go to: http://www.amex.com/othProd/prodInf/opPiIndComp.jsp?prod_Symbol=GDM.

Approximately one fourth of the included companies are large cap, about the same amount are medium cap, and the remainder small and micro cap.

The 5 largest companies account for about 40% of the total index weighting. Roughly 96% of the index resources are in gold and about 4% in silver.

A good way to invest in this index is via the Market Vectors Gold Miners ETF (GDX) listed on the New York Stock Exchange.

SPTGD is the symbol for the S&P/TSX Global Gold Index and is another modified market capitalization index of 19 precious metals mining companies with a minimum market capitalization of close to a quarter billion dollars. More than three quarters are large cap and most of the rest are mid cap. The three largest cap companies dominate the index with greater than 50% of the weighted value. The 5 largest companies account for about two thirds of the total index weight. Nearly 100% of index resources are in gold.

 To find weekly weighting updates go to:
http://.ca.ishares.com/product_info/fund_holdings.do?ticker=XGD.
A good way to track the returns of this index is via the iShares CDN Gold Sector Index ETF (XGD). Another is the Claymore S&P/TSX Global Mining ETF (CMW). Both trade on the Toronto Stock exchange. There is not a great deal of diversity between the four indexes listed above. The two below do offer some difference.

The symbol for the S&P/TSX Venture Composite Index is **CDNX**. This index consists of over 500 micro-cap companies. The average company capitalization is in the neighborhood of $25 million. Nearly two thirds are involved in natural resource extraction in one form or another. Slightly less than half actually mine, produce, or explore for gold or silver. Perhaps one in five is an oil and gas company. This is the only index of the six that is comprised of almost all micro cap companies. To get updates to the index see:
ftp.cdnx.com/SPCDNXIndex/Components.txt.

The **GSCI** index is the newest of the six and includes a variety of small, mid, and large cap enterprises. 22% of the companies are large-cap. 17% are mid/small-cap and 61% are micro/nano-caps. The GSCI contains gold and silver miners and royalty companies that trade on U.S. and Canadian stock exchanges. It is ideal for tracking the performance of the full spectrum of gold and silver mining and royalty companies trading in Canada and the USA.

Which index should you follow?

The HUI and the XAU are the most widely followed by industry personnel, just like the DOW and Nasdaq are for the broader markets.

Follow the XAU to follow the gold market leaders.

Follow the HUI for a mix of large and medium sized companies.

Follow the GDM for a good cross-sectional view of large, mid, and small companies.

Follow the SPTGD to follow only gold companies.

Follow the CDNX for a broader look at resource stocks as a sector.

Follow the GSCI if interested primarily in smaller companies.

Chapter 10
Summary and Conclusion

- **Gold IS Money**. We know that gold is money because every Central Bank in the world carries gold on their balance sheets as 'an official reserve asset'.
- Gold is the most conservative investment one can make. It is no-one else's liability. There is no counterparty risk.
- Gold is in limited supply. Currency is not. Both the amount of above ground gold and the world population in general increase at an annual rate of 1-2%. Therefore, its monetary value is stable (No inflation). There is a finite amount of gold but an infinite amount of dollars.
- Gold is the only major asset class that is inversely correlated to all others (Real Estate, Bonds, Equities, Currencies, etc.) and the only that has risen every year since 2001.
- The Precious Metals markets are small. Only 3-9% of investors have some precious metal exposure in any form. Eventually most will but at a higher cost.
- The total value of all precious metal mining stock is less than that of Exxon.
- Currencies are easily destroyed. Gold and silver are not.
- Currencies are inflating at 10-30+% per year. Gold is inflating at about 1.6% currently.
- Gold is the ultimate form or money and the ultimate form of financial insurance.
- At all times and in all circumstances gold and silver have remained money because their value has been recognized by the masses.

Take away points:
- Recognize that the paradigm has changed. The world is a different place going forward than what we have become accustomed to. We're not in Kansas anymore.
- Currency printing has gone exponential in many, if not most, countries.
- Use metal for long term wealth preservation; not currency, or bonds, or any form of paper.
- Metal will not be available in a crisis. Panic early and avoid the rush.
- If no metal is available, get other tangible assets.
- The metals markets are very volatile. They will not go straight up or down. Have an eye to the long term.
- Do not put all of your assets in only one place.
- Do as 'They' (The smart money) do.

Got Gold Yet?

182

Appendices:

Appendix A
A Reading List of Gold Books with Author and Publisher

Buy Gold Now – Shayne McGuire (Wiley)

The Collapse of the Dollar and How to Profit from it – James Turk and John Rubino (Broadway Business)

The Coming Economic Collapse – Stephen Leeb

Commodities for Every Portfolio – Emanuel Balarie

Crash Proof: How to Profit from the Coming Economic Collapse - Peter Schiff (Wiley)

The Creature from Jekyll Island - G. Edward Griffin (Amer Media)

Empire of Debt: The Rise of an Epic Financial Crisis - William Bonner and Addison Wiggin (Wiley)

End the Fed - Ron Paul

The Ethics of Money Production - Jörg Guido Hülsmann (Von Mises)

Fiat Paper Money: The History and Evolution of our Currency - Ralph T. Foster

Financial Armageddon: Protecting Your Future - Michael Panzner

Get the Skinny on Silver Investing - David Morgan

Gold: The Once and Future Money – Nathan Lewis (Wiley)

Gold Trading Boot Camp –Gregory T. Weldon (Wiley)

Gold Wars - Ferdinand Lips (FAME)

Good as Gold?: How We Lost Our Gold Reserves and Destroyed The Dollar - Christopher Weber

The Great Credit Contraction – Trace Mayer

Honest Money – Douglas V. Gnazzo

Mining Explained: A Layman's Guide - (Northern Miner)

The Mystery of Banking - Murray Rothbard - mises.org/Books/mysteryofbanking.pdf

Pieces of Eight: The Monetary Powers and Disabilities of the United States Constitution - Edwin Vieira

Precious Metals Investing For Dummies – Paul Mladjenovic

Rich Dad's Advisors: Guide to Investing In Gold and Silver - Michael Maloney

Ruff's Little Book of Big Fortunes in Gold & Silver - Howard Ruff

Secrets of the Federal Reserve - Eustace Mullins

This Time Is Different: Eight Centuries of Financial Folly - Reinhart & Rogoff

What has Government Done to Our Money? - Murray Rothbard

When Giants Fall – Michael Panzner

Appendix B
A List of Links to Articles about the Precious Metals Markets

Options for Storing Precious Metals - Austin Fitts and Betts - 8/10
http://www.silverbearcafe.com/private/08.10/options.html

Bullion As An Alternative To Shorting (Part II) - Nielson - 8/10
http://www.gold-eagle.com/editorials_08/nielson082110.html

Gold Meltdown or Mania - Batten Down the Hatches - James - 8/10
http://news.goldseek.com/GoldSeek/1280948950.php

Yes, You Can Time The Market - Here's How! - Wilson - 7/10
http://www.gold-eagle.com/editorials_08/wilsonl072510.html

The Enigmatic Silver Miners - Nielson - 7/10
http://www.gold-eagle.com/editorials_08/nielson072510.html

Why Bullion is Outperforming Mining Stocks - Barisheff - 7/10
http://news.goldseek.com/GoldSeek/1279204500.php

The Prospect Generator Model: A Primer for the Lay Investor - Fulp -
7/10
http://news.goldseek.com/GoldSeek/1278959657.php

Historical Silver: Gold Ratio Suggests Parabolic Top For Silver of Over $100
per Ounce!   - Wilson - 7/10
http://www.silverbearcafe.com/private/07.10/parabolic.html

Inventory-Fraud Increases In Silver Market - Nielson - 7/10
http://www.gold-eagle.com/editorials_08/nielson070110.html

Why Many Analysts See Gold Going As High As $10,000 - Wilson -
6/10
http://www.gold-eagle.com/editorials_08/wilsonl062310.html

The 5 Worst Ways to Buy Gold - Kristof - 6/10
http://www.silverstrategies.com/story.aspx?local=0&id=20353

Finding the Best Precious Metals Price Forecasters - MineFund - 6/10
http://www.resourceinvestor.com/News/2010/6/Pages/Finding-the-
Best-Precious-Metals-Price-Forecasters.aspx

Give Unto Caesar – What to Pay when You're Selling - Clark - 6/10
http://news.goldseek.com/GoldSeek/1275501483.php

The Silver Price Spiral Part II: Paper "Inventories" - Nielson - 5/10
http://www.gold-eagle.com/editorials_08/nielson050110.html

The Silver Price Spiral Part III: Tomorrow - Nielson - 5/10
http://www.gold-eagle.com/editorials_08/nielson050310.html

Gold and 'The' Parabolic Peak - Baker - 4/10
http://news.goldseek.com/GoldSeek/1272548046.php

How to Buy Real Gold - Lewis - 4/10
http://www.silverstrategies.com/story.aspx?local=0&id=19718

How to corner the Gold Market - Tavakoli - 3/10
www.tavakolistructuredfinance.com/Gold.pdf

Gold 1500 - Klein - 3/10
http://www.gold-eagle.com/editorials_08/klein032510.html

The Silver Report - CanadianFinancing.com - 3/10
http://www.canadianfinancing.com/silver_report.pdf

The Gold Silver Ratio - McCoach - 3/10
http://www.silverstrategies.com/story.aspx?local=0&id=19444

Gold: The End of "Seasons" - Nielson - 3/10
http://www.gold-eagle.com/editorials_08/nielson031610.html

The Top 10 Potential Takeover Candidates in the Mining Industry -
Hyperinflation - 3/10
http://seekingalpha.com/article/194090-the-top-10-potential-
takeover-candidates-in-the-mining-industry

New ETFs: Bullion Equivalent or Metal Facade? - Barry - 3/10
http://www.financialsense.com/fsu/editorials/barry/2010/0312.html

Silver is the Best Investment in the World - Mason - 3/10
http://www.silverbearcafe.com/private/03.10/investment.html

More IMF Gold Propoganda - Nielson - 2/10

http://www.gold-eagle.com/editorials_08/nielson021810.html

Modern Day Alchemy - Long - 2/10
http://www.silverbearcafe.com/private/02.10/alchemy.html

Will the COMEX Keep Pace - Mclagan - 2/10
http://news.goldseek.com/RickAckerman/1266418260.php

Breakdown in the Gold Market - Willie - 2/10
http://news.goldseek.com/GoldenJackass/1265248800.php

Gold Stocks Versus Gold Bullion - Saville - 2/10
http://news.goldseek.com/SpeculativeInvestor/1265094540.php

Billion-ETF Shrinkage Good for Sector - Nielson - 2/10
http://www.gold-eagle.com/editorials_08/nielson020110.html

What's a Company's Gold Worth? - James & Dashkov - 1/10
http://www.financialsense.com/editorials/casey/2010/0129.html

The Outlook for 2010 - Turk - 1/10
http://www.fgmr.com/january-2-2010-outlook-for-2010.html

Welcome to Stage Two of Gold's Bull Market - Turk - 11/09
http://www.fgmr.com/stage-two-of-golds-bull-market.html

This Little-Known Rule Could Send Gold to $10,000 - Stansberry - 12/09
http://www.kitco.com/ind/stansberry/dec022009.html

Just like the Old Days - Katz - 12/09
http://www.321gold.com/editorials/katz/katz122809.html

Gold: Going Higher Or About To Pop? - Summers - 12/09
http://www.gold-eagle.com/editorials_08/summers122209.html

The Fractional Reserve Aspects of Gold ETFs
http://www.fgmr.com/fractional-reserve-aspects-of-gold-etfs.html

Extereme Speculation - Butler - 12/09
http://news.silverseek.com/SilverSeek/1260816780.php

Gold Bears Continue To Contradict Each Other - Nielson - 12/09 http://www.gold-eagle.com/editorials_08/nielson120909.html

Buying Silver and Gold in China - Pharaoh - 12/09
http://www.istockanalyst.com/article/viewarticle/articleid/3695713

Why the Gold Bears are Wrong Once Again - Degraaf 12/09
http://www.gold-eagle.com/editorials_08/degraaf120809.html

Tax implications of owning gold - Biller 12/09
http://www.christianpost.com/blogs/investing/2009/12/tax-implications-of-owning-gold-04/

Gold is a Bubble - Brochert - 12/09
http://news.goldseek.com/GoldSeek/1259936419.php

Gold Buyer's Checklist - Tustain - 11/09
http://news.goldseek.com/BullionVault/1259517231.php

The United States Lost Decade & Gold - Kilbach - 11/09
http://news.goldseek.com/GoldSeek/1259337900.php

Miners say they're running out of gold - Brisbane Times - 11/09
http://www.brisbanetimes.com.au/business/miners-were-running-out-of-gold-20091125-jqqy.html

Next Station Approaches - Charnock - 11/09
http://news.goldseek.com/GoldSeek/1259074800.php

Gold's Price is Not a Bubble Price - Rozeff - 11/09
http://news.goldseek.com/LewRockwell/1259056800.php

Peak Silver and Mining by a Falling EROI - St. Angelo - 11/09
http://www.marketoracle.co.uk/Article14756.html

Looking Back at Peak Global Production of…Gold - The Oil Drum - 11/09
http://www.theoildrum.com/node/5960

Ganesha and the Price of Gold - Hera - 11/09
http://news.goldseek.com/GoldSeek/1258146000.php

On Doing God's Work - Kirby - 11/09
http://news.goldseek.com/GoldSeek/1258049769.php

Mining Services - Kupperman - 11/09
http://news.goldseek.com/GoldSeek/1258009500.php

Gold... Do We Finally Have Your Attention? - Sutton - 11/09
http://news.goldseek.com/GoldSeek/1258039701.php

The Day the Bears Lost Control of Gold - Downey - 11/09
http://news.goldseek.com/GoldSeek/1257778800.php

Gold Market Reaching the Breaking Point - deCarbonnel - 11/09
http://www.gold-eagle.com/editorials_08/decarbonnel110609.html

Investment Checklist for Precious Metals Miners (part 1) - Nielson - 10/09
http://www.gold-eagle.com/editorials_08/nielson102709.html

Investment Checklist for Precious Metals Miners (part 2) - Nielson - 10/09
http://www.gold-eagle.com/editorials_08/nielson103009.html

Gold Bug Bit the Tudor - Mayer - 11/09
http://news.goldseek.com/GoldSeek/1257177900.php

Silver Wheaton (SLW): The Safe Alternative to SLV - Nielson - 9/09
http://www.gold-eagle.com/editorials_08/nielson091609.html

Ten Thousand Reasons to Buy Silver - Cook - 9/09
http://www.investmentrarities.com/best_of_jim_cook09-11-09.shtml

Your ETF Silver is for Sale - Nielson - 9/09
http://www.gold-eagle.com/editorials_08/nielson091409.html

The Super Bubble to Come - Butler - 9/09
http://www.gold-eagle.com/editorials_08/butler090909.html

Massive Institutional Gold Market Change
http://news.goldseek.com/GoldSeek/1251815214.php

"Gold Is Pale Because It Has So Many Thieves Plotting Against It" - Fekete - 8/09
http://news.goldseek.com/GoldSeek/1251468000.php

Gold Wars Part 1: Central Banks Supreme - Nielson - 8/09
http://www.gold-eagle.com/editorials_08/nielson082509.html

Something for Nothing - Katz - 8/09
http://news.goldseek.com/GoldSeek/1249906640.php

The Spot Price - Stott - 8/09
http://www.silverbearcafe.com/private/08.09/spot.html

Global Gold Production - Wright - 7/09
http://news.goldseek.com/Zealllc/1249056776.php

Gold $1000 Quest - Hamilton - 7/09
http://news.goldseek.com/Zealllc/1248451691.php

Morgan Stanley pays damages for Precious Metals Fraud - Nielson -
7/09
http://www.silverbearcafe.com/private/07.09/damages.html

Silver Stocks 3 - Wright - 7/09
http://www.gold-eagle.com/gold_digest_08/wright070309.html

What can ever beat the gold and silver cartel? - Douglas 7/09
http://news.goldseek.com/GATA/1246860420.php

Next Stop for Gold is $2,100 Not $1,300 - Roy-Byrne - 7/09
http://news.goldseek.com/GoldSeek/1246542892.php

Preserve Your Wealth with Precious Metals - Barisheff - 7/09
http://news.goldseek.com/GoldSeek/1246582800.php

The 21st Century Gold Rush - Gofsky - 12/03
http://www.financialsense.com/fsu/editorials/2003/1209.html

Turning Bling into Ka-Ching - Casey - 4/09
http://www.silverbearcafe.com/private/04.09/bling.html

Gold & Silver... How Do I Own Thee?
... Let Me Count The Ways - Macfarland - 4/09
http://www.gold-eagle.com/editorials_08/macfarlane040609.html

Gold and Silver... How Do I Own Thee?... Let Me Count The Ways: Part II -
Macfarland 4/09
http://www.safehaven.com/article-13013.htm

Gold:Gold Stock Index Ratio Analysis - Wilson - 4/09
http://www.gold-eagle.com/editorials_08/wilsonl040609.html

Why the Gold Price is not yet Soaring - Iacono Research - 3/09
http://news.goldseek.com/GoldSeek/1238002413.php

Gold Buying Opportunity of a Lifetime - Schoon - 3/09
http://news.goldseek.com/GoldSeek/1237382162.php

Gold & Gold Stocks During Periods of Deflation and Inflation - Roy-
Byrne - 3/09
http://www.gold-eagle.com/editorials_08/roy-byrne031709.html

Reserves and Resources: A Primer for the Lay Investor - Fulp - 9/08
http://www.theaureport.com/pub/na/1623

Gold Indexes: Comparing and Evaluating the HUI, XAU, GDX, XGD
and CDNX - Wilson - 3/09
http://news.goldseek.com/GoldSeek/1236751860.php

Metals & Mining - Agricole 1/06
http://www.gata.org/files/CheuvreuxGoldReport.pdf

HUI Gold Stocks – Wright - 2/09
http://news.goldseek.com/Zealllc/1235753400.php

Ten Reasons to Avoid the Gold ETF - Seeking Alpha - 2/09
http://seekingalpha.com/article/121121-ten-reasons-to-avoid-the-
gold-etf

Riding the Golden Bull - Field - 2/09

Gold Drivers 2009 – Extraordinary Bullish Outlook for Gold – Update -
Hommelberg - 2/09
http://news.goldseek.com/EricHommelberg/1233939600.php

Why Juniors? Why Now? - Maund 2/09
http://www.321gold.com/editorials/maund/maund020509.html

Red Alert: Gold Backwardation!!! - Fekete - 12/08
http://news.goldseek.com/GoldSeek/1228499200.php

Is the End of the COMEX nigh? - Hoffman 11/08
http://news.goldseek.com/GoldSeek/1228061100.php

The Great Deception as Gold Hit All Time Highs - Greene - 11/08
http://news.goldseek.com/ThunderCapitalManagement/1227123024
.php

Last Chance to Trade your Paper Gold and Silver for Physical -
Greene - 9/08
http://www.gold-eagle.com/editorials_08/greene091708.html

Silver Mining Share Value Strategy: Revisited Fall 2008 - Hansen -
9/08
http://www.safehaven.com/article-11273.htm

The Law of Supply and Demand is Dead for Gold and Silver - Kim -
9/08
http://seekingalpha.com/article/95496-the-law-of-supply-and-
demand-is-dead-for-gold-and-silver

Gold Mining Challenges 2 - Wright - 9/08
http://news.goldseek.com/Zealllc/1220631230.php

Silver End Game? - Kovaka - 9/08
http://www.financialsense.com/fsu/editorials/2008/0904.html

Gold Supply and Demand - Saville - 9/08
http://news.goldseek.com/SpeculativeInvestor/1220359279.php

Gold Fundamentals Still Pointing Towards $2000+ - Hommelberg -
9/08
http://news.goldseek.com/EricHommelberg/1220359803.php

Gold Production and Reserves 2 - Wright - 8/09
http://news.goldseek.com/Zealllc/1220026615.php

Once-Upon-A-Time, In 'Never-Never' Land, There Were Two
Competing Silver Prices - Degraaf - 8/08
http://news.silverseek.com/SilverSeek/1219793829.php

Where's the Gold? - West - 8/08
http://news.goldseek.com/GoldSeek/1219676400.php

Amateur Hour in the Precious Metals Markets - Greene - 8/08
http://news.goldseek.com/ThunderCapitalManagement/1219385040
.php

Silver has Run Out, Now! - Hommel - 8/08
http://news.silverseek.com/GoldIsMoney/1219250737.php

The Disconnect Between Supply and Demand in Gold & Silver Markets
- Conrad - 8/08
http://seekingalpha.com/article/91357-the-disconnect-between-
supply-and-demand-in-gold-silver-markets

Paper prices no longer rule the precious metals markets - Sanders
8/08
http://www.gata.org/node/6492

A Fabrication Bottleneck or Something More - Turk - 8/08
http://www.goldmoney.com/en/commentary/2008-08-17.html

21st Century Gold Rush Re-Examined - Baltin - 8/08
http://www.gold-eagle.com/editorials_08/baltin081708.html

Let's Be Hunts - Bond - 8/08
http://news.silverseek.com/SilverSeek/1219028976.php

Silver Shortage Causes Price Disconnect - Hommel - 8/08
http://news.silverseek.com/GoldIsMoney/1219027615.php

The AMEX Gold Bugs Index (HUI): Again a Golden Opportunity to Buy
Gold Shares? - Zihlmann - 8/08
http://www.safehaven.com/article-10965.htm

Gold Bull Seasonals 3 - Hamilton - 8/08
http://www.gold-eagle.com/gold_digest_08/hamilton080808.html

Precious Metal's Relativity to Shine - Captain Hook - 7/08
http://www.financialsense.com/fsu/editorials/petch/2008/0714.html

Three-Digit Silver Ahead - Rakhimov - 7/08
http://www.silverstrategies.com/story.aspx?local=0&id=901

Elliot Wave Gold Update 20 - Field - 7/08
http://news.goldseek.com/AlfField/1215005723.php

A Hidden Silver Default? - 6/08
http://www.silver-investor.com/pdf/ADB%20061908%20-%20Issue%2037.pdf

Gold Stocks Gearing Up for a Big Rally - Swanson - 6/08
http://www.gold-eagle.com/editorials_08/swanson063008.html

Too Late to Buy Gold? - Ash - 6/08
http://www.gold-eagle.com/editorials_08/ash062708.html

The Truth about Gold - Orlandini - 6/08
http://www.gold-eagle.com/editorials_08/orlandini062608.html

Explosive Upside potential - Nichols - 6/08
http://www.gold-eagle.com/editorials_08/nichols062608.html

Precious metals Timing - Rosen - 6/08
http://www.gold-eagle.com/editorials_08/rosen062608.html

Another Gold Attack, Then 'North' to $2000/oz! - Wallenwein - 6/08
http://www.gold-eagle.com/editorials_08/wallenwein062308.html

Breakout! - Degraaf - 6/08
http://news.goldseek.com/GoldSeek/1213978750.php

Silver – Two Sides of the Story - Morgan - 6/08
http://news.silverseek.com/SilverInvestor/1213979107.php

SLV Silver EFT - Hamilton - 6/08
http://www.gold-eagle.com/gold_digest_08/hamilton062008.html

Not All Metals are Created Equal (part 1) - Lee - 6/08
http://www.gold-eagle.com/editorials_08/lee061908.html

The Bursting Commodities Bubble - Galland - 6/08
http://news.goldseek.com/DougCasey/1213899980.php

Silver Bulls Predict Price Bounce - Won - 6/08

http://www.theglobeandmail.com/servlet/story/LAC.20080617.RSIL
VER17/TPStory/Business

Is the World Really Short of Silver? - Frisby - 6/08
http://www.silverstrategies.com/story.aspx?local=0&id=752

A "Lot of Money" Heading back into Gold? - Ash - 6/08
http://news.goldseek.com/GoldSeek/1213810744.php

Silver Shorts Reported - Hommel - 6/08
http://news.silverseek.com/GoldIsMoney/1213796934.php

Precious Metals Market Timing - Rosen - 6/08
http://www.gold-eagle.com/editorials_08/rosen061608.html

A hidden Silver Default? - Butler - 6/08
http://news.silverseek.com/TedButler/1213640342.php

Precious Metal Stock Review - Bevan - 6/08
http://news.goldseek.com/GoldSeek/1213596210.php

Silver… Still No Respect - Morgan - 6/08
http://www.silverbearcafe.com/private/6.08/respect.html

Will the Hunts buy Silver again after Selling Hunt Petroleum? - Cooper
- 6/08
http://www.silverbearcafe.com/private/6.08/hunts.html

Dynamics of the Silver Price Revolution - Bressler - 6/08
http://www.gold-eagle.com/editorials_08/bressler061508.html

Why Gold could Hit $8500 an Ounce - Frisby - 6/08
http://www.silverbearcafe.com/private/6.08/gold.html

Gold Stocks – Ready to Rumble! - Wallenwein - 6/08
http://www.safehaven.com/article-10496.htm

The Real Speculators - Butler - 6/08
http://www.silverbearcafe.com/private/6.08/speculators.html

Silver Delivery "Delays" - Kovaka - 6/08
http://silverbearcafe.com/private/6.08/delays.html

Commodities Correct as Dollar Outlook Improves - Martens 6/08
http://www.gold-eagle.com/editorials_08/martens060508.html

So, you want to Sell your Gold Stocks... - Greene 6/08
http://www.financialsense.com/fsu/editorials/greene/2008/0604.html

Silver Big Bang - Montana - 5/08
http://silverstrategies.com/story.aspx?local=0&id=568

Silver Stocks 2 -Wright - 5/08
http://www.gold-eagle.com/gold_digest_08/wright053008.html

Silver Shortages Misunderstood - Hommel - 5/08
http://www.gold-eagle.com/editorials_08/hommel052808.html

Gold Benefits Versus Mining Costs - Willie - 5/08
http://www.gold-eagle.com/editorials_08/willie052808.html

Humanoid - Goldrunner 5/08
http://www.gold-eagle.com/editorials_08/goldrunner052808.html

Silver Technicals 2 - Hamilton 5/08
http://www.gold-eagle.com/gold_digest_08/hamilton052308.html

Inflation and Gold-Silver Breakout - Willie 5/08
http://www.gold-eagle.com/editorials_08/willie052208.html

Long-Term Direction of Gold Remains Very Clear - Taylor 5/08
http://www.gold-eagle.com/gold_digest_08/taylor052008.html

Predicting the Silver Top - Watson 3/08
http://news.silverseek.com/SilverSeek/1204596000.php

Bullion or Mining Stocks - Barisheff - 2/08
http://www.financialsense.com/fsu/editorials/bms/2008/0213.html

The Surrender of the Silver Shorts - Watson - 2/08
http://news.silverseek.com/SilverSeek/1202394061.php

Gold – Bullion is Safer than Gold Stocks - Petrov - 2/08
http://www.financialsense.com/editorials/petrov/2008/0225.html

Gold – How High will it go? _ Petrov - 2/08
http://www.financialsense.com/editorials/petrov/2008/0219.html

Profit? - Stott - 2/08
http://www.silverbearcafe.com/private/2.08/profit.html

Investing in the XAU and HUI for Small Investors - Urban - 2/08
http://www.financialsense.com/fsu/editorials/urban/2008/0214.html

Silver in Surplus? - Watson - 1/08
http://www.gold-eagle.com/editorials_08/watson012808.html

Gold EFT Impact 3 - Hamilton - 11/07
http://www.zeallc.com/2007/gldetf3.htm

Gold's Strange Behaviour During Financial Crisis - Speck - 11/07
http://www.financialsense.com/fsu/editorials/2007/1126.html

Silver Lagging Gold - Hamilton - 10/07
http://www.zeallc.com/2007/silvlag.htm

Why Silver will Outperform Gold 400% - Sanders - 2006
http://the-moneychanger.com/articles_files/mmm_files/silver_files/silver_will_outperform.php

Appendix C
A List of Links to Articles on the Fundamentals of Gold

The Coming Crash: Usury and the Irrelevant Church - Vrabel - 5/10
http://www.silverbearcafe.com/private/05.10/usury.html

U.S. Dollar is the new 'Tulip" - Nielsen - 5/10
http://www.gold-eagle.com/editorials_08/nielson050910.html

Gold and Silver Equal Future Purchasing Power - Wesley - 4/10
http://www.silverbearcafe.com/private/04.10/power.html

Chasing Gelten Shadows - Towne - 1/10
http://news.goldseek.com/GoldSeek/1262591760.php

The World's First and Best Central Bank - Souleles - 12/09

http://www.gold-eagle.com/editorials_08/souleles122009.html

Gold Suppression is Public Policy and Public Record, Not 'Conspiracy Theory' - Powell - 11/09
http://news.goldseek.com/GATA/1257721500.php

Fort Knox, Fort Hocks, or Fort Shocks: Three U.S. Gold Scenarios - Dougherty - 7/09
http://news.goldseek.com/GoldSeek/1248373722.php

The Goldsmiths – Part LXXXIX (1933 Confiscation) - Bradshaw - 7/09
http://news.goldseek.com/GoldSeek/1247205780.php

Fiat Money History in the U.S.
http://www.kwaves.com/fiat.htm

The Money Matrix – Who Owns the Fed - Mayer - 6/09
http://news.goldseek.com/GoldSeek/1245647789.php

The Nature of Money and Our Monetary System - Silver Bear - 2004
http://www.silverbearcafe.com/private/natureofmoney.html

A Novice Guide to Precious Metals (part 1) - Nielson - 5/09
http://www.gold-eagle.com/editorials_08/nielson052709.html

How Much Money Should there Be? – Shostak – 10/2001
http://mises.org/story/797

A Short History of the Gold Cartel – Turk – 4/09
http://news.goldseek.com/JamesTurk/1241449200.php

A New Monetary System for the USA - Weir - 3/09
http://news.goldseek.com/GoldSeek/1238191282.php

How to Buy Gold and Other Metals with a Self-Directed IRA - 3/09
http://www.prweb.com/pdfdownload/2252974/pr.pdf

The Confiscation Threat - Turk - 12/03
http://www.fgmr.com/confiscation.htm

About Safes - Anonymous - 3/09
http://www.321gold.com/info/030609_safes.html

Gold and Economic Freedom - Greenspan - 1966
http://www.dollardaze.org/blog/?post_id=00527

Restoring Sound Money in America - Turk - 1/09
http://news.goldseek.com/JamesTurk/1232989200.php

A New Summary of GATAs Work - Powell - 12/08
http://www.silverbearcafe.com/private/12.08/gata.html

Inflatino Rate is 5.6%...and Other Nonsense - Suprynowicz - 8/08
http://news.goldseek.com/LewRockwell/1219755900.php

Truth in the Coin Shop - Tucker - 8/08
http://mises.org/story/3073

A Golden Parachute with a Silver Lining - Schoon - 7/08
http://news.goldseek.com/GoldSeek/1216731828.php

Frequently Asked Question - Hommel - 7/08
http://www.silverstrategies.com/story.aspx?local=1&id=935

History has a way of Repeating: The Gold Price will Run - Stanczyk - 7/08
http://www.silverbearcafe.com/private/7.08/repeating.html

Crisis Memo to ICMA - Savoie - 7/08
http://news.goldseek.com/GoldSeek/1215005580.php

The Federal Reserve & Central Bank Gold Sales - Gnazzo - 7/08
http://news.goldseek.com/GoldSeek/1215005580.php

Fate of Paper Money - Hewitt - 6/08
http://news.goldseek.com/GoldSeek/1214842037.php
Sinking Currencies - Hewitt - 6/08
http://news.goldseek.com/GoldSeek/1214584561.php

Three Things Every American should Know - 6/08
http://www.silverbearcafe.com/private/6.08/threethings.html

Fed Meeting: The Long-Lasting Costs of Inflation - Ash - 6/08
http://www.gold-eagle.com/editorials_08/ash062408.html

The United States Fiat Money and the Federal Reserve System -
Schoon - 6/08
http://news.goldseek.com/GoldSeek/1214201040.php

Silver, Gold and the IRS - Brownfield - 6/08
http://www.silverbearcafe.com/private/6.08/irs.html

Why the Sun Rises - Mathid - 6/08
http://www.321gold.com/editorials/mathid/mathid061708.html

Roosevelt and Gold Confiscation (Final Part) - Gnazzo - 6/08
http://www.gold-eagle.com/gold_digest_08/gnazzo061708.html

Roosevelt and Gold Confiscation - Gnazzo - 6/08
http://www.gold-eagle.com/gold_digest_08/gnazzo061308.html

90% U.S. Silver Coin Bags, $1000 Face - Hommel - 6/08
http://news.silverseek.com/GoldIsMoney/1212338328.php

Why does a Mint Lease out Gold/Silver - Schwensen - 5/08
http://www.kitco.com/ind/schwensen/may292008.html

Hyperinflation Special Report - Williams - 4/08
http://www.shadowstats.com/article/292

Chaos Chronicled - Field - 4/08
http://news.goldseek.com/AlfField/1207839600.php

The Power to Create Money - Montana - 2/08
http://www.silverstrategies.com/publications/The_Power_to_Creat
e_Money.pdf

10 Gold / Silver Ratios - Chaize - 2/08
http://www.kitco.com/ind/Chaize/feb202008.html

Illusionomics - Mathid - 2/08
http://www.321gold.com/editorials/mathid/mathid020508.html

Will Gold Crash in a Recession - Conrad & Galland - 1/08
http://www.321gold.com/editorials/casey/casey012808.html

Find Your Local Coin Shop - Hommel - 2008
http://www.find-your-local-coin-shop.com/

Everybody Wants It - Degraaf - 8/07
http://www.pdegraaf.com/articles/everybodywantsit.html

Why Silver will Outperform Gold 400% - Sanders - 2006
http://the-moneychanger.com/articles_files/mmm_files/silver_files/silver_will_outperform.php

Buy Silver or Gold? - North - 2006
http://www.lewrockwell.com/north/north436.html

Gold's Hidden Secret - Gnazzo - 12/05
http://www.honestmoneyreport.com/archives/2005/1215.html

Gold Investing 101 - Hamilton - 5/02
http://www.zeallc.com/2002/gold101.htm

Fiat Currency: Using the Past to See into the Future - The Daily Reckoning
http://dailyreckoning.com/rpt/fiathistoryWP.html

Value of Silver vs. Value of the Dollar - The Daily Reckoning
http://www.dailyreckoning.com/rpt/SilverValueVSDollarValue.html

Investing in Silver - The Daily Reckoning
http://dailyreckoning.com/rpt/Investing-In-Silver.html

Honest Money - Gnazzo
http://www.honestmoneyreport.com/bookIntro.pdf

The Ten Commandments of Gold & Silver Buying - Sanders
http://the-moneychanger.com/commandments.phtml

What You Need to Know Before You Buy Numismatics - Sanders
http://the-moneychanger.com/numismatic_files/numismatic.phtml

Bimetallism: The Only Enduring Standard - Sanders
http://the-moneychanger.com/articles_files/mmm_files/gold_files/enemy_in_mirrow.phtml

The Nature of Money and our Monetary System - Silverbear

http://www.silverbearcafe.com/private/2.08/natureofmoney.html

The Hunt Brothers and the Silver Bubble - Trumbore
http://www.buyandhold.com/bh/en/education/history/2000/hunt_br
os.html

The Federal Reserve – Its Origins, History, & Current Strategy -
Krautkramer
http://news.goldseek.com/GoldSeek/1095269452.php

Appendix D
A List of Links to Classic Articles on Gold

Guernsey's Monetary Experiment - Even - 2004
http://www.silverbearcafe.com/private/8.08/guernsey.html

The War Against Specie Money & How we can Win it at Face Value -
Sanders - 7/09
http://www.321gold.com/editorials/sanders/sanders072809.html

"The Hunts' Tried to Corner the Silver Market" Myth - Gallup - 6/09
http://www.silverbearcafe.com/private/06.09/hunts.html

The Essays of James Turk
http://goldmoney.com/en/essays-archive.html

What is a Dollar? - Vieira - 1994
http://www.fame.org/HTM/Vieira_Edwin_What_is_a_Dollar_EV-002.HTM

Gold and Economic Freedom - Greenspan - 1966
http://www.silverbearcafe.com/private/01.09/greenspan66.html

Stealth Bankruptcy - Di Lorenzo - 12/08
http://www.silverbearcafe.com/private/12.08/stealth.html

4 Fundamentals of the Silver Price - Hommel - 6/08
http://news.silverseek.com/GoldIsMoney/1212701763.php

Gold's Hidden Secret - Gnazzo - 12/05
http://www.honestmoneyreport.com/archives/2005/1215.html

One Dozen Silver Investor Mistakes - Kanarowski - 2005
http://www.financialsense.com/fsu/editorials/2005/0106.html

Numismatic Coins - Sanders - 2003
http://www.silver-investor.com/misc_articles/numi.htm

Gold and Silver Could Replace all National Currencies - Sanders
http://www.silver-investor.com/misc_articles/Sanders.htm

70 Approaching Forces for Higher Silver Prices - Kanarowski
http://www.gold-eagle.com/editorials_03/kanarowski072303.html

Better to Light a Candle than to Curse the Darkness - Silverbear
http://www.silverbearcafe.com/liteacandle.html

The Economy - Sanders & Exter - 1991
http://the-
moneychanger.com/articles_files/mmm_files/economy/exter.phtml

Appendix E
A List of Links to Articles on Gold Money and the Collapsing Dollar

A Gold Economy Begins - Sardi - 6/10
http://www.silverbearcafe.com/private/06.10/economy.html

Dangerous Paper Bubble Dynamics - Brochert - 4/10
http://news.goldseek.com/GoldSeek/1272374657.php

Hyperinflation Looms – The Dollar Arrives at Its 'Havenstein Moment' -
Turk - 4/10
http://www.fgmr.com/hyperinflation-looms-dollar-arrives-at-its-
havenstein-moment.html

Gold Is Money - Barisheff - 3/10
http://news.goldseek.com/GoldSeek/1268756265.php

U.S. Hyperinflation Possible by 2015 - NIA - 3/10
http://www.silverbearcafe.com/private/03.10/hyperinflation.html

Desperate Times and Desperate Measures - Brochert - 2/10
http://news.goldseek.com/GoldSeek/1266504452.php

Living in a Powder Keg and Giving Off Sparks - FOFOA - 2/10
http://www.silverbearcafe.com/private/02.10/powderkeg.html

The Big Picture - Katz - 12/09
http://news.goldseek.com/GoldSeek/1260802800.php

GOLD IS NOT GOING UP – PAPER MONEY IS GOING DOWN - von Greyerz - 12/09
http://www.gold-eagle.com/editorials_08/greyerz120709.html

Cold Turkey Thanksgiving 2009 - Schoon
http://news.goldseek.com/GoldSeek/1259046480.php

Zimbabwe: A Fresh Start - Field - 11/09
http://www.321gold.com/editorials/field/field111109.html

Gold Becoming Money Once Again - deCarbonnel - 1/09
http://www.marketskeptics.com/2009/01/gold-becoming-money-once-again.html

Gold is Money - Caravan - 9/09
http://news.goldseek.com/LewRockwell/1253111287.php

Confiscation Anatomy - A Different View - FOFOA - 8/09
http://www.silverbearcafe.com/private/08.09/confiscation.htm

Gold and Why Gold Now - Schoon - 8/09
http://www.321gold.com/editorials/schoon/schoon081709.html

The Mystery of the Disappearing SDR Certificates - FreeMarket Gold&Money Report - 2001
http://www.fgmr.com/sdr.htm

Bernanke's Collectivism - Rozeff - 7/09
http://news.goldseek.com/LewRockwell/1249050701.php

The Day the Dollar Died - Downey 7/09
http://www.gold-eagle.com/editorials_08/downey072609.html

How the Elites always Destroy the Paper Money they Value - Turk - 7/09
http://www.thedailybell.com/bellPage.asp?nid=4388&fl=

Fiat money in Death Throes - Fekete - 7/09
http://news.goldseek.com/GoldSeek/1246862700.php

A New Monetary System for the USA - Weir - 3/09
http://news.goldseek.com/GoldSeek/1238191282.php

The New Global Currency Franchise - Kovaka – 4/09
http://www.financialsense.com/fsu/editorials/2009/0423.html

Gold Versus Paper – Brochert – 4/09
http://news.goldseek.com/GoldSeek/1240988400.php

Current Dollar Currency Controls - Mayer - 6/09
http://news.goldseek.com/GoldSeek/1244642250.php

Printing Debt not Money - Brochert - 6/09
http://news.goldseek.com/GoldSeek/1244642400.php

Define the Dollar or Else - Mayer - 5/09
http://news.goldseek.com/GoldSeek/1243429238.php

The Real Enemies of Capitalism - Baltin 5/09
http://www.gold-eagle.com/editorials_08/baltin051409.html

Long Gold During Deflation? - Brochert - 5/09
http://news.goldseek.com/GoldSeek/1242306000.php

Globl Economy on Tilit – How to Protect Your Ass(ets) – Clark/Casey
Research
http://www.silverbearcafe.com/private/05.09/tilt.html

Gold – The Apex of the Pyramid - Brochert – 4/09
http://news.goldseek.com/GoldSeek/1241372765.php

Gold-Exchange Standard, Gold, and Monetary Freedom - Rozeff –
5/09
http://news.goldseek.com/LewRockwell/1241445854.php

The Significance of the Gold Standard – Fekete - 4/09
http://news.goldseek.com/GoldSeek/1239903849.php

Can the Zimbabwean School of Economics Save the World? - Maund
- 3/09
http://news.goldseek.com/CliveMaund/1238163082.php

The Effects of Dollar Inflation - Goldrunner - 3/09

http://www.gold-eagle.com/editorials_08/goldrunner032509.html

Is Gold Money? - Rees-Mogg - 3/09
http://www.lewrockwell.com/orig10/rees-mogg3.html

Grand Illusion – The Federal Reserve - Quinn - 3/09
http://www.financialsense.com/editorials/quinn/2009/0311.html

Paper Tiger Preying on Gold Bugs - Fekete - 2008
http://www.professorfekete.com/articles/AEFPaperTigerPreyingOn
GoldBugs.pdf

Lessons from the London Gold Pool - Judge - 2001
http://www.gold-eagle.com/editorials_01/judge052101.html

The Six Biggest Myths about Gold - Barisheff - 11/08
http://news.goldseek.com/GoldSeek/1227164640.php

Is Gold Money? - Blumen - 9/08
http://www.financialsense.com/editorials/blumen/2008/0922.html

Government Money or Sound Money - Turk - 9/08
http://www.financialsense.com/editorials/turk/2008/0922.html

Cut Off Your Tail to Save My Face! - Fekete - 9/08
http://www.financialsense.com/editorials/fekete/2008/0902.html

Gold & the Collapse of Paper Money - Schoon - 9/08
http://www.financialsense.com/fsu/editorials/schoon/2008/0902.ht
ml

Gold Clauses in Contracts - Wallenwein - 8/08
http://www.gold-eagle.com/editorials_08/wallenwein083108.html

How Low Will Gold Go? - Wallenwein - 8/08
http://www.gold-eagle.com/gold_digest_08/wallenwein081708.html

The Great Gold Robbery of 1933 - Woods - 8/08
http://news.goldseek.com/GoldSeek/1218647442.php

What is Money? - Turk - 8/08
http://news.goldseek.com/DollarCollapse/1218142611.php

Silver and Monetary Considerations - Morgan - 7/08
http://news.silverseek.com/SilverInvestor/1217482877.php

A Chart of Gold vs. the World - Van Vredenburch - 7/08
http://www.gold-eagle.com/editorials_08/vredenburch070408.html

Dollar's Doomsday - Field - 7/08
http://news.goldseek.com/AlfField/1215529200.php

US Dollar on Edge, Gold on Verge - Willie - 7/08
http://news.goldseek.com/GoldenJackass/1215028634.php

Local Communities Returning to Silver as money - Herpel - 6/08
http://www.americanchronicle.com/articles/64315

On the Precipice - Turk - 6/08
http://www.goldmoney.com/en/commentary.php

Common Misconceptions about the Fed & Gold - Sobolev - 6/08
http://www.gold-eagle.com/editorials_08/sobolev062908.html

Mining Mergers & Three Wealth Creation Tools - Amerman - 6/08
http://www.financialsense.com/fsu/editorials/amerman/2008/0624.html

Central Bank Gold Agreement - Phillips - 6/08
http://news.goldseek.com/GoldForecaster/1214233613.php

Something[s] that need to be Said - Kirby - 6/08
http://www.financialsense.com/fsu/editorials/kirby/2008/0619.html

Rime to "Wheedle and Cajole" - Turk - 6/08
http://www.goldmoney.com/en/commentary.php#current

Tracking the Re-Monetization of Silver - Bressler - 6/08
http://news.silverseek.com/SilverSeek/1212414200.php

It's not a Dollar Crisis: It's a Gold Crisis - Fekete - 6/08
http://news.goldseek.com/GoldSeek/1212681600.php

'Gold as Money"... - Stanczyk - 6/08
http://www.silverbearcafe.com/private/6.08/goldismoney.html

Returning to Gold Money - Saville - 6/08
http://news.goldseek.com/SpeculativeInvestor/1213682700.php

Waiting for the Dollars Next New Low - Turk - 6/08
http://www.goldmoney.com/en/commentary/2008-06-01.html

A 4-Month Review - Turk - 5/08
http://www.goldmoney.com/en/commentary/2008-05-01.html

The Death of the "Dollar" - Stang - 3/08
http://www.newswithviews.com/Stang/alan39.htm

How Low can the Dollar Go? Zero Value - Rogers - 3/08
http://www.gold-eagle.com/editorials_08/rogers031008.html

Why you must buy Gold, or even better, Silver, now - Stansberry - 2/08
http://www.silverbearcafe.com/private/2.08/mustbuygold.html

Gold – a Better Inflation Hedge than Real Estate - Petrov - 2/08
http://www.financialsense.com/editorials/petrov/2008/0211.html

Gold: A "Bridge Over Troubled Water" - Dienhart - 11/07
http://news.goldseek.com/GoldSeek/1195750644.php

The Dollar's Coming Collapse - Turk & Sanders - 2004
http://the-moneychanger.com/goldmoney/dollar_collapse.phtml

The Enemy in the Mirror - Sanders
http://the-moneychanger.com/articles_files/mmm_files/gold_files/enemy_in_mirrow.phtml

Appendix F
A List of Links to Articles on the Coming Economic Collapse
The Global Economic Crisis: Riots, Rebellion and Revolution - When Empire Hits Home - Marshall - 4/10
http://www.silverbearcafe.com/private/04.10/hitshome.html

The 21st Centruy Bank Run - FOFOA - 4/10
http://www.silverbearcafe.com/private/04.10/bankrun.html

The Most Important chart of the century - Martin - 3/10
http://www.silverbearcafe.com/private/03.10/chart.html

It's Going To Implode: Buy Physical Gold – NOW - Gekko - 3/10
http://news.goldseek.com/GoldSeek/1268425088.php

Young Greenspan and Gold - Nielson - 3/10
http://www.gold-eagle.com/editorials_08/nielson031310.html

Living in a Powder Keg and Giving Off Sparks - FOFOA - 2/10
http://www.silverbearcafe.com/private/02.10/powderkeg.html

Beware Counterfeiters - Bambrough and Franklin - 1/10
http://www.sprott.com/Docs/MarketsataGlance/01_10%20Beware%20Counterfeiters.pdf

Don't Bank on the Banks - Vallee - 12/09
http://www.silverbearcafe.com/private/12.09/banks.html

2010 Ready Or Not Here It Comes - Schoon - 12/09
http://news.goldseek.com/GoldSeek/1260169740.php

A Shocking Fall - von Greyerz - 8/09
http://www.gold-eagle.com/editorials_08/greyerz082709.html

The Royal Scam - Of Two Minds - 8/09
http://www.oftwominds.com/blogaug09/KaPoom2CHS.htm

Where do WE go from here? - Richter - 8/09
http://www.silverbearcafe.com/private/08.09/decisions.html

A Tremendous Secret – Rubino - 7/09
http://news.goldseek.com/DollarCollapse/1247638020.php

Hey You! - Katz - 5/09
http://news.goldseek.com/GoldSeek/1242657880.php

The Theft of a Nation – Dougherty – 4/09
http://www.321gold.com/editorials/dougherty/dougherty041009.html

Gold: Musings & Peptalk - Willie - 2/09
http://news.goldseek.com/GoldenJackass/1235754000.php

The Collapse of Capitalism and the Safety Net of Gold - Schoon -
1/09
http://news.goldseek.com/GoldSeek/1232546472.php

The Year Ahead: 2009 - Allport - 12/08
http://www.silverbearcafe.com/private/12.08/ahead.html

Headed for a Sudden Stop - Janszen - 10/08
http://news.goldseek.com/GoldSeek/1222841580.php

Credit Crisis II… A World Financial Armageddon? - Laird - 8/08
http://www.gold-eagle.com/editorials_08/laird082508.html

Don't Cry for Me Argentina - 8/08 - Schoon
http://news.goldseek.com/GoldSeek/1219644120.php

Wag the Dog: How to Conceal Massive Economic Collapse - Brown -
8/08
http://www.gold-eagle.com/editorials_08/brown081408.html

The Sad Road to Socialism - Loeffler - 7/08
http://www.financialsense.com/editorials/loeffler/2008/0718.html

The Winds of change - Depression 2009/10 - Baltin - 7/08
http://www.gold-eagle.com/editorials_08/baltin071008.html

Road to Roota II - Weir - 6/08
http://news.goldseek.com/GoldSeek/1214492700.php

The Crack-Up Boom, Part !!! - Andros - 6/08
http://news.goldseek.com/GoldSeek/1214492400.php

The Thin Red White & Blue Line - Macfarlane - 6/08
http://www.321gold.com/editorials/macfarlane/macfarlane062308.h
tml

Failed States: Mexico & California - Willie - 6/08
http://news.goldseek.com/GoldenJackass/1213983840.php

Will You Outlive Your Money? - Kidd - 6/08

http://www.silverbearcafe.com/private/6.08/outlive.html

The Bilderbergers: Paper Money & Paper Tigers - Schoon - 6/08
http://news.goldseek.com/GoldSeek/1213682580.php

$1.14 Quadrillion in Derivatives – What Goes Up… - DeMeritt - 6/08
http://www.gold-eagle.com/editorials_08/demeritt061608.html

The International Forecaster - Bob Chapman - 6/08
http://news.goldseek.com/InternationalForecaster/1213250760.php

The Crack-Up Boom: Part II - Andros - 6/08
http://news.goldseek.com/GoldSeek/1213212128.php

Florida at the Precipice of Economic Collapse - Morgan - 6/08
http://www.silverbearcafe.com/private/6.08/crystalball.html

They're Getting Worse - Martens 6/08
http://www.gold-eagle.com/editorials_08/martens060508.html

It's Only Going to get Worse - Lindsey 6/08
http://www.silverbearcafe.com/private/6.08/getworse.html

The Biggest Debt beat of All Buckler 6/08
http://www.investmentrarities.com/thebestofbb.html

Curse of the paper Dollar - Berry 6/08
http://www.investmentrarities.com/thebestofmberry.html

The Return of the Creature from Jekyll Island - Pugsley 6/08
http://www.investmentrarities.com/thebestofjpugsley.html

Global Financial Meltdown ahead - West 6/08
http://www.gold-eagle.com/editorials_08/west060408.html

Is this the Big One? - Faux 5/08
http://www.silverbearcafe.com/private/5.08/bigone.html

Sunday Sermon - Rosen 5/08
http://www.gold-eagle.com/editorials_08/rosen052508.html

The Chickens Coming Home to Roost - Baltin - 5/08
http://www.gold-eagle.com/editorials_08/baltin052408.html

Hyperinflation Special Report - Williams - 4/08
http://www.shadowstats.com/article/292

The Financial Tsunami Part IV…   - Engdahl - 2/08
http://www.321gold.com/editorials/engdahl/engdahl020808.html

The Financial Tsunami Part V…   - Engdahl - 2/08
http://www.321gold.com/editorials/engdahl/engdahl022508.html

The Yellow Brick Road to Armageddon - Baltin - 2/08
http://www.gold-eagle.com/editorials_08/baltin030708.html

It's all Downhill from here Folks - Whitney - 2/08
www.informationclearinghouse.info/article19307.htm

Into the Abyss - Field - 1/08
http://news.goldseek.com/AlfField/1199651180.php

Paradise Lost - Silver Bear - 1/05
http://silverbearcafe.com/private/paradiselost.html

Appendix G
A List of Links to Articles on the Economy

"Quantitative Easing" and Market Lies - Nielson - 6/10
http://www.gold-eagle.com/editorials_08/nielson062010.html
If The Money Supply Is Exploding Why Are We Not Seeing Rampant Inflation?
- Economic Collapse - 3/10
http://www.silverbearcafe.com/private/03.10/rampant.html

What if It Was All Just a Big Bubble? - Iacono - 3/10
http://news.goldseek.com/GoldSeek/1269458303.php

Something is VERY Wrong with Treasuries - Summers - 2/10
http://www.gold-eagle.com/editorials_08/summers022510.html

The ABCs of ETFs - Investing primer: The pros and cons of different
funds - Katusa - 2/10
http://news.goldseek.com/GoldSeek/1266604597.php

Hedging Non-Gold Investments with Gold - Fekete - 2/10

http://news.goldseek.com/GoldSeek/1266595200.php

The Next Stage of the Credit Crisis - Aaronson & Markowitz - 1/10
http://news.goldseek.com/GoldSeek/1263580700.php

How to Inflation-Proof Your Portfolio – Part 2 - Barisheff - 11/09
http://news.goldseek.com/GoldSeek/1259200800.php

Reply to Paul Krugman - Katz - 11/09
http://news.goldseek.com/GoldSeek/1258985917.php

Four Reasons Hyperinflation Hasn't Hit the U.S. Economy Yet - Fitz-Gerald - 11/09
http://www.silverbearcafe.com/private/11.09/reasons.html

The Federal Reserve's Self-Imposed Dilemma – North – 2/09
http://news.goldseek.com/LewRockwell/1233759640.php

Defending the Fed's Power with Myths - Rozeff - 4/09
http://news.goldseek.com/LewRockwell/1240320060.php

The Effects of Dollar Inflation - Goldrunner - 4/09
http://www.gold-eagle.com/editorials_08/goldrunner041309.html

Lack of Transparency = Shareholders Get Ratcheted - Sprott - 6/08
http://www.sprott.com/pdf/marketsataglance/MAAG.pdf

USFed Blinks: Propoganda & Bluffs - Willie - 6/08
http://news.goldseek.com/GoldenJackass/1214503996.php

Is the Party Over? - Kasun - 6/08
http://www.gold-eagle.com/editorials_08/kasun062508.html

Old Keynesian Dogs, Old Fiscal Tricks - North - 6/08
http://www.silverbearcafe.com/private/6.08/olddogs.html

Dow & Gold: Very Different 'Bull' Markets - Tanashian - 6/08
http://www.gold-eagle.com/editorials_08/tanashian062408.html

We May be Facing a Fall Stock Market Disaster - Swanson - 6/08
http://www.gold-eagle.com/editorials_08/swanson062308.html

The Spin Stops Here - Baltin - 6/08

http://www.gold-eagle.com/editorials_08/baltin062108.html

The Fed Unreserved - Schiff - 6/08
http://news.goldseek.com/EuroCapital/1213980391.php

Fed-Ache - Wallenwein - 6/08
http://www.small-business-goldmine.com/fed-ache.html

Dangers – Danger Period 2008 and 2009 - Laird - 6/08
http://www.financialsense.com/fsu/editorials/laird/2008/0619.html

RBS issues global stock and credit crash alert - Evans-Pritchard -
6/08
http://www.silverbearcafe.com/private/6.08/alert.html

A New Socio-Economic Era - Bloom - 6/08
http://www.gold-eagle.com/editorials_08/bloom061608.html

Discombobulated - Norcini - 6/08
http://www.silverbearcafe.com/private/6.08/discombobulated.html

Because Uncle Ben is one of Them - Chapman 6/08
http://www.silverbearcafe.com/private/6.08/uncleben.html

The Treasury Yield Curve & Gold - Willie - 6/2008
http://news.goldseek.com/GoldenJackass/1213293600.php

Grasping at Straws - Baltin - 6/08
http://www.gold-eagle.com/editorials_08/baltin060708.html

WOW! What a Week! - Taylor - 6/08
http://www.gold-eagle.com/gold_digest_08/taylor060808.html

The Story No One is Talking About - Sutton 6/08
http://www.silverstrategies.com/story.aspx?local=1&id=669

The U.S. Economic Recession - Buckler - 6/08
http://www.321gold.com/editorials/buckler/buckler060408.html

The Shell Game - Schoon - 5/08
http://www.gold-eagle.com/editorials_08/schoon052608.html

The New Era - Mathid - 3/08

www.321gold.com/editorials/mathid/mathid031708.html

The Realities of this Secular Bull Market in Commodities - Roulston - 2/08
http://www.kitco.com/ind/Resopp/roulston_jan122008.html

Let's Legalize Competing Currencies - Paul - 2/08
http://news.goldseek.com/RonPaul/1203089229.php

Is the Commodity Super Cycle under Threat? - McKillop - 2/08
http://www.financialsense.com/editorials/mckillop/2008/0211.html

Appendix H
A List of Links to Articles about the World Geo-Political Order and Gold

The Goldsmiths—Part CLIII - Bradshaw - 8/10
http://news.goldseek.com/GoldSeek/1281074580.php

A Plague Upon The World: The USA is a "Failed State" - Roberts - 6/10
http://www.silverbearcafe.com/private/06.10/plague.html

The Ten Benefits of Expatriation - Casey Research - 6/10
http://news.goldseek.com/GoldSeek/1276030841.php

Gold & Money: More than Meets the Eye - Aristotle - 1999
http://www.24hgold.com/english/printarticle.aspx?pagedest=571432&langue=en&viewarticle=True

Hunt Brothers Demanded Physical Delivery Too - Matonis - 3/10
http://news.silverseek.com/SilverSeek/1268779599.php

Gold & the New World Order - Roache - 2/10
http://www.321gold.com/editorials/roache/roache021610.html

The United States of America - An American Tragedy - Schoon - 1/10
http://news.goldseek.com/GoldSeek/1262599200.php

The Old Order Changeth - Katz - 1/10
http://news.goldseek.com/GoldSeek/1262616338.php

Killing the Currency - Murphy - 12/09

http://www.silverbearcafe.com/private/12.09/currency.html

Accidental American Patriot - Sardi - 12/09
http://www.silverbearcafe.com/private/12.09/patriot.html

The Second Wave of The Financial Tsunami - Chang - 11/09
http://www.silverbearcafe.com/private/11.09/secondwave.html

A Case for a Rise in the FRN Dollar - Mayer - 8/09
http://news.goldseek.com/GoldSeek/1250692777.php

The Royal Scam - Of Two Minds - 8/09
http://www.oftwominds.com/blogaug09/KaPoom2CHS.htm

Why the Fed is Depreciating the Currency - Katz - 7/09
http://news.goldseek.com/GoldSeek/1246892860.php

R.I.P. – The London Gold Pool, 1961-1968 - Towne - 6/09
http://news.goldseek.com/GoldSeek/1245046140.php

The Silver phoenix Rises from the Ashes of the American Revolution - Stoddard - 5/09
http://news.silverseek.com/SilverSeek/1242252457.php

U.S. Global Hegemony – The Beginning …and the End - hoffman - 4/09
http://news.goldseek.com/GoldSeek/1240158180.php

Civilization at the Crossroads - Meyer - 4/09
http://www.silverbearcafe.com/private/04.09/crossroads.html

The Financial New World Order: Towards a Global Currency and World Government – Marshall – 4/09
http://www.silverbearcafe.com/private/04.09/nwo.html

Operation Meltdown, part III - Ash - 9/08
http://news.goldseek.com/GoldSeek/1220634000.php

Operation Meltdown, part II - Ash - 8/08
http://news.goldseek.com/GoldSeek/1220031650.php

Fate of Paper Money - Hewitt - 6/08
http://news.goldseek.com/GoldSeek/1214842037.php

The Dow-Crash, The Dollar, Gold, and WAR! - Wallenwein - 6/08
http://www.gold-eagle.com/editorials_08/wallenwein062808.html

Another China Syndrome - Bond - 6/08
http://news.goldseek.com/GoldSeek/1214579213.php

Exchange Controls are Proposed for the U.S.A. - Phillips - 6/08
http://news.goldseek.com/GoldForecaster/1214325973.php

Tribute Paid in Oil - Price - 6/08
http://www.financialsense.com/editorials/salinasprice/2008/0620.html

Illegal Rationing of US Siver Eagles - Hommel - 6/08
http://www.silverbearcafe.com/private/6.08/eagles.html

How Safe is My Gold? - Shedlock - 6/08
http://www.silverbearcafe.com/private/6.08/safe.html

The Shrinking U.S. Global Reach - Buckler - 6/08
http://www.321gold.com/editorials/buckler/buckler060208.html

IMF Gold: Bring it on! - Schoon - 3/08
http://news.goldseek.com/GoldSeek/1204527960.php

Year of the Rat - Rodgers - 2/08
http://www.numismaster.com/ta/numis/Article.jsp?ad=article&Artic
leId=3809

Uncle Sam Crying "Uncle!" - Fekete - 2/08
http://www.gold-eagle.com/gold_digest_08/fekete020908.html

The Double Whammy - Fekete - 1/08
http://www.321gold.com/editorials/fekete/fekete013108.html

Appendix I
A List of Links to Articles about Gold Market Manipulation and Conspiracy

Real World Solutions to Economic Tyranny - Bruno - 9/10
http://silverbearcafe.com/private/09.10/tyranny.html
The Failure of the Second London Gold Pool - Douglas - 8/10
http://news.goldseek.com/GATA/1282198140.php

The Great American Disaster: How Much Gold Remains In Fort Knox? -
Weber - 8/10 http://www.silverbearcafe.com/private/08.10/fortknox.html

US Prepares For Gold Standard - Weir - 8/10
http://news.goldseek.com/GoldSeek/1282111440.php

FLOATING EXCHANGE RATES: SCHEME TO EMBEZZLE
THE DOLLAR BALANCES OF SURPLUS COUNTRIES -
Fekete - 7/10
http://www.gold-eagle.com/gold_digest_08/fekete070510.html

End Game: Gold Investors Destroyed - Moore - 6/10
http://www.financialsense.com/fsu/editorials/moore/2010/0615.html

The BIS: The Banker's Money Launderer - Neilson 6/10
http://www.silverbearcafe.com/private/06.10/launderer.html

Dark Days for the Realists - Nielson - 5/10
http://www.gold-eagle.com/editorials_08/nielson052510.html

Gold: Why the Bankers Need the Miners - Nielson - 5/10
http://www.gold-eagle.com/editorials_08/nielson051810.html

Forget the Politicians... - Carlin
http://www.silverbearcafe.com/private/05.10/carlin.html

IMF can't explain gold sales now without revealing squeeze -
Douglas - 5/10
http://news.goldseek.com/GATA/1273161575.php

Dear Gold and Silverbugs: Shut your Pieholes and Stop Whining - Galt
- 4/10
http://www.silverbearcafe.com/private/04.10/piehole.html

Golden Road - Weir - 4/10
http://news.goldseek.com/GoldSeek/1271262840.php

Fake Silver "Moly-Bars"? - Weir - 3/10
http://www.silverbearcafe.com/private/03.10/molybars.html

The 10 Step Final Countdown To Retirement Plan Nationalization -
Holland - 3/10
http://www.silverbearcafe.com/private/03.10/nationalize.html

Precious Metals & Rigged Markets - Nielson - 3/10
http://www.gold-eagle.com/editorials_08/nielson031910.html

SULTANS OF SWAP: Smoking Guns & the Sting! - Long - 3/10
http://www.gold-eagle.com/editorials_08/long031510.html

Building a Future without the New World Order - Bruno - 3/10
http://www.silverbearcafe.com/private/03.10/future.html

More IMF Gold Propoganda - Nielson - 2/10
http://www.gold-eagle.com/editorials_08/nielson021810.html

Will the COMEX Keep Pace - Mclagan - 2/10
http://news.goldseek.com/RickAckerman/1266418260.php

Gold and the Road to Roota Theory - Weir - 2/10
http://news.goldseek.com/GoldSeek/1266416387.php

All Roads Lead to Goldman Sachs - Kirby - 2/10
http://news.goldseek.com/GoldSeek/1266345000.php

Is it all just a Ponzi Scheme? - Sprott - 12/09
www.sprott.com/Docs/MarketsataGlance/12_2009_MAAG.pdf

How Would Anyone Know if the Comex is Lying Too? - GATA - 12/09
http://news.goldseek.com/GATA/1262118153.php

Gold and Silver: Why they are Important, and Why They are Often
Manipulated - Bruno - 12/09
http://www.silverbearcafe.com/private/12.09/manipulated.html

What's Really in Fort Knox? - Long - 12/09
http://www.financialsense.com/fsu/editorials/long/2009/1214.html

Appendix J

A Listing of 36 of the Largest and best known National and International
Precious Metal Retailers with links to Company Websites

- A-Mark Precious Metals   amark.com
- American Precious Metals Exchange   apmex.com

- Anglo Far East   anglofareast.com
- ASI   assetstrategies.com
- BlanchardOnline   blanchardonline.com
- Border Gold   bordergold.com
- Brinks   brinks.com
- Bullion Direct   BullionDirect.com
- Bullionvault.com   bullionvault.com
- California Numismatic Investments   golddealer.com
- CMI Gold & Silver   cmi-gold-silver.com
- Coin Agent, The   thecoinagent.com
- e-gold   e-gold.com
- Fidelitrade   fidelitrade.com
- First Majestic   firstmajestic.com
- Goldline   goldline.com
- GoldMoney   goldmoney.com
- Handy & Harman   handyharmancanada.com
- Investment Rarities   investmentrarities.com
- Johnson Matthey   matthey.com/about/preciousmetals.htm
- Kitco   kitco.com
- Liberty Dollar   libertydollar.org
- Miles Franklin   milesfranklin.com
- Monex Precious Metals   monex.com
- Northwest Territorial Mint   nwtmint.com
- Perth Mint   perthmint.com.au
- Rocklin Coin Shop   rocklincoinshop.com
- Royal Canadian Mint   mint.ca
- Royal Mint, The (UK)   royalmint.com
- SeekBullion   seekbullion.com
- Scotiabank   scotiabank.com

- The Silver Exchange   thesilverxchange.com
- Tulving   tulving.com
- United States Mint   usmint.gov
- USAGold   usagold.com
- Wexford Coin   wexfordcoin.com

Appendix K
A Listing of 42 of the Most Prominent Gold Advisory Subscription Services and their Websites

- 49 North Resource Fund   www.fnr.ca
- American Precious Metals Advisors   www.nicholsongold.com
- Bottom Fishing Report   www.kaiserbottomfish.com
- Bullion Management Group   www.bmginc.ca
- Butler Research   www.butlerresearch.com
- Casey Research   www.caseyresearch.com
- Deepcaster   www.deepcaster.com
- Dines Letter   www.dinesletter.com
- Diploma Technical Analysis   www.clivemaund.com
- Discovery Investing   www.discoveryinvesting.com
- Gold and Oil Guy, The   www.thegoldandoilguy.com
- Gold Drivers   www.golddrivers.com
- Gold Forecaster   www.goldforecaster.com
- Gold Newsletter   www.goldnewsletter.com
- Gold Oz   goldoz.com.au
- Gold Speculator, The   www.thegoldspeculator.com
- Gold Stock Analyst   www.goldstockanalyst.com
- Graceland Updates   www.gracelandupdates.com
- Hard Rock Analyst   www.hraadvisory.com

- Hat Trick Letter, The   www.goldenjackass.com
- Institutional Advisors   www.institutionaladvisors.com
- International Forecaster   www.theinternationalforecaster.com
- J.   Taylor's   Gold,   Energy,   &   Tech   Stocks www.miningstocks.com
- Lemetropole Café   www.lemetropolecafe.com
- Merv's Precious Metals Central   preciousmetalscentral.com
- Midas Letter   www.midasletter.com
- Mining Speculator, The   www.miningspeculator.com
- One-Handed Economist, The   www.thegoldspeculator.com
- Precious Metals Warrants   www.preciousmetalswarrants.com
- Privateer, The   www.the-privateer.com
- Prudent Squirrel, The   www.prudentsquirrel.com
- Resource Opportunities   www.resourceopportunities.com
- Rule, Rick   www.gril.net
- Ruff Times   www.rufftimes.com
- Schultz, Harry   www.hsletter.com
- Silver Investor   www.silver-investor.com
- Silver Stock Report   www.silverstockreport.com
- Speculative Investor, The   www.speculative-investor.com
- Sunshine Profits   www.sunshineprofits.com
- Trader Tracks   www.tradertracks.com
- Willie, Jim   goldenjackass.com
- Zeal Intelligence   www.zealllc.com

Appendix L

A Listing of 35 Recommended Authors who write about Gold and the Websites where you can read their Free Postings

- Katherine Austin-Fitts gata.org
- Nick Barisheff bmginc.ca bmgbullionbars investinpreciousmetals.ca
- Bill Buckler the-privateer.com
- Ted Butler butlerresearch.com
- Doug Casey caseyresearch.com
- Bob Chapman theinternationalforecaster.com
- John Doody goldstockanalyst.com
- Adrian Douglas gata.org lemetropolecafe.com
- John Embry sprott.com
- Antal Fekete professorfekete.com goldisfreedom.com goldstandardinstitute.com
- Alf Field Posts on Numerous Sites
- Goldrunner Posts at gold-eagle.com
- Jason Hommel silverstockreport.com
- Howard Katz thegoldbug.net
- Rob Kirby kirbyanalytics.com
- Bill Murphy gata.org lemetropolecafe.com
- Jeff Nielson Posts at Gold-eagle.com
- Dan Norcini jsmineset.com
- Julian D.W. Phillips Posts on Numerous Sites
- John Pugsley biorationalinstitute.com
- Jim Puplava financialsense.com
- Howard Ruff rufftimes.com
- Rick Rule gril.net
- Hugo Salinas Price Posts on Numerous Sites
- Franklin Sanders the-moneychanger.com
- Darryl Robert Schoon Posts on Numerous Sites
- Harry Schultz hsletter.com
- Johnny Silverbear silverbearcafe.com

- Jim Sinclair   jsmineset.com

- Ed Steer   gata.org   www.caseyresearch.com

- Jay Taylor   miningstocks.com

- Stewart Thompson   gracelandupdates.com

- James Turk   goldensextant.com   goldmoney.com   fgmr.com

- Edwin Vieira   Various Books and Writings

- Jim Willie   goldenjackass.com

Appendix M
A Listing of 55 Recommended Gold Analysis and Editorial WebSites

- 24hgold   24hgold.com

- 24hPM   24hPM.com

- 321Energy   321energy.com

- 321Gold   321gold.com

- The au Report   theaureport.com

- BullionDesk   thebulliondesk.com

- Bullionvault.com   bullionvault.com

- Cambridge House   cambridgehouse.ca

- Casey Research   caseyresearch.com

- CPM Group   cpmgroup.com

- Daily Reckoning   thedailyreckoning.com

- Dollar Collapse   dollarcollapse.com

- e-gold   e-gold.com

- Financial Sense   financialsense.com

- Free Gold Money Report   fgmr.com

- Free-Market News Network   freemarketnews.com

- Gold Anti-Trust Action Committee   gata.org

- Gold Drivers   golddrivers.com

- Gold Eagle   gold-eagle.com
- Goldensextant   goldensextant.com
- GoldMoney   goldmoney.com
- Gold Report, The   theaureport.com
- Goldseek   goldseek.com
- Graceland Updates   gracelandupdates.com
- Investment Rarities   investmentrarities.com
- Jim Sinclair's Mineset   jsmineset.com
- Kitco   kitco.com
- Korelin Economics Report   kereport.com
- Lemetropole Café   lemetropolecafe.com
- Lew Rockwell   lewrockwell.com
- London Bullion Market Association   lbma.org.uk
- Ludwig von Mises Institute   mises.org
- Mining Company Report   miningcompanyreport.com
- MineWeb   mineweb.com
- MiningMX   miningmx.com
- MoneyChanger   the-moneychanger.com
- Privateer   the-privateer.com
- Resource Investor   resourceinvestor.com
- Run to Gold   runtogold.com
- Shadow Stats   shadowstats.com
- Safehaven   safehaven.com
- Silver Axis   silveraxis.com
- Silverbear Cafe   silverbearcafe.com
- Silver Institute   silverinstitute.org
- Silver Investor   silver-investor.com
- Silverseek   silverseek.com
- Silver Strategies   silverstrategies.com

- SilverStockReport   silverstockreport.com
- Silver Valley Mining Journal   silverminers.com
- Sovereign Society   sovereignsociety.com
- Sprott Assett Management   sprott.com
- Stock House   stockhouse.com
- World Gold Council   gold.org
- Zeal Intelligence   zealllc.com

Appendix N
A Listing of 26 Recommended Research Sites on the Web. Mining Company Directories, Metal Calculators, Charts, and other goodies.

- **24hgold Directory**   The most comprehensive searchable database of PM companies on the Web.   24hgold.com

- **The AuReport**   Coverage of Precious Metals Companies. theaureport.com

- **The AuReport Silver Directory**   Directory of Silver Mining Companies. theaureport.com/pub/htdocs/silver.html

- **Bullion Bulls Canada**   Database of Junior PM Companies. bullionbullscanada.com

- **CoinInfo.com**   Look for a Coinshop Near You. coininfo.com/index.php?op=searchDealers

- **Coin Specs**   Major gold coins with their weights, diameters and thicknesses._onlygold.com/TutorialPages/Coin_specsFulScreenVersion.htm

- **eBay Gold Premiums**   How much more do I have to pay over the spot price for physical gold on eBay? 24hgold.com/english/buy_sell_gold_coins.aspx?co_id=0

- **eBay Silver Premiums**   How much more do I have to pay over the spot price for physical silver on eBay? 24hgold.com/english/buy_sell_silver_coins.aspx?co_id=0

- **Federal Reserve Inflation Calculator**   Calculate Inflation over time using CPI Data. minneapolisfed.org/research/data/us/calc

- **Gold Fields Mineral Services**   An independent, London-based Consultancy and Research Company, focused on the International gold and silver markets.   gfms.co.uk

- **Gold Price Charts**   A wealth of gold related chart and information. goldprice.org

- **Gold Ratios**   Updated gold related ratios.   runtogold.com/key-ratios

- **Gold Sheet Mining Directory**   goldsheetlinks.com

- **How much is that rock worth?**   Subscription Required. caseyresearch.com

- **Insider Insights**   Tracks the buying and selling of corporate insiders of junior mining and natural resource companies.   insiderinsights.com

- **Kitco**   Real Time Precious Metals Spot Price 24/7 and historical charts. kitco.com

- **London Metal Exchange**   Find Amount of Non-Ferrous Base Metal Stored in World Warehouses   lme.co.uk

- **Metal Augmentor**   metalaugmentor.com

- **Miningpedia**   Comprehensive Searchable Database of Mining Companies. miningpedia.com

- **New York Mercantile Exchange**   COMEX Inventories and Commitment of Traders Data   nymex.com

- **Precious Metals Warrants**   Database for all warrants trading on the natural resource companies of the U.S. and Canada. preciousmetalswarrants.com

- **Resource Stock Guide**   Searchable Database of Selected Mining Companies.   resourcestockguide.com

- **Silver Strategies**   Profiles of Junior Silver Companies. silverstrategies.com

- **StockCharts**   Create your own Historical Charts.   stockcharts.com

- **U.S. Silver Coin Calculator**   "The U.S. Silver Coin Calculator lets you determine the value of silver within circulating coins quickly and easily. Simply enter the quantity of coins in the yellow boxes, adjust the silver spot price (if you wish), or even the default bid/ask spread percentage. The Silver Coin Calculator does all the rest!"   silvercoinstoday.com/silver-calculators/us-silver-coin-calculator

- **Yahoo Finance**   Look for Stock Quotes or Ticker Symbols. finance.yahoo.com

Other books by Jerry Western:

The Precious Metals Mining Company Directory:
A Who's Who Guide of the Leading Gold and Silver Mining Plays

ISBN-10: 1461097967
ISBN-13: 978-1461097969

http://www.amazon.com/Precious-Metals-Mining-Company-Directory/dp/1461097967/ref=sr_1_10?s=books&ie=UTF8&qid=1305825659&sr=1-10#_

The Precious Metals Bull Market Model Portfolio: Investment Options for Riding the Silver and Gold Bull Market

ISBN-10: 146111148X
ISBN-13: 978-1461111481

http://www.amazon.com/Precious-Metals-Market-Model-Portfolio/dp/146111148X/ref=sr_1_9?s=books&ie=UTF8&qid=1305825805&sr=1-9

The Precious Metals Investment Guide: A Directory of Securities offering Investment Opportunities in Gold, Silver, and other Precious Metals

ISBN-10: 1461139503
ISBN-13: 978-1461139508

http://www.amazon.com/Precious-Metals-Investment-Guide-Opportunities/dp/1461139503/ref=sr_1_11?s=books&ie=UTF8&qid=1305825860&sr=1-11

###